Recent Advances in the Diagnosis and Treatment of Chronic Liver Diseases

Recent Advances in the Diagnosis and Treatment of Chronic Liver Diseases

Editor

Hirayuki Enomoto

MDPI • Basel • Beijing • Wuhan • Barcelona • Belgrade • Manchester • Tokyo • Cluj • Tianjin

Editor
Hirayuki Enomoto
Division of Hepatobiliary and
Pancreatic Disease, Department
of Internal Medicine
Hyogo College of Medicine
Nishinomiya
Japan

Editorial Office
MDPI
St. Alban-Anlage 66
4052 Basel, Switzerland

This is a reprint of articles from the Special Issue published online in the open access journal *International Journal of Molecular Sciences* (ISSN 1422-0067) (available at: www.mdpi.com/journal/ijms/special_issues/liver_diseases).

For citation purposes, cite each article independently as indicated on the article page online and as indicated below:

LastName, A.A.; LastName, B.B.; LastName, C.C. Article Title. *Journal Name* **Year**, *Volume Number*, Page Range.

ISBN 978-3-0365-2993-6 (Hbk)
ISBN 978-3-0365-2992-9 (PDF)

© 2022 by the authors. Articles in this book are Open Access and distributed under the Creative Commons Attribution (CC BY) license, which allows users to download, copy and build upon published articles, as long as the author and publisher are properly credited, which ensures maximum dissemination and a wider impact of our publications.
The book as a whole is distributed by MDPI under the terms and conditions of the Creative Commons license CC BY-NC-ND.

Contents

Preface to "Recent Advances in the Diagnosis and Treatment of Chronic Liver Diseases" . . . vii

Susumu Hamada-Tsutsumi, Masaya Onishi, Kentaro Matsuura, Masanori Isogawa, Keigo Kawashima and Yusuke Sato et al.
Inhibitory Effect of a Human MicroRNA, miR-6133-5p, on the Fibrotic Activity of Hepatic Stellate Cells in Culture
Reprinted from: *Int. J. Mol. Sci.* **2020**, *21*, 7251, doi:10.3390/ijms21197251 1

Tatsuo Kanda, Reina Sasaki, Ryota Masuzaki, Hiroshi Takahashi, Taku Mizutani and Naoki Matsumoto et al.
Co-Occurrence of Hepatitis A Infection and Chronic Liver Disease
Reprinted from: *Int. J. Mol. Sci.* **2020**, *21*, 6384, doi:10.3390/ijms21176384 15

Yi-Shan Tsai, Ming-Lun Yeh, Pei-Chien Tsai, Ching-I Huang, Chung-Feng Huang and Meng-Hsuan Hsieh et al.
Clusters of Circulating let-7 Family Tumor Suppressors Are Associated with Clinical Characteristics of Chronic Hepatitis C
Reprinted from: *Int. J. Mol. Sci.* **2020**, *21*, 4945, doi:10.3390/ijms21144945 33

Kazuya Takemura, Etsuko Takizawa, Akihiro Tamori, Mika Nakamae, Hiroshi Kubota and Sawako Uchida-Kobayashi et al.
Post-Treatment M2BPGi Level and the Rate of Autotaxin Reduction are Predictive of Hepatocellular Carcinoma Development after Antiviral Therapy in Patients with Chronic Hepatitis C
Reprinted from: *Int. J. Mol. Sci.* **2020**, *21*, 4517, doi:10.3390/ijms21124517 47

Leona Osawa, Nobuharu Tamaki, Masayuki Kurosaki, Sakura Kirino, Keiya Watakabe and Wan Wang et al.
Wisteria floribunda Agglutinin-Positive Mac-2 Binding Protein but not -fetoprotein as a Long-Term Hepatocellular Carcinoma Predictor
Reprinted from: *Int. J. Mol. Sci.* **2020**, *21*, 3640, doi:10.3390/ijms21103640 63

Yoshimitsu Fukasawa, Shinichi Takano, Mitsuharu Fukasawa, Shinya Maekawa, Makoto Kadokura and Hiroko Shindo et al.
Form-Vessel Classification of Cholangioscopy Findings to Diagnose Biliary Tract Carcinoma's Superficial Spread
Reprinted from: *Int. J. Mol. Sci.* **2020**, *21*, 3311, doi:10.3390/ijms21093311 75

Hirayuki Enomoto, Nobuhiro Aizawa, Kunihiro Hasegawa, Naoto Ikeda, Yoshiyuki Sakai and Kazunori Yoh et al.
Possible Relevance of PNPLA3 and TLL1 Gene Polymorphisms to the Efficacy of PEG-IFN Therapy for HBV-Infected Patients
Reprinted from: *Int. J. Mol. Sci.* **2020**, *21*, 3089, doi:10.3390/ijms21093089 89

Preface to "Recent Advances in the Diagnosis and Treatment of Chronic Liver Diseases"

Dear readers,

It is my great pleasure and honor to publish a book entitled Advances in the Diagnosis and Treatment of Chronic Liver Diseases. Chronic liver diseases develop from a wide range of causes, including hepatitis B virus (HBV) infection, hepatitis C virus (HCV) infection, alcoholic-related liver disease, non-alcoholic fatty liver disease (NAFLD), and autoimmune liver diseases. Recent advances in molecular and cellular techniques have succeeded in providing new aspects in the diagnosis and treatment of chronic liver diseases. This book includes seven state-of-the-art studies on chronic liver diseases.

I believe that the present special collection would be beneficial for a wide range of readers. Sincerely,

Hirayuki Enomoto
Editor

Article

Inhibitory Effect of a Human MicroRNA, miR-6133-5p, on the Fibrotic Activity of Hepatic Stellate Cells in Culture

Susumu Hamada-Tsutsumi [1], Masaya Onishi [1], Kentaro Matsuura [2], Masanori Isogawa [1], Keigo Kawashima [1], Yusuke Sato [3] and Yasuhito Tanaka [1,4,*]

1. Department of Virology and Liver Unit, Nagoya City University Graduate School of Medical Sciences, Nagoya 467-8601, Japan; tsutsumi@med.nagoya-cu.ac.jp (S.H.-T.); om19840905@gmail.com (M.O.); misogawa@med.nagoya-cu.ac.jp (M.I.); keepitgood0110@yahoo.co.jp (K.K.)
2. Department of Gastroenterology and Metabolism, Nagoya City University Graduate School of Medical Sciences, Nagoya 467-8601, Japan; matsuura@med.nagoya-cu.ac.jp
3. Laboratory of Innovative Nanomedicine, Faculty of Pharmaceutical Sciences, Hokkaido University, Sapporo 060-0812, Japan; y_sato@pharm.hokudai.ac.jp
4. Department of Gastroenterology and Hepatology, Faculty of Life Sciences, Kumamoto University, Kumamoto 860-8556, Japan
* Correspondence: ytanaka@kumamoto-u.ac.jp; Tel.: +81-96-373-5146

Received: 30 July 2020; Accepted: 28 September 2020; Published: 1 October 2020

Abstract: Background: We recently identified 39 human microRNAs, which effectively suppress hepatitis B virus (HBV) replication in hepatocytes. Chronic HBV infection often results in active, hepatitis-related liver fibrosis; hence, we assessed whether any of these microRNAs have anti-fibrotic potential and predicted that miR-6133-5p may target several fibrosis-related genes. Methods: The hepatic stellate cell line LX-2 was transfected with an miR-6133-5p mimic and subsequently treated with Transforming growth factor (TGF)-β. The mRNA and protein products of the *COL1A1* gene, encoding collagen, and the *ACTA2* gene, an activation marker of hepatic stellate cells, were quantified. Results: The expression of *COL1A1* and *ACTA2* was markedly reduced in LX-2 cells treated with miR-6133-5p. Interestingly, phosphorylation of c-Jun N-terminal kinase (JNK) was also significantly decreased by miR-6133-5p treatment. The expression of several predicted target genes of miR-6133-5p, including *TGFBR2* (which encodes Transforming Growth Factor Beta Receptor 2) and *FGFR1* (which encodes Fibroblast Growth Factor Receptor 1), was also reduced in miR-6133-5p-treated cells. The knockdown of *TGFBR2* by the corresponding small interfering RNA greatly suppressed the expression of *COL1A1* and *ACTA2*. Treatment with the JNK inhibitor, SP600125, also suppressed *COL1A1* and *ACTA2* expression, indicating that TGFBR2 and JNK mediate the anti-fibrotic effect of miR-6133-5p. The downregulation of *FGFR1* may result in a decrease of phosphorylated Akt, ERK (extracellular signal-regulated kinase), and JNK. Conclusion: miR-6133-5p has a strong anti-fibrotic effect, mediated by inactivation of TGFBR2, Akt, and JNK.

Keywords: liver fibrosis; hepatic stellate cells; TGF-β; JNK signaling pathway

1. Introduction

The progression of liver fibrosis often leads to fatal outcomes, such as the development of cirrhosis and hepatocellular carcinoma. Infections with viruses such as the hepatitis B virus (HBV) and hepatitis C virus are the major causes of liver fibrosis and contributed to around 50% of cirrhosis and hepatocellular carcinoma cases in 2017 [1]. Approximately 250 million people worldwide were infected with hepatitis viruses, resulting in nearly 1.4 million deaths in 2016, which is more than those caused by human immunodeficiency virus infection or tuberculosis [2]. Therefore, the development of novel treatment options to prevent the progression of liver fibrosis is important for reducing risks to health.

Hepatic stellate cells (HSCs) are major producers of extracellular matrix proteins, such as collagen fibers, during the development of fibrosis. HSCs are activated by fibrogenic cytokines, such as Transforming growth factor (TGF)-β, angiotensin II, and leptin, induced by liver injury [3]. Once activated, HSCs proliferate and differentiate into myofibroblasts and start to produce α-smooth muscle actin (α-SMA). Although extensive efforts have revealed that various signaling molecules such as Akt and c-Jun N-terminal kinase (JNK) control the activation and fibrogenesis of HSCs [4–8], the molecular processes involved in HSC activation are not entirely understood [9].

MicroRNAs (miRNAs) are small non-coding RNAs, 21–25 nucleotides in length, encoded in the human genome. Each miRNA targets hundreds of mRNAs and downregulates them post-transcriptionally by base pairing with their 3'-untranslated regions (3'-UTRs) [10,11]. Extensive studies have revealed that miRNAs regulate various biological and cellular processes, including proliferation, differentiation, cell behavior, and cancer development [12–17]. The involvement of miRNAs in fibrosis of the liver and other organs also has been reported [18–22].

Recently, by screening a human miRNA mimic library, we identified 39 miRNAs that effectively suppress HBV replication [23]. A significant portion of chronically HBV-infected patients suffer from progression of liver fibrosis toward cirrhosis [24]. Hence, we investigated whether any of these miRNAs have additional effects related to fibrosis and found that one of them, miR-6133-5p, potentially targets several fibrosis-related genes. Interestingly, miR-6133 greatly suppressed not only the *COL1A1* gene that encodes the α-chain of collagen type I (collagen Iα1), the major component of fibrous tissue in the liver, but also the *ACTA2* gene, which encodes α-SMA, indicating its anti-fibrotic potential. In the present study, we explored the molecular mechanisms by which miR-6133-5p suppresses the fibrotic activity of hepatic stellate cells.

2. Results

2.1. MiR-6133-5p Suppresses the Synthesis of α-Chain of Collagen Type I and α-Smooth Muscle Actin in LX-2 Cells

To explore the role of miR-6133-5p in HSC functions, we transfected an miR-6133-5p mimic or a negative control miRNA mimic (hereafter referred to as miControl) into a human HSC line, LX-2, 24 h before treatment with 5 ng/mL of recombinant human transforming growth factor β1 (rhTGF-β1), a strong inducer of fibrogenesis. RNA and protein were collected at each time point, as indicated in Figure 1A. As shown in Figure 1B, in the miControl-treated cells, rhTGF-β1 treatment dramatically increased the expression of *COL1A1* and *ACTA2*. Interestingly, the levels of *COL1A1* and *ACTA2* were significantly decreased in the miR-6133-5p-treated cells, irrespective of rhTGF-β1 treatment, indicating that miR-6133 has strong anti-fibrotic property. Western blot analyses showed that the amounts of collagen Iα1 and α-SMA were also decreased in the miR-6133-5p-transfected cells, with or without rhTGF-β1 treatment (Figure 1C). It was noted that the amount of α-SMA protein increased only 72 h after rhTGF-β1 treatment.

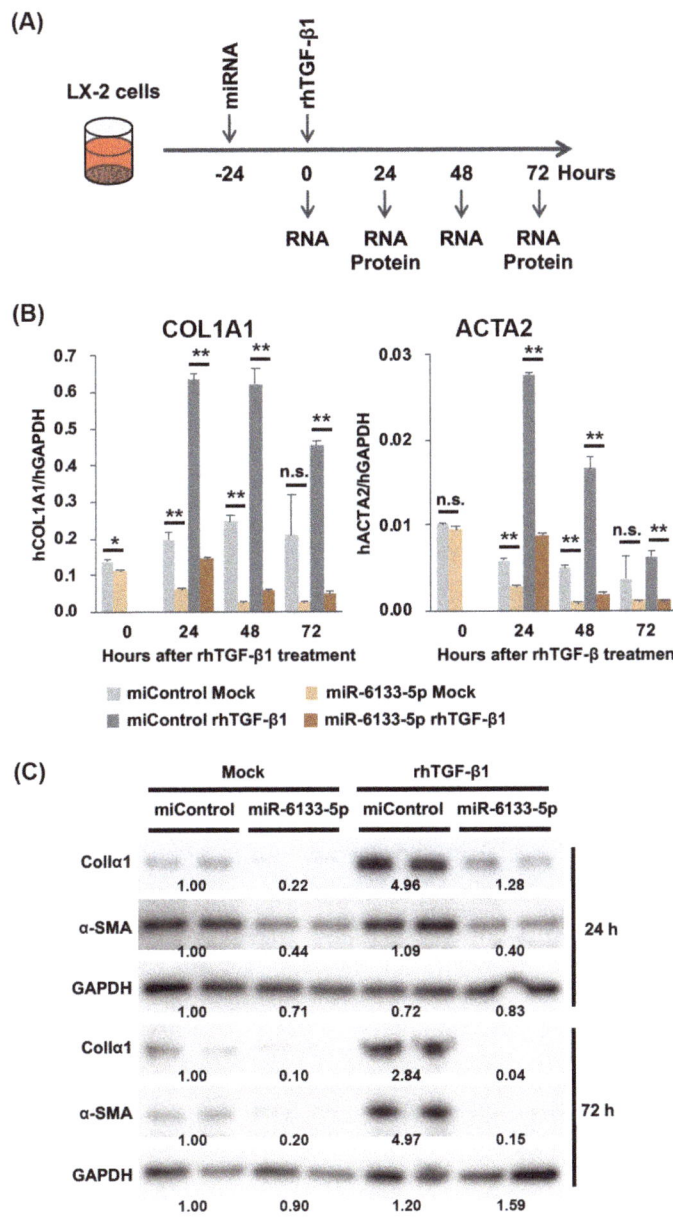

Figure 1. The impact of miR-6133 on the anti-fibrotic activity of LX-2 cells. (**A**) LX-2 cells were transfected with a miR-6133-5p mimic or a negative control microRNA mimic (miControl) at a final concentration of 20 nM, 24 h before treatment with recombinant human transforming growth factor β1 (rhTGF-β1, 5 ng/mL). Total RNA and proteins were extracted from the cells collected at the time points indicated. (**B**) The expression of the *COL1A1* gene encoding collagen Iα1, and the *ACTA2* gene encoding α-smooth muscle actin was determined by RT-qPCR. (**C**) The amounts of α-chain of collagen type I (collagen Iα1) and α-smooth muscle actin (α-SMA) were determined by Western blot analysis. Error bars represent means ± standard deviations (n = 3). * $p <$ 0.05; ** $p <$ 0.01., n.s. not significant.

To identify the molecular mechanisms by which miR-6133-5p suppressed *COL1A1* and *ACTA2*, we performed an RNAseq analysis to compare gene expression patterns of the cells transfected with miR-6133-5p with those transfected with miControl, 24 h after rhTGF-β treatment. Several genes ($n = 373$) were downregulated by more than 50%, with statistical significance (Figure 2A). Among them, 36 genes were also found among the putative target genes of miR-6133-5p predicted by TargetScanHuman v7.2 (total 438 genes, http://www.targetscan.org/vert_72/) [11]. We then examined the role of each gene on the expression of *COL1A1* and *ACTA2* by transfecting with the corresponding small interfering RNAs (siRNA). As shown in Figure 2B, only knockdown of the *TGFBR2* gene, which encodes a component of the human TGF-β receptor, downregulated *COL1A1* and *ACTA2* more than 20%, compared with cells treated with a non-targeting control siRNA (siControl), with statistical significance. However, suppression of *COL1A1* and *ACTA2* by miR-6133-5p was also observed in the absence of rhTGF-β. Moreover, miR-6133 did not alter rhTGF-β-induced phosphorylation of Smad2/3, indicating the presence of TGFBR2-Smad independent pathways (Figure 3A).

By analyzing the RNAseq data in terms of gene ontology, we found that several genes encoding extracellular matrix proteins and genes involved in epithelial-to-mesenchymal transition, such as *CTGF* (connective tissue growth factor), *COL1A2* (collagen Iα2), *COL5A3* (collagen Vα3), *LOX* (Lysyl oxidase), *SNAI2* (Snail 2), and *CDH2* (Cadherin 2), were also significantly downregulated in the miR-6133-5p-treated group (Supplementary Tables S1 and S2). These results indicated that miR-6133-5p partially affects the activation and fibrotic function of LX-2 cells.

2.2. MiR-6133 Decreased Phosphorylation of Akt, ERK, and JNK

We then examined the impact of miR-6133 on the major cellular signaling pathways mediated by the serine/threonine kinases, Akt, ERK (extracellular signal-regulated kinase), JNK, and p38. Surprisingly, the amounts of phosphorylated forms of Akt, ERK, and JNK, but not p38, were smaller in the miR-6133-treated LX-2 cells than the miControl-treated cells, 24 h after rhTGF-β treatment (Figure 3A). Moreover, these differences were also observed in the mock-treated groups (Figure 3A). To determine whether the inhibition of phosphorylation of any of these kinases affected the expression of *COL1A1* and *ACTA2*, we used siRNAs targeting the *SMAD2*, *SMAD3*, and *SMAD4* genes, which are the central mediators of canonical TGF-β signaling and those targeting the *AKT1*, *AKT2*, and *AKT3* genes; and chemical inhibitors of MEK (MAPK/ERK kinase), JNK, and p38.

As shown in Figure 3B, treatment with SMAD2/3/4 siRNAs slightly decreased *COL1A1* and *ACTA2*, but without statistical significance, indicating that *COL1A1* and *ACTA2* are not solely regulated by the canonical TGF-β-Smad2/3/4 pathway. The knockdown of *AKT1/2/3* decreased the level of *COL1A1*, but not *ACTA2*. Treatment with the MEK inhibitor, U0126, which inhibits phosphorylation of ERK by the upstream kinase MEK, slightly increased the levels of *COL1A1* and *ACTA2*. In contrast, inhibition of JNK and p38 by their corresponding inhibitors (SP600125 and SB203580, respectively) significantly suppressed *COL1A1* and *ACTA2* expression (Figure 3B). Collectively, these results suggested that Akt may partially account for the suppression of *COL1A1* by miR-6133-5p and, similarly, JNK may partially account for the suppression of both *COL1A1* and *ACTA2* by miR-6133-5p.

We next investigated the relationship between the suppression of the *TGFBR2* gene and that of Akt, ERK, and JNK phosphorylation using an siRNA targeting the *TGFBR2* gene (siTGFBR2). As shown in Figure 4A, the amount of collagen Iα1 was greatly decreased and that of α-SMA was slightly decreased in the LX-2 cells treated with siTGFBR2 compared with the siControl-treated cells. While the amount of phosphorylated forms of Smad2/3 and Akt was also significantly decreased by siTGFBR2, it had no impact on the amounts of phosphorylated ERK, JNK, and p38 (Figure 4A). These results indicated that the suppression of JNK by miR-6133 is independent of TGFBR2.

(A)

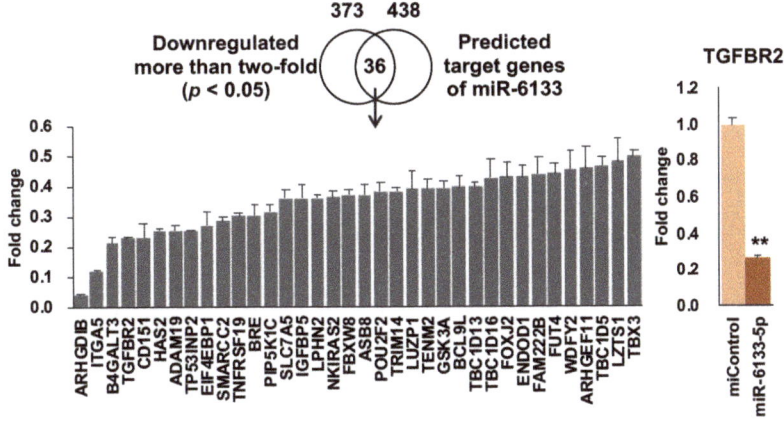

(B)

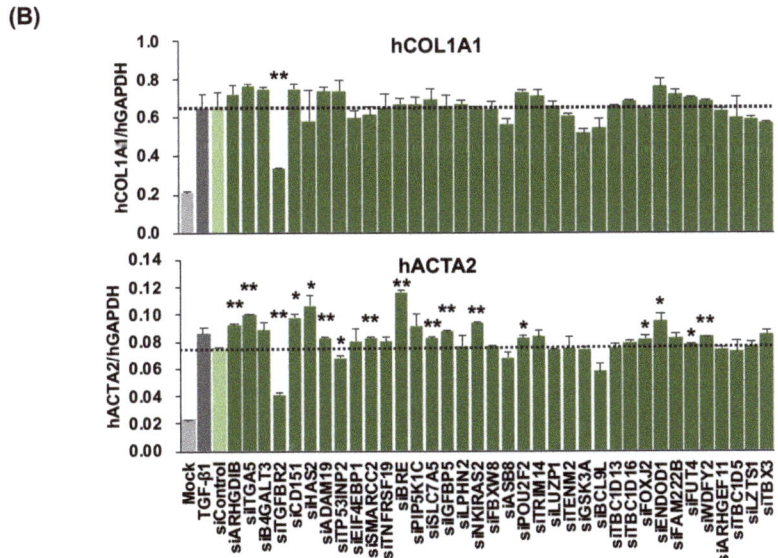

Figure 2. The impact of miR-6133 target genes on the anti-fibrotic activity of LX-2 cells. (**A**) RNAseq analysis revealed that 373 genes were downregulated in miR-6133-treated LX-2 cells compared with those treated with miControl, with statistical significance ($p < 0.05$). Thirty-six of these genes were also among 438 putative miR-6133-5p target genes predicted by TargetScanHuman v7.2. The levels of *TGFBR2* (which encodes Transforming Growth Factor Beta Receptor 2) in the miR-6133-treated and miControl-treated LX-2 cells ($n = 3$) were determined by RT-qPCR. (**B**) LX-2 cells were transfected with small interfering RNAs (siRNAs) corresponding to each of the 36 genes or a non-targeting control siRNA (siControl) at a final concentration of 20 nM, 24 h before treatment with rhTGF-β1 (5 ng/mL). The expression of *COL1A1* and *ACTA2* was determined by RT-qPCR. Fold change was calculated as the ratio over the expression in the siControl-treated sample (indicated by a dotted line). Error bars represent means ± standard deviations ($n = 3$). * $p < 0.05$; ** $p < 0.01$.

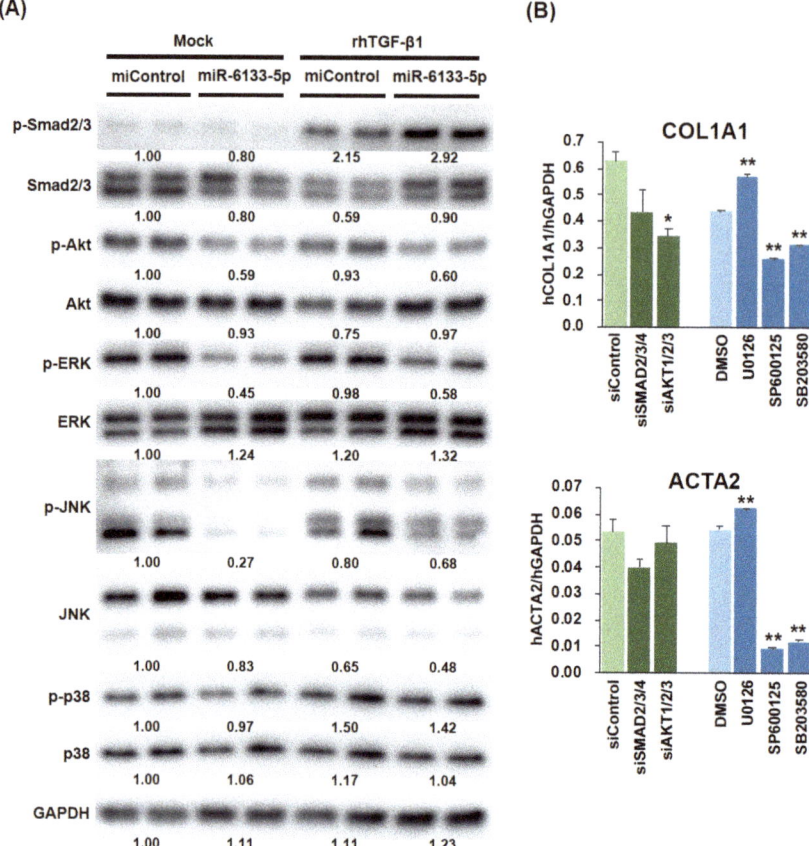

Figure 3. The effect of miR-6133 on the activation of intracellular signaling pathways. (**A**) The amounts of phosphorylated-Smad2/3 (p-Smad2/3), total Smad2/3, p-Akt, Akt, p-ERK (extracellular signal-regulated kinase), ERK, p-JNK (c-Jun N-terminal kinase), JNK, p-p38, p38, and GAPDH (glyceraldehyde-3-phosphate dehydrogenase) were determined by western blot analysis, using the LX-2 extracts collected 24 h after rhTGF-β1 treatment. (**B**) LX-2 cells were treated with a mixture of siRNAs corresponding to the *SMAD2*, *SMAD3*, and *SMAD4* genes (siSMAD2/3/4), a mixture of siRNAs corresponding to the *AKT1*, *AKT2*, and *AKT3* genes (siAKT1/2/3), or siControl, at a final concentration of 30 nM (10 nM for individual siRNA), 24 h before treatment with rhTGF-β1 (5 ng/mL). LX-2 cells were also treated side by side with an MEK (MAPK/ERK kinase) inhibitor (U0126), a JNK inhibitor (SP600125), a p38 inhibitor (SB203580), or DMSO (dimethylsulfoxide), 24 h before rhTGF-β1 treatment. Total RNA was extracted from the samples collected 24 h after rhTGF-β1 treatment and the expression of COL1A1 and ACTA2 was determined by RT-qPCR analysis. Error bars represent means ± standard deviations ($n = 3$). * $p < 0.05$; ** $p < 0.01$.

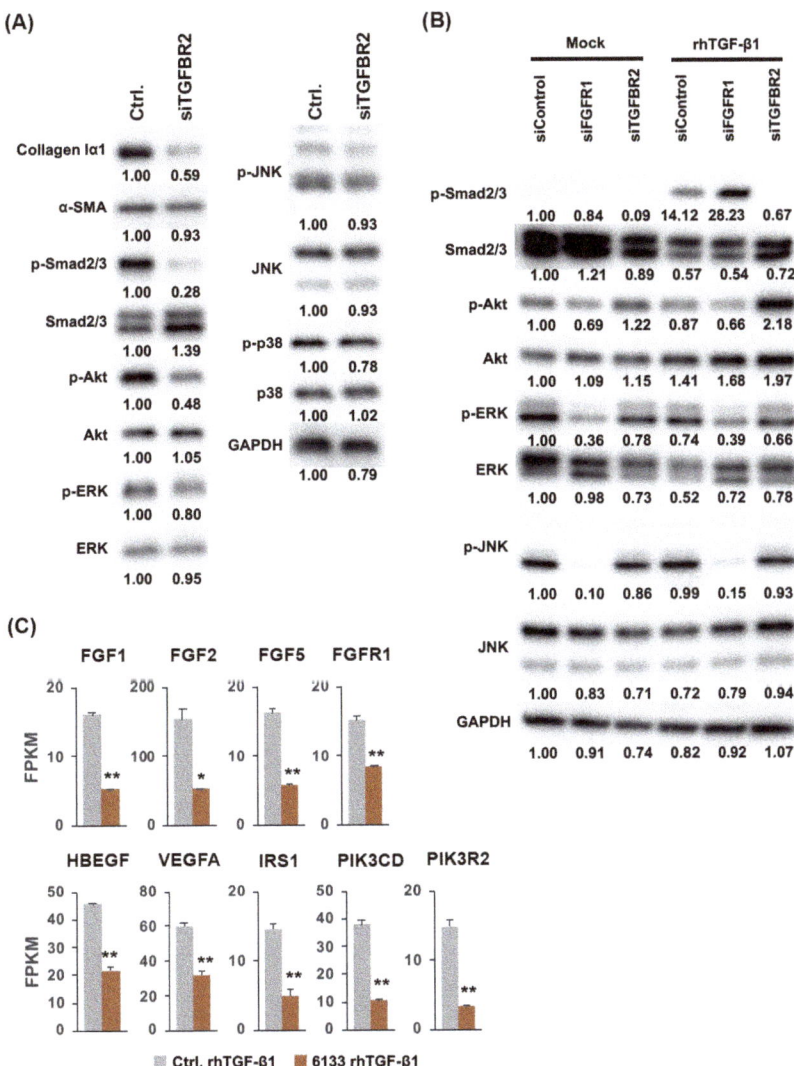

Figure 4. The effect of knockdown of *TGFBR2* and *FGFR1* (which encodes Fibroblast Growth Factor Receptor 1), on the activation of intracellular signaling pathways. (**A**) LX-2 cells were treated with an TGFBR2 siRNA or siControl at a final concentration of 20 nM, 24 h before treatment with rhTGF-β1 (5 ng/mL). Protein extracts were prepared from the samples collected 24 h after rhTGF-β1 treatment and subjected to Western blot analysis. (**B**) LX-2 cells were treated with an FGFR1 siRNA, TGFBR2 siRNA, or siControl at a final concentration of 20 nM, 24 h before treatment with rhTGF-β1. The lysates were analyzed by Western blot analysis. (**C**) Values of fragments per kilobase of exon per million reads mapped (FPKM) for *FGF1*, *FGF2*, *FGF5*, *FGFR1*, *HBEGF*, *VEGFA*, *IRS1*, *PIK3CD*, and *PIK3R2* genes, deduced from the RNAseq analysis comparing samples treated with miR-6133-5p and miControl. Error bars represent means ± standard deviations ($n = 3$). * $p < 0.05$; ** $p < 0.01$.

2.3. Possible Involvement of the Fibroblast Growth Factor Receptor 1 (FGFR1) Gene in the Suppression of JNK Phosphorylation by MiR-6133-5p

Next, to further elucidate the mechanism by which miR-6133-5p suppressed the phosphorylation of Akt, ERK, and JNK, we performed gene set enrichment analysis (GSEA) and constructed miRNA-mRNA networks from RNAseq data. By analyzing GSEA of gene ontology (GO) gene sets in the miR-6133-5p-treated LX-2 cells, we found that a group of genes annotated as 'extracellular matrix organization' were significantly downregulated in the miR-6133-5p-treated cells (Supplementary Figure S1A,B). From the putative miR-6133-target genes predicted by TargetScanHuman v7.2 and experimentally validated miR-6133-5p target genes listed in miRTarBase v8.0 (http://mirtarbase.cuhk.edu.cn/php/index.php) [25], we selected 98 genes whose expression was significantly lower in the miR-6133-5p-treated LX-2 cells (fold change in log2 ratio > 0.8, $p < 0.05$, fold discovery rate < 0.01; Supplementary Figure S1C). Among them, we found the *FGFR1* gene annotated in 'extracellular matrix organization', which is known to transmit a signal to the PI3K-Akt and ERK/JNK/p38 signaling pathways upon activation by its ligands, fibroblast growth factors [26]. As shown in Figure 4B, knockdown of *FGFR1* by the corresponding siRNA significantly decreased the phosphorylated form of JNK. It also decreased phosphorylated forms of Akt and ERK to some extent. These results suggested that the anti-fibrotic function of miR-6133-5p may partially be mediated by the FGFR-Akt/ERK/JNK axis. In contrast, knockdown of *FGFR1* increased the amount of phosphorylated form of Smad2/3 (Figure 4B), indicating that FGFR1 acts inhibitory to the TGF-β pathway, including Smad2/3, as reported by Li et al. [27]. Interestingly, the levels of expression of genes encoding FGFR ligands (*FGF1*, *FGF2*, and *FGF5*) were also reduced in the miR-6133-5p-treated cells. The level of genes involved in other growth factor signaling pathways, such as *HBEGF* (the epidermal growth factor signaling pathway), *VEGFA* (the vascular endothelial growth factor signaling pathway), and *IRS1*, *PIK3CD*, *PIK3R2* (the IGF-PI3K signaling pathway), were also significantly decreased (Figure 4C).

3. Discussion

Recently, we reported that the human miRNA, miR-6133-5p, has strong antiviral activity against HBV replication [23]. In this study, we found that miR-6133-5p effectively suppressed *COL1A1* and *ACTA2*—the main component of fibrous tissue in the liver and a representative marker of HSC activation, respectively. An RNAseq analysis also revealed that several genes encoding other extracellular matrix proteins and those involved in epithelial-to-mesenchymal transition were significantly downregulated in the miR-6133-5p-treated cells, suggesting that miR-6133-5p has strong, but partial, anti-fibrotic property when introduced in HSCs. Functional analyses revealed that siRNA-mediated knockdown of *TGFBR2* and *AKT1/2/3*, and inhibition of JNK by an appropriate chemical, suppressed *COL1A1* and *ACTA2* expression, suggesting that the anti-fibrotic effects of miR-6133-5p may be mediated by TGFBR2, Akt, and JNK (Figure 5).

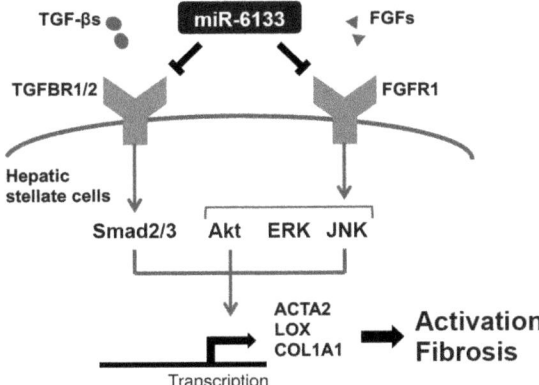

Figure 5. Schema of anti-fibrotic mechanisms via miR-6133-5p. TGF-β signaling mediated by the receptor TGFBR2 and its receivers, Smad2/3, control, *COL1A1*, and *ACTA2*. miR-6133-5p directly suppresses the expression of *TGFBR2*. miR-6133-5p decreases phosphorylation (activation) of Akt, ERK, and JNK, possibly by targeting *FGFR1* which results in the suppression of FGF/FGFR axis. Akt and JNK regulate *COL1A1* and *ACTA2* expression.

The decrease of phosphorylated Akt, ERK, and JNK in the miR-6133-treated LX-2 cells could be due to the downregulation of *FGFR1*, a target gene of miR-6133-5p. Several reports have shown that Akt is involved in collagen synthesis and the activation of HSCs [4,5]. JNK has also been reported to regulate collagen synthesis and the activation of HSCs [6–8]. A chemical compound, GS-444217, that specifically inhibit ASK1 (Apoptosis signal-regulating kinase 1), a protein kinase upstream of JNK and p38, has been reported to reduce liver fibrosis in a mouse model with a *Nlrp3* (NLR family pyrin domain containing 3) loss-of-function mutation [28]. These findings, together with our present study, indicate that signaling pathways including Akt and JNK are therapeutic targets for the control of liver fibrosis.

The roles of endogenous miR-6133-5p in humans are largely unknown. miR-6133-5p is expressed in almost all tissues, including the liver. One report revealed that the amount of urinary exosomal miR-6133-5p was increased in type II diabetic nephropathy patients [29]. On the other hand, we found that the level of miR-6133-5p was not altered in the rhTGF-β1-treated LX-2 cells, compared with the control (data not shown), indicating that endogenous level of miR-6133 have no impact on the fibrogenic function of HSCs.

miR-6133-5p is found in the genome of several primates. Although it is important to determine whether miR-6133-5p effectively ameliorates liver fibrosis in vivo, at present, we could not employ physiologically relevant small animal models for evaluating the effect of primate-restricted miRNA such as miR-6133-5p on liver fibrosis in vivo. Chimeric mice, with liver repopulated with human hepatocytes, were frequently used to study HBV replication in vivo [30]. The development of similar experimental animal models such as small animals harboring human HSCs in the liver would help to examine the effect of reagents on liver fibrosis in future studies.

Some issues remain to be addressed. While the expression of *ACTA2* was induced by rhTGF-β1 and peaked 24 h after treatment, the increase of α-SMA protein became obvious only 72 h after rhTGF-β1 treatment (Figure 1B,C). Similarly, while knockdown of *TGFBR2* greatly suppressed *ACTA2* expression 24 h after rhTGF-β1 treatment, the amount of α-SMA protein was not decreased so much (Figures 2B and 4A). This could be due to the balance between the efficiency of translation and the degradation of α-SMA protein, which may cause a delay in the outcome of the increase/decrease of *ACTA2* mRNA and changes in the amount of its protein product.

On the other hand, knockdown of *TGFBR2* by the corresponding siRNA greatly decreased the phosphorylated form of Smad2/3. However, although miR-6133-5p treatment also suppressed *TGFBR2* effectively, it had no impact on the amount of phosphorylated Smad2/3. The amount of phosphorylated Smad2/3 was increased by the knockdown of *FGFR1* (Figure 4B); hence, it is possible that the downregulation of *FGFR1* by miR-6133 may partially cancel the suppressive effect by the downregulation of *TGFBR2* in terms of the level of phosphorylation of Smad2/3.

Our results showed that the inhibition of p38 by its inhibitor, SB203580, also effectively suppressed *COL1A1* and *ACTA2* expression (Figure 3B). On the other hand, miR-6133-5p had no impact on the phosphorylation of p38 in LX-2. JNK and p38 are differently regulated by upstream kinases (MKK4 (mitogen-activated protein kinase kinase 4)/MKK7 and MKK3/MKK6, respectively); hence, miR-6133-5p could selectively inhibit JNK without affecting p38 and it is sufficient for the suppression of *COL1A1* and *ACTA2* in LX-2 cells.

A comprehensive transcriptome analysis covering many time points is needed in a future study to dissect the effect of miR-6133-5p from the immediate-early suppression of direct target genes, middle-stage changes of signaling pathways, and late-stage changes, such as the downregulation of *COL1A1* and *ACTA2*. The role of miR-6133-5p in the fibrosis of other organs or tissues has also not been documented; further studies will be required to examine the effect of miR-6133-5p in various fibroblast cells of different organ origins.

In conclusion, we found that miR-6133-5p has strong anti-fibrotic effect which could be mediated by inactivation of TGFBR2, Akt, and JNK.

4. Materials and Methods

4.1. Cell Culture and Transfection

LX-2 cells were cultured in Dulbecco's modified Eagle's medium (Thermo Fisher Scientific, Waltham, MA, USA) supplemented with 1% antibiotic antimycotic solution and 2% heat-inactivated fetal bovine serum (Thermo Fisher Scientific). MiRIDIAN MicroRNA miR-6133-5p Mimic and MiRIDIAN MicroRNA Mimic Negative Control #1 (miControl) were purchased from Horizon Discovery Group plc. (Cambridge, UK). ON-TARGETplus siRNA SMARTpools targeting *SMAD2*, *SMAD3*, *SMAD4*, *AKT1*, *AKT2*, *AKT3*, and *FGFR1*; and ON-TARGETplus Non-targeting Pool (siControl) were purchased from Horizon Discovery Group plc. Each SMARTpool contains four independent siRNA molecules to ensure efficient gene knockdown. Silencer Select siRNA reagents corresponding to 36 predicted target genes of miR-6133-5p and Silencer Select negative control siRNA were purchased from Thermo Fisher Scientific. Two independent Silencer Select siRNA molecules for each gene were mixed equally and used in the following assay to ensure efficient gene knockdown. The sequence information of the siRNAs used in this study was shown in Supplementary Table S4.

miRNAs or siRNAs were introduced into LX-2 cells at a final concentration of 20 nmol/L using Lipofectamine RNAiMAX Reagent (Thermo Fisher Scientific), according to the manufacturer's instructions. Twenty-four hours after transfection, the cells were further cultured with medium containing 5 ng/mL of rhTGF-β1. The cells were then harvested and subjected to RNA and protein extraction at the time points indicated in Figure 1A.

4.2. Gene Expression Analysis by RT-qPCR

Total RNA was extracted using ISOGEN (Nippon Gene, Toyama, Japan). Gene expression was determined by RT-qPCR using StepOne Plus (Thermo Fisher Scientific). The primer–probe sets for RT-qPCR analysis of human *COL1A1*, *ACTA2*, *TGFBR2*, *FGFR1*, and *GAPDH* genes were purchased from Thermo Fisher Scientific.

4.3. Quantification of Protein

Cell lysates were prepared using a lysis buffer containing 1% Nonidet P40, 150 mM sodium chloride, and 50 mM Tris-Cl buffer (pH 7.4). A cOmplete Mini EDTA-free tablet and a PhosSTOP tablet (Roche diagnostics, Basel, Switzerland) were added to each 10 mL of the lysis buffer immediately before use. Western blot analyses were performed by a routine procedure using the primary antibodies listed below with the species, target, company, catalogue number, and dilution: mouse anti-collagen Iα1 (sc-293182, Santa Cruz, Dallas, TX, USA, 1:1000); rabbit anti-α-SMA (GTX100034, GeneTex, Irvine, CA, USA, 1:1000); rabbit anti-phospho-Smad2/3 (#8828, Cell Signaling Technology, Danvers, MA, USA, 1:2000); rabbit anti-Smad2/3 (#8685, Cell Signaling Technology, 1:2000); rabbit anti-phospho-Akt (#9271, Cell Signaling Technology, 1:2000); rabbit anti-Akt (#9272, Cell Signaling Technology, 1:2000); mouse anti-phospho-ERK (#9106, Cell Signaling Technology, 1:2000); rabbit anti-ERK (#9102, Cell Signaling Technology, 1:2000); rabbit anti-phospho-JNK (#9251, Cell Signaling Technology, 1:2000); rabbit anti-JNK (#9252, Cell Signaling Technology, 1:2000); rabbit anti-phospho-p38 (#9211, Cell Signaling Technology, 1:2000); rabbit anti-p38 (#9212, Cell Signaling Technology, 1:2000); mouse anti-GAPDH (ab8245, Abcam, Cambridge, UK, 1:10,000). The intensity of the bands was calculated using ImageJ v1.8.0 (https://imagej.nih.gov/ij/index.html).

4.4. RNAseq Analysis

Total RNA samples collected from miR-6133-5p- and miControl-treated LX-2 cells ($n = 2$) 24 h after rhTGF-β1 treatment were subjected to an RNAseq analysis. PolyA + RNA was extracted, fragmented, and reverse-transcribed to yield a single-stranded cDNA mixture. Double-stranded DNA was then synthesized using the cDNA mixture as a template. The ends of the product were blunted, phosphorylated, followed by addition of 3'-deoxyadenosine, and ligated with adapter DNA fragments containing an index sequence unique to each sample. After amplification by PCR, the resultant sequencing libraries were subjected to pair-end sequencing (sequence length = 150 bases) using NovaSeq 6000, NovaSeq 6000 S4 Reagent Kit, and NovaSeq Xp 4-Lane Kit (Illumina Inc., San Diego, CA, USA). The reads were mapped and annotated using GeneData Profiler Genome v11.0.4a (GeneData, Basel, Switzerland) and STAR v2.5.3a (https://github.com/alexdobin/STAR). *Homo sapiens* genome assembly GRCh37 (hg19) was used as the reference. The number of reads and the percentage of mapped reads for each sample are shown in Supplementary Table S3. Read counts underwent the trimmed mean of M values (TMM) normalization and log2 computes counts per million (CPM) transformation using the edgeR software v3.30.3 [31]. Differences in gene expression between miR-6133-5p and miControl were tested by a quasi-likelihood test function (glmQLFit). We set a false-discovery rate (FDR) threshold of 0.01 to correct for multiple testing and set a log-fold change (Log2FC) threshold of 0.8. The RNAseq data were deposited in the Gene Expression Omnibus database (accession number: GSE158478, https://www.ncbi.nlm.nih.gov/geo/).

To functionally characterize miR-6133-5p, we performed a pathway analysis using the GSVA R package (https://www.bioconductor.org/packages/release/bioc/html/GSVA.html) [32]. The gene sets used were the Kyoto Encyclopedia of Genes and Genomes (KEGG) pathway and all GO gene sets from the Broad Institute's Molecular Signatures Database (MSigDB) v7.1. The top differentially enriched pathways were yielded along with *p*-values adjusted for multiple testing correction using the Benjamini–Hochberg FDR controlling procedure. Cytoscape software v3.6.2 [33] was employed to construct the miRNA–mRNA gene network. All data were analyzed in R (http://www.r-project.org/).

4.5. Statistical Analysis

The student's *t*-test was performed using Microsoft Excel. Data are depicted as the mean ± standard deviation, and *p*-values < 0.05 were considered significant: * $p < 0.05$, ** $p < 0.01$.

Supplementary Materials: Supplementary materials can be found at http://www.mdpi.com/1422-0067/21/19/7251/s1. Table S1: Downregulated genes listed in the gene set 'Extracellular matrix'; Table S2: Downregulated genes listed in the gene set 'Hallmark epithelial mesenchymal transition'; Table S3: The RNAseq Results; Table S4: Sequence information of the siRNAs used in this study; Figure S1: Characterization of genes controlled by miR-6133-5p.

Author Contributions: Conceptualization, Y.T.; investigation, S.H.-T., M.O., K.M., M.I., and K.K.; resources, Y.S.; writing—original draft preparation, S.H.-T.; writing—review and editing, Y.T.; project administration, Y.T.; funding acquisition, Y.T. All authors have read and agreed to the published version of the manuscript.

Funding: This study was partly supported by the Research Program on Hepatitis from the Japan Agency for Medical Research and Development (AMED), Grant Numbers JP20fk0210048 and JP20fk0310101.

Acknowledgments: We are grateful to Kyoko Ito for gene expression analyses and Mayumi Hojo for Western blot analyses.

Conflicts of Interest: The authors declare no conflict of interest.

Abbreviations

HBV	hepatitis B virus
HSCs	hepatic stellate cells
TGF-β	transforming growth factor β
α-SMA	α-smooth muscle actin
miRNA	microRNA
3'-UTRs	3'-untranslated regions
ERK	extracellular signal-regulated kinase
JNK	c-Jun N-terminal kinase
FGFR1	fibroblast growth factor 1
siRNA	small interfering RNA
GSEA	gene set enrichment analysis
GO	gene ontology

References

1. Sepanlou, S.G.; Safiri, S.; Bisignano, C.; Ikuta, K.S.; Merat, S.; Saberifiroozi, M.; Poustchi, H.; Tsoi, D.; Colombara, D.V.; Abdoli, A.; et al. The global, regional, and national burden of cirrhosis by cause in 195 countries and territories, 1990-2017: A systematic analysis for the Global Burden of Disease Study 2017. *Lancet Gastroenterol. Hepatol.* **2020**, *5*, 245–266. [CrossRef]
2. Graber-Stiehl, I. The silent epidemic killing more people than HIV, malaria or TB. *Nature* **2018**, *564*, 24–26. [CrossRef] [PubMed]
3. Bataller, R.; Brenner, D.A. Liver fibrosis. *J. Clin. Investig.* **2005**, *115*, 209–218. [CrossRef]
4. Cai, C.X.; Buddha, H.; Castelino-Prabhu, S.; Zhang, Z.; Britton, R.S.; Bacon, B.R.; Neuschwander-Tetri, B.A. Activation of Insulin-PI3K/Akt-p70S6K Pathway in Hepatic Stellate Cells Contributes to Fibrosis in Nonalcoholic Steatohepatitis. *Dig. Dis. Sci.* **2017**, *62*, 968–978. [CrossRef] [PubMed]
5. Reif, S.; Scanga, A.E.; Brenner, D.A.; Rippe, R.A. The role of AKT in hepatic stellate cell activation. *YGAST* **2001**, *120*, A27.
6. Schnabl, B.; Bradham, C.A.; Bennett, B.L.; Manning, A.M.; Stefanovic, B.; Brenner, D.A. TAK1/JNK and p38 have opposite effects on rat hepatic stellate cells. *Hepatology* **2001**, *34*, 953–963. [CrossRef]
7. Anania, F. Aldehydes potentiate α2(I) collagen gene activity by JNK in hepatic stellate cells. *Free Radic. Biol. Med.* **2001**, *30*, 846–857. [CrossRef]
8. Kluwe, J.; Pradere, J.P.; Gwak, G.Y.; Mencin, A.; De Minicis, S.; Österreicher, C.H.; Colmenero, J.; Bataller, R.; Schwabe, R.F. Modulation of Hepatic Fibrosis by c-Jun-N-Terminal Kinase Inhibition. *YGAST* **2010**, *138*, 347–359. [CrossRef]
9. Higashi, T.; Friedman, S.L.; Hoshida, Y. Hepatic stellate cells as key target in liver fibrosis. *Adv. Drug Deliv. Rev.* **2017**, *121*, 27–42. [CrossRef]
10. Krol, J.; Loedige, I.; Filipowicz, W. The widespread regulation of microRNA biogenesis, function and decay. *Nat. Rev. Genet.* **2010**, *11*, 597–610. [CrossRef]
11. Agarwal, V.; Bell, G.W.; Nam, J.-W.; Bartel, D.P. Predicting effective microRNA target sites in mammalian mRNAs. *Elife* **2015**, *4*, 101. [CrossRef] [PubMed]

12. Alvarez-Garcia, I.; Miska, E.A. MicroRNA functions in animal development and human disease. *Development* **2005**, *132*, 4653–4662. [CrossRef] [PubMed]
13. Ivey, K.N.; Srivastava, D. microRNAs as Developmental Regulators. *Cold Spring Harb. Perspect. Biol.* **2015**, *7*, a008144. [CrossRef] [PubMed]
14. Baltimore, D.; Boldin, M.P.; O'Connell, R.M.; Rao, D.S.; Taganov, K.D. MicroRNAs: New regulators of immune cell development and function. *Nat. Immunol.* **2008**, *9*, 839–845. [CrossRef]
15. Gailhouste, L.; Histopathol, T.O.H. Cancer-related microRNAs and their role as tumor suppressors and oncogenes in hepatocellular carcinoma. *Histol. Histopathol.* **2013**, *28*, 437–451.
16. Chuma, M.; Toyoda, H.; Matsuzaki, J.; Saito, Y.; Kumada, T.; Tada, T.; Kaneoka, Y.; Maeda, A.; Yokoo, H.; Ogawa, K.; et al. Circulating microRNA-1246 as a possible biomarker for early tumor recurrence of hepatocellular carcinoma. *Hepatol. Res.* **2019**, *49*, 810–822. [CrossRef]
17. Zheng, Z.; Wen, Y.; Nie, K.; Tang, S.; Chen, X.; Lan, S.; Pan, J.; Jiang, K.; Jiang, X.; Liu, P.; et al. Construction of a 13-microRNA-based signature and prognostic nomogram for predicting overall survival in patients with hepatocellular carcinoma. *Hepatol. Res.* **2020**, *50*, hepr.13538. [CrossRef]
18. Roderburg, C.; Urban, G.W.; Bettermann, K.; Vucur, M.; Zimmermann, H.; Schmidt, S.; Janssen, J.; Koppe, C.; Knolle, P.; Castoldi, M.; et al. Micro-RNA profiling reveals a role for miR-29 in human and murine liver fibrosis. *Hepatology* **2011**, *53*, 209–218. [CrossRef]
19. Ogawa, T.; Iizuka, M.; Sekiya, Y.; Yoshizato, K.; Ikeda, K.; Kawada, N. Suppression of type I collagen production by microRNA-29b in cultured human stellate cells. *Biochem. Biophys. Res. Commun.* **2010**, *391*, 316–321. [CrossRef]
20. Oba, S.; Kumano, S.; Suzuki, E.; Nishimatsu, H.; Takahashi, M.; Takamori, H.; Kasuya, M.; Ogawa, Y.; Sato, K.; Kimura, K.; et al. miR-200b Precursor Can Ameliorate Renal Tubulointerstitial Fibrosis. *PLoS ONE* **2010**, *5*, e13614. [CrossRef]
21. Hyun, J.; Wang, S.; Kim, J.; Rao, K.M.; Park, S.Y.; Chung, I.; Ha, C.-S.; Kim, S.-W.; Yun, Y.H.; Jung, Y. MicroRNA-378 limits activation of hepatic stellate cells and liver fibrosis by suppressing Gli3 expression. *Nat. Commun.* **2016**, *7*, 10993. [CrossRef] [PubMed]
22. Matsuura, K.; De Giorgi, V.; Schechterly, C.; Wang, R.Y.; Farci, P.; Tanaka, Y.; Alter, H.J. Circulating let-7 levels in plasma and extracellular vesicles correlate with hepatic fibrosis progression in chronic hepatitis C. *Hepatology* **2016**, *64*, 732–745. [CrossRef] [PubMed]
23. Naito, Y.; Hamada-Tsutsumi, S.; Yamamoto, Y.; Kogure, A.; Yoshioka, Y.; Watashi, K.; Ochiya, T.; Tanaka, Y. Screening of microRNAs for a repressor of hepatitis B virus replication. *Oncotarget* **2018**, *9*, 29857–29868. [CrossRef]
24. McMahon, B.J. The natural history of chronic hepatitis B virus infection. *Hepatology* **2009**, *49*, S45–S55. [CrossRef] [PubMed]
25. Huang, H.-Y.; Lin, Y.-C.-D.; Li, J.; Huang, K.-Y.; Shrestha, S.; Hong, H.-C.; Tang, Y.; Chen, Y.-G.; Jin, C.-N.; Yu, Y.; et al. miRTarBase 2020: Updates to the experimentally validated microRNA-target interaction database. *Nucleic Acids Res.* **2020**, *48*, D148–D154. [CrossRef]
26. Turner, N.; Grose, R. Fibroblast growth factor signalling: From development to cancer. *Nat. Rev. Cancer* **2010**, *10*, 116–129. [CrossRef] [PubMed]
27. Li, J.; Shi, S.; Srivastava, S.P.; Kitada, M.; Nagai, T.; Nitta, K.; Kohno, M.; Kanasaki, K.; Koya, D. FGFR1 is critical for the anti-endothelial mesenchymal transition effect of N-acetyl-seryl-aspartyl-lysyl-proline via induction of the MAP4K4 pathway. *Cell Death Dis.* **2017**, *8*, e2965. [CrossRef]
28. Schuster-Gaul, S.; Geisler, L.J.; McGeough, M.D.; Johnson, C.D.; Zagorska, A.; Li, L.; Wree, A.; Barry, V.; Mikaelian, I.; Jih, L.J.; et al. ASK1 inhibition reduces cell death and hepatic fibrosis in an Nlrp3 mutant liver injury model. *JCI Insight* **2020**, *5*, 3030. [CrossRef]
29. Delić, D.; Eisele, C.; Schmid, R.; Baum, P.; Wiech, F.; Gerl, M.; Zimdahl, H.; Pullen, S.S.; Urquhart, R. Urinary Exosomal miRNA Signature in Type II Diabetic Nephropathy Patients. *PLoS ONE* **2016**, *11*, e0150154. [CrossRef]
30. Dandri, M.; Burda, M.R.; Török, E.; Pollok, J.M.; Iwanska, A.; Sommer, G.; Rogiers, X.; Rogler, C.E.; Gupta, S.; Will, H.; et al. Repopulation of mouse liver with human hepatocytes and in vivo infection with hepatitis B virus. *Hepatology* **2001**, *33*, 981–988. [CrossRef]
31. Robinson, M.D.; McCarthy, D.J.; Smyth, G.K. edgeR: A Bioconductor package for differential expression analysis of digital gene expression data. *Bioinformatics* **2010**, *26*, 139–140. [CrossRef] [PubMed]

32. Hänzelmann, S.; Castelo, R.; Guinney, J. GSVA: Gene set variation analysis for microarray and RNA-seq data. *BMC Bioinform.* **2013**, *14*, 7–15. [CrossRef] [PubMed]
33. Shannon, P.; Markiel, A.; Ozier, O.; Baliga, N.S.; Wang, J.T.; Ramage, D.; Amin, N.; Schwikowski, B.; Ideker, T. Cytoscape: A software environment for integrated models of biomolecular interaction networks. *Genome Res.* **2003**, *13*, 2498–2504. [CrossRef] [PubMed]

© 2020 by the authors. Licensee MDPI, Basel, Switzerland. This article is an open access article distributed under the terms and conditions of the Creative Commons Attribution (CC BY) license (http://creativecommons.org/licenses/by/4.0/).

Review

Co-Occurrence of Hepatitis A Infection and Chronic Liver Disease

Tatsuo Kanda *, Reina Sasaki, Ryota Masuzaki, Hiroshi Takahashi, Taku Mizutani, Naoki Matsumoto, Kazushige Nirei and Mitsuhiko Moriyama

Division of Gastroenterology and Hepatology, Department of Medicine, Nihon University School of Medicine, 30-1 Oyaguchi-kamicho, Itabashi-ku, Tokyo 173-8610, Japan; sasaki.reina@nihon-u.ac.jp (R.S.); masuzaki.ryota@nihon-u.ac.jp (R.M.); hiroshi.t.215@gmail.com (H.T.); mattakunotaku1981@yahoo.co.jp (T.M.); matsumoto.naoki@nihon-u.ac.jp (N.M.); nirei.kazushige@nihon-u.ac.jp (K.N.); mizutani.taku@nihon-u.ac.jp (M.M.)
* Correspondence: kanda.tatsuo@nihon-u.ac.jp; Tel.: +81-3-3972-8111

Received: 10 August 2020; Accepted: 1 September 2020; Published: 2 September 2020

Abstract: Hepatitis A virus (HAV) infection occasionally leads to a critical condition in patients with or without chronic liver diseases. Acute-on-chronic liver disease includes acute-on-chronic liver failure (ACLF) and non-ACLF. In this review, we searched the literature concerning the association between HAV infection and chronic liver diseases in PubMed. Chronic liver diseases, such as metabolic associated fatty liver disease and alcoholic liver disease, coinfection with other viruses, and host genetic factors may be associated with severe hepatitis A. It is important to understand these conditions and mechanisms. There may be no etiological correlation between liver failure and HAV infection, but there is an association between the level of chronic liver damage and the severity of acute-on-chronic liver disease. While the application of an HAV vaccination is important for preventing HAV infection, the development of antivirals against HAV may be important for preventing the development of ACLF with HAV infection as an acute insult. The latter is all the more urgent given that the lives of patients with HAV infection and a chronic liver disease of another etiology may be at immediate risk.

Keywords: HBV; HCV; HIV; acute liver failure; nonalcoholic fatty liver diseases; NASH; GRP78

1. Introduction

Liver failure is a common disease with high mortality, and its incidence is increasing with the use of alcohol and the prevalence of obesity and diabetes [1–3]. It has also been reported that the prognosis of acute hepatitis or acute liver injury was affected by the preexistence of chronic liver diseases and cirrhosis [1,2], extrahepatic diseases, such as metabolic, malignant, and psychiatric diseases [4], and host factors, such as older age and obesity [3,5,6], although the etiology of acute insults is one of the most important risk factors for the development of severe liver diseases [1,7].

Hepatitis A virus (HAV) infection is still one of the major causes of acute hepatitis worldwide. HAV infection occasionally causes acute liver failure [4,8]. It has been reported that a superinfection of HAV in patients with a chronic hepatitis C virus (HCV) infection is associated with fulminant hepatitis [9], although much research denies this association [5,10]. HAV infection rarely causes acute liver failure in patients without underlying chronic liver diseases [9].

There are excellent, safe, and effective HAV vaccines to prevent HAV infection. However, HAV vaccination costs a lot. As no universal vaccination program against HAV infection exists in certain countries, such as Japan, it may be important to develop potential drugs against HAV infection [11].

In this review, we searched the recent literature concerning the association between HAV infection and chronic liver diseases, including metabolic associated fatty liver disease (MAFLD), in PubMed. We also discussed the mechanism of severe acute hepatitis A.

2. Acute-On-Chronic Liver Failure with HAV Infection as an Acute Insult

Acute-on-chronic liver diseases include acute-on-chronic liver failure (ACLF) and non-ACLF [12]. ACLF, which presents acutely with multiple organ failure and is precipitated by an acute insult, has high short-term mortality [2,13]. In general, the prognosis of ACLF is worse than that of acute liver failure. ACLF is a distinct concept, where acute hepatic decompensation occurs in patients with chronic liver disease or cirrhosis in encountering an acute insult, leading to high short-term mortality [2]. In Asian countries, hepatitis viruses are important factors of acute insults, unlike in European countries and the United States [2], and HAV is one of the acute insults of ACLF [1,12,14–17].

HAV superinfection was found to be the most common etiology (42%) of acute deterioration in children with ACLF in India [15]. ACLF in adults was found to be due to HEV, HAV, or both in 61%, 27%, and 6% of cases [1], respectively, although HAV infections occur in childhood, and HAV infection as an acute insult in adult ACLF is relatively uncommon in India [17]. Agrawal et al. reported an adult patient with ACLF and HAV as an acute insult who had an underlying cirrhotic liver due to nonalcoholic steatohepatitis (NASH) [17]. Among the children and adults with ACLF, acute insults caused by both HAV and HEV are important. It may be important to consider them in order to improve the prognosis of ACLF by developing a treatment for HAV infection.

3. HAV Infection and Metabolic Associated Fatty Liver Disease (MAFLD)

ACLF may occur among patients with chronic liver diseases or cirrhosis due to nonalcoholic fatty liver diseases (NAFLD), including NASH and alcoholic liver diseases (ALD), in eastern and western countries [2,13]. NASH is the most rapidly increasing etiology for ACLF [18]. Agrawal et al. reported a nonobese 34-year-old man presenting ACLF with acute HAV infection superimposed on NASH without cirrhosis [17] (Table 1). Kahraman et al. also reported a human immunodeficiency virus (HIV)-positive case presenting ACLF with acute HAV infection superimposed on cirrhosis due to NASH [19]. NASH is also observed among people less than 40 years old, and acute-on-chronic liver diseases may have an atypical course among these patients [20].

Table 1. Acute-on-chronic liver failure with hepatitis A virus (HAV) infection in patients with nonalcoholic steatohepatitis (NASH) or chronic alcoholic liver diseases (ALD).

Authors (Year) [References]	N	Acute Insults	Underlying CLD	Prognosis
Agrawal S, et al. (2018) [17]	1	HAV	NASH	Recovered
Kahraman A, et al. (2006) [19]	1	HAV	NASH and HIV	Died
Lefillatre P, et al. (2000) [21]	1	HAV	ALD	Died
Spada E, et al. (2005) [22]	2	HAV	ALD and HCV	Died

CLD, chronic liver diseases; HIV, human immunodeficiency virus; ALD, alcoholic liver disease; HCV, hepatitis C virus.

Fatty liver diseases associated with metabolic dysfunction are common and have a heterogeneous genetic predisposition, metabolic syndrome, and environmental factors [23]. Recently, experts suggested "MAFLD" should replace NAFLD/NASH [23]. The diagnosis of MAFLD is based on the detection of liver steatosis in the presence of overweight or obesity, diabetes mellitus, and/or clinical evidence of metabolic abnormalities, such as hypertension, dyslipidemia, and hyperglycemia.

A Japanese nationwide survey of ALF and late-onset hepatic failure (LOHF) caused by HAV infection suggested that diabetic mellitus was more common among deceased patients than among rescued patients (29% vs. 8%; $p < 0.05$), excluding patients with liver transplantations, and that diabetic mellitus was independently associated with the outcome [24]. Patients with diabetes are at risk of developing severe hepatitis [25].

We observed that HAV HA11-1299 genotype IIIA strain replication is enhanced by the accumulation of lipids or high-concentration glucose in the human hepatoma cell line, Huh7 [26–28]. Hyperglycemia or the accumulation of lipids induces an endoplasmic reticulum (ER) stress response in human hepatocytes. HAV replicates in the ER of human hepatocytes and induces an ER stress response. The ER stress response is mediated by the sensor molecules, inositol-requiring enzyme 1α (IRE1α), PKR-like ER kinase (PERK), and activating transcription factor 6 (ATF6), which are usually associated with molecular chaperone glucose-regulated protein 78 (GRP78) [27]. GRP78 is a negative regulator of ER stress response. We also observed that the overexpression of GRP78 could inhibit HAV replication, while the knockdown or knockout of GRP78 enhanced HAV replication [26,28]. In sum, GRP78 is an antiviral protein against HAV replication [28].

4. HAV Infection and Alcoholic Liver Diseases (ALD)

There are several factors affecting the severity of HAV infection and the rates of fulminant hepatic failure [29]. These important factors include older age, concomitant virus infection, chronic liver disease, sexual orientation, intravenous drug use, and alcohol abuse [6,29]. Feller et al. reported that 12 patients developed hepatic encephalopathy, ascites, or both, among 20 patients with alcoholic cirrhosis and a superimposed episode of acute viral hepatitis [30]. HAV infection was excluded in only three of these patients [30].

Lefilliatre et al. reported that three patients with fulminant hepatitis A had preexisting liver diseases, and one of the three had biopsy-proven alcoholic cirrhosis [21] (Table 1). Spada et al. reported that two individuals were HCV-coinfected alcohol abusers, had underlying liver cirrhosis, and died of acute liver failure due to HAV infection [22] (Table 1).

While the direct effects of alcohol on HAV replication is unknown, excess alcohol intake (binge drinking) could induce hepatic fibrosis. As only alcohol intake is responsible for worsening ACLF with alcoholic chronic liver diseases and alcoholic cirrhosis [31], HAV may have an additive responsibility for worsening ACLF with ALD.

5. Coinfection of HAV with HIV

In Japan, where no universal vaccination programs against HAV infection exist, 10–20% of those with HIV infection tested positive for immunoglobulin G (IgG) anti-hepatitis A (HA) antibodies [32–35]. This prevalence is similar to that of IgG anti-HA in those without HIV infection [36,37], although a higher prevalence area can also be observed in Japan [38]. In general, individuals of high-risk groups, such as healthcare workers, sewage workers, and drug addicts, have ~60% of IgG anti-HA worldwide [39,40]. The seroprevalence of IgG anti-HA is relatively higher in people living with HIV worldwide [41–43].

HIV infection has also been reported as a cause of liver damage in patients infected with HIV [40]. Thus, it is as important to consider patients with HIV infection as those with chronic liver disease. Not only chronic viral hepatitis B or C but also drug-induced liver injury induced by the antiretroviral drugs, NAFLD and ALD, has also been observed in people with HIV [40].

HAV infection in patients with chronic liver diseases and coinfected with HIV are shown in Table 2 [21,22,44,45]. Prolonged HAV infection was also reported in an HIV-seropositive patient [44]. It was reported that the recovery of immunity through recently developed anti-HIV therapies may lead to more severe hepatocellular damage in patients with HAV infection [45].

HAV infects humans through fecal–oral routes, when HAV-contaminated water and food are consumed. Among men who have sex with men (MSM), HAV is sexually transmitted [46], and HAV outbreaks have been observed [47–55]. It is noteworthy that acute hepatitis A among MSM is one of the male-dominant diseases, although, in general, no gender difference exists in patients with an HAV infection caused by HAV-contaminated water and food. While HAV may cause severe hepatitis in people living with HIV, two doses of an HAV vaccine are more effective for them to achieve a sustained HAV seroresponse than a single dose of an HAV vaccine [56].

Table 2. Coinfection with hepatitis A virus (HAV) and human immunodeficiency virus (HIV).

Authors (Year) [References]	N	Acute Insults	Underlying CLD	Prognosis
Lefillatre P, et al. (2000) [21]	1	HAV	HBV, HCV, and HIV	Died
Spada E, et al. (2005) [22]	1	HAV	HCV and HIV	Died
Costa-Mattioli et al. (2002) [44]	1	HAV	HIV	Alive; HAV RNA detected in 256 days
Maki Y, et al. (2020) [45]	1	HAV	HIV	Died

CLD, chronic liver diseases; HBV, hepatitis B virus; HCV, hepatitis C virus.

6. Coinfection of HAV with HBV

Several cases of ACLF with HAV as an acute insult and chronic hepatitis or cirrhosis due to HBV, as well as cases with a superinfection of HAV in patients with HBV, have been reported (Table 3) [9,21,57–62]. A superinfection of HBsAg carriers with HAV seems not to cause more severe conditions [57]. Patients with HBV plus HAV infection had a less advanced baseline liver disease and a better prognosis than those with HBV plus hepatitis E virus infection [60].

Table 3. Acute-on-chronic liver failure and/or superinfection of hepatitis virus (HAV) in patients with hepatitis B virus (HBV).

Authors (Year) [References]	N	Acute Insults	Underlying CLD	Prognosis
Tassopoulos N, et al. (1985) [57]	10	HAV	HBV	Recovered
Vento S, et al. (1998) [9]	10	HAV	HBV	Recovered (marked cholestasis, 1)
Lefillatre P, et al. (2000) [21]	1	HAV	HBV	Died
Cooksley WGE, et al. (2000) [58]	27,346	HAV	HBV	Died, 15 (0.05%)
Sagnelli E, et al. (2006) [59]	13	HAV	HBV	Recovered (severe hepatitis, 1)
Zhang X, et al. (2010) [60]	52	HAV	HBV	Died, 1 (1.9%) [Hepatic failure, 6 (11.5%)]
Fu J, et al. (2016) [61]	35	HAV	HBV	Recovered
Beisei C, et al. (2020) [62]	1	HAV	HBV	Recovered (seroconversion of HBeAg to anti-HBe)
Lefillatre P, et al. (2000) [21]	1	HAV	HBV, HCV, and HIV	Died

CLD, chronic liver diseases; HCV, hepatitis C virus; HIV, human immunodeficiency virus; HBeAg, hepatitis B virus e antigen.

Vento et al. reported that, among 10 patients with an acquired HAV superinfection and chronic HBV infection, one (10%), who had cirrhosis, had marked cholestasis [9]. Pramoolsinsap et al. evaluated acute superinfection with HAV in 20 HBV asymptomatic carriers and fulminant hepatitis or submassive hepatitis in 11 (55%) of 20 HBsAg carriers [63]. A superinfection of HAV in patients with HBV occasionally leads to critical conditions in HBV carriers with or without cirrhosis, although patients with advanced fibrosis or cirrhosis are more susceptible to severe conditions [9,21,57–63].

A total of 310,746 cases with acute hepatitis A were observed during the Shanghai hepatitis A epidemic [58]. A total of 47 fatal cases (0.015%) were reported. Fatality rates were 0.05% (15/27,346) and 0.009% (25/283,400) in patients with or without HBV infection, respectively. It is worth noting that there were 5.6-fold greater fatality rates in patients with HBV infection than in those without [58]. Cooksley et al. reported that patients infected with HBV who have raised ALT levels and high HBV levels have a higher risk of liver failure following HAV superinfection [58]. HAV vaccination seems to be effective in preventing liver failure associated with HAV in patients with or without HBV infection [64–67]. However, HAV vaccination may not be necessary in the case of countries in which HAV is endemic, such as India [68,69].

It has been reported that the transient suppression of HBV replication and the disappearance of HBV DNA with the seroconversion of HBeAg were observed in several cases of double infections with HAV and HBV carries [57]. Beisel et al. also reported that an HBsAg carrier case with HAV superinfection presented the seroconversion of HBsAg, suggesting that unspecific immunological responses to HAV could lead to a functional cure of HBV [62]. It was reported that the sharp peak in interferon-gamma production induced by a superinfection of HAV may lead to the suppression of HBV replication in patients with chronic hepatitis B [70]. This peak in interferon-gamma production occurred just before the rise in serum transaminase activity, resulting in a decrease in HBV DNA and HBeAg.

Berthillon et al. infected the human hepatoma cell line, PLC/PRF/5 [71], which integrates HBV DNA and produces HBsAg, with the HAV CF53 strain [72]. The inhibition of HBsAg production in PLC/PRF/5 cells infected with HAV was observed, compared with those without HAV infection, demonstrating that HAV interferes with the expression of HBsAg from hepatocytes harboring integrated HBV DNA sequences [71]. We also infected HepG2.2.15, which produces HBV virion or HepG2 cells, with the HAV HA11-1299 strain. We demonstrated that the HAV replication is similar between HepG2.2.15 and HepG2, 96 h after HAV infection. However, HBV replication is inhibited in HAV-infected HepG2.2.15, compared to HepG2.2.15 without HAV infection [73].

We also observed that the replication of both HAV and HBV is suppressed in human hepatocyte PXB cells superinfected with HAV and HBV, compared to those mono-infected with HAV or HBV [73]. Thus, HAV infection seems to inhibit HBV replication. Further studies are required to support this point, although it indicates that the existence of cirrhosis or advanced liver fibrosis should cause severe hepatitis in the superinfection of HAV in patients with HBV.

7. Coinfection of HAV with HCV

In general, HCV is a rare cause of fulminant hepatitis or acute liver failure [74,75]. We did not identify any cases of fulminant hepatitis with HCV RNA in 82 cases of fulminant hepatitis and late-onset hepatic failure from 1986 to 2001, which were examined at Chiba University School of Medicine, Japan [74]. There were several reports that HAV infection in patients with chronic hepatitis C is associated with increased mortality [9,21,22,76], although several contrary opinions exist [59,77] (Table 4).

Table 4. Acute-on-chronic liver failure (ACLF) and/or the superinfection of hepatitis virus (HAV) in patients with hepatitis C virus (HCV).

Authors (Year) [References]	N	Acute Insults	Underlying CLD	Prognosis
Vento S, et al. (1998) [9]	17	HAV	HCV	Recovered, 10; fulminant hepatitis, 7
Sagnelli E, et al. (2006) [59]	8	HAV	HCV	Recovered
Deterding K, et al. (2006) [77]	17	HAV	HCV	Fulminant hepatitis, 0
Spada E, et al. (2005) [22]	1	HAV	HCV and ALD	Died
Spada E, et al. (2005) [22]	1	HAV	HCV and HIV	Died
Lefillatre P, et al. (2000) [21]	1	HAV	HBV plus HCV and HIV	Died

CLD, chronic liver diseases; HBV, hepatitis B virus; ALD, alcoholic liver disease; HIV, human immunodeficiency virus.

Vento et al. reported that, among 17 patients with an acquired HAV superinfection with chronic hepatitis C, seven patients (41.2%) possessed fulminant hepatic failure, and six (85.7%) of those seven patients died [9]. It is interesting to note that antinuclear antibodies, anti-smooth-muscle antibodies, and/or anti-asialoglycoprotein receptor antibodies were detected in five of seven patients with fulminant hepatitis (71.4%) [9]. Moreover, six of these seven patients possessed chronic active hepatitis, and one patient recovered from fulminant hepatitis and was treated with methylprednisolone [9]. There are some reports indicating a higher fatality rate of HAV superinfection in patients with chronic HCV infection, not considering those with or without cirrhosis [21]. However, it is unclear whether the high fatality rates were due to severe underlying liver damage or not [21,22].

It was reported that the superinfection of HAV is associated with decreased HCV replication, which may lead to a clearance of HCV [77,78]. Esser-Nobis et al. found that Huh7-Lunet cells supported HAV and HCV replication with similar efficacy and limited interference with each other [79].

In fact, as several severe hepatitis A cases have been observed in patients with chronic HCV infection, clinicians should pay attention to HAV infection in HCV-infected individuals [80]. At present, although direct-acting antivirals against HCV can lead to a higher sustained virological response with less adverse events, no effective HCV vaccines are available. Thus, HAV vaccination should be considered for HCV-infected patients, especially those with cirrhosis or advanced fibrosis [81–88].

8. HAV and Other Chronic Liver Diseases

It was reported that a prospective study of 31 children in the age group of 1–16 years, who fulfilled the criteria for ACLF of the Asian Pacific Association for the Study of the Liver (APASL) 2008 consensus, found 13 ACLF cases of HAV as an acute insult and autoimmune hepatitis or Wilson disease as causes of chronic liver disease [15]. In children, acute-on-chronic liver diseases, HEV, and HAV are more frequently causes of acute insults and Wilson disease, while autoimmune liver disease and primary sclerosing cholangitis are more frequently causes of chronic liver disease [12]. It is possible that HAV infection, as an acute insult, could result in ACLF in patients with any chronic liver disease, especially cirrhosis. Careful attention should also be paid to HAV infection in adults and children who have certain chronic liver diseases.

9. Host Genetic Factors in HAV Infection

Acute insults in ACLF are different, depending on the country in which they are found [2]. In Asian countries, European countries, and the United States, hepatic, hepatic, and extrahepatic or infection (extrahepatic) causes, respectively, are representative acute insults in the definition of the APASL, EASL, and NACSELD ACLF guidelines [2,89–91]. Of course, not only a sanitary environment but also host genetic factors are different in these different regions. Among Mexican Americans, transforming growth factor beta 1 (TGFB1) rs1800469 (adjusted odds ratio (OR), 1.38; 95% confidence interval (CI), 1.14–1.68; P value adjusted for false discovery rate (FDR-P) = 0.017) and X-ray repair cross complementing 1 (XRCC1) rs1799782 (OR, 1.57; 95% CI, 1.27–1.94; FDR-P = 0.0007) were associated with an increased risk of HAV infection [92]. ATP-binding cassette subfamily B member 1 (ABCB1) rs1045642 (OR, 0.79; 95% CI, 0.71–0.89; FDR-P = 0.0007) was associated with a decreased risk [92]. Host genetic factors may also play an important role in determining the differential susceptibility to HAV infection [92–94].

10. Prevention of HAV Infection in Patients with Chronic Liver Diseases

10.1. HAV Vaccination

HAV vaccination may be important for patients with chronic liver diseases, especially those with cirrhosis [81–88]. While a universal vaccination program against HAV seems to be the most effective solution for the prevention of HAV infection, it may be difficult to carry out this program worldwide due to the high costs of HAV vaccine production and its low effectiveness in certain countries in which the infection is endemic [88,95]. HAV vaccination targeting certain populations may also be effective and important in this regard [96]. Antivirals against HAV infection may also be needed (Figure 1). The unknown causes for chronic injury constitute only 5–15% of cases of ACLF [2].

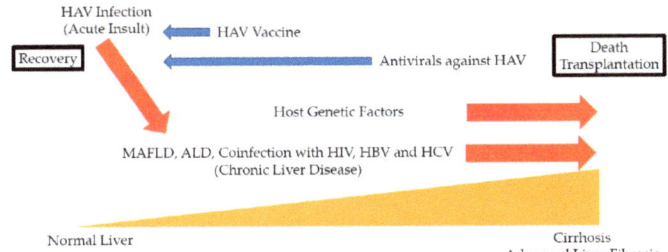

Figure 1. Effects of hepatitis A infection (HAV) on the prognosis of chronic liver disease. Possible acceleration and inhibition of the disease progression of hepatitis A are indicated by red and blue arrows, respectively. MAFLD, metabolic associated fatty liver disease; ALD, alcoholic liver disease; HIV, human immunodeficiency virus; HBV, hepatitis B virus; HCV, hepatitis C virus.

10.2. Japanese Rice-Koji Miso Extracts and Zinc Sulfates Could Inhibit HAV Replication with the Enhancement of GRP78 Expression

Japanese rice-koji miso extracts enhanced GRP78 expression and inhibited HAV HA11-1299 genotype IIIA strain replication in the human hepatocytes, Huh7 and PXB cells [97]. We investigated the effect of miso extracts on virus replication in HepG2.2.15 cells infected with the HAV HA11-1299 strain [73]. It is noteworthy that miso extracts have an inhibitory effect on HAV replication but no inhibitory effect on HBV replication. Japanese rice-koji miso extracts may have an inhibitory effect on HAV replication in patients superinfected with HAV and HBV.

The zinc homeostasis pathway was identified as a key pathway of the antiviral activity of Japanese rice-koji miso against HAV infection using transcriptome-sequencing analysis [98]. We also demonstrated that zinc sulfate has an inhibitory effect on HAV HA11-1299 replication in human hepatocytes with the enhancement of GRP78 expression [98]. As Japanese miso soup and zinc sulfate are traditional foods and drugs, respectively, they induce GRP78 expression and are useful and safe antiviral compounds against HAV, with fewer adverse events. Gut dysbiosis and increased permeability cause pathological bacterial translocation and endotoxemia, which play an important role in the development of ACLF [2]. HAV infects the liver by the gut-portal vein–liver axis through fecal–oral routes. The digestion and absorption of Japanese rice-koji miso extracts and zinc sulfate may be used through similar routes.

10.3. Candidates of Antivirals against HAV in Chronic Liver Diseases

The inhibitory effects of interferon-alpha, interferon-gamma, interferon-lambda, ribavirin, amantadine, sirtinol, and AZD1480 as host-targeting drugs and HAV 3C cysteine protease inhibitors, as well as small interfering RNAs against HAV, as antivirals that directly act on HAV replication, have been reported [11,46,99]. Interferon has antiviral potential against HAV [100,101], but it is difficult to use interferon in patients with ACLF, as interferon generally has cytotoxicity. Peginterferon-lambda has fewer side effects than peginterferon-alpha and may be useful in some patients with HAV infection. Amantadine is a broad-spectrum antiviral and has an inhibitory effect on HAV replication through the targeting of HAV internal entry site (IRES) activity [100,102,103]. The sirtuin inhibitor, sirtinol, also inhibits HAV replication by inhibiting HAV IRES activity [104]. Further studies on the mechanism of the sirtuin inhibitor and JAK pathways in HAV replication are needed [104,105]. In patients with chronic liver diseases or ACLF, these drugs should be improved, and more safe drugs are needed and should be explored. It has been reported that HCV receptor candidates, such as HAV cellular receptor 1 (HAVcr-1), integrin β1, and gangliosides, are the entry receptor candidates for HAV. Further studies in this vein are needed [106–108]. Gangliosides seem to function as endosome receptors for infection using both naked and quasi-enveloped HAV virions [108]. Blocking the cellular entry of HAV is also an attractive drug target for combating HAV infection.

10.4. HAV Infection Is Associated with the Activation of the Host Immune System and Severe Systemic Inflammation

Acute hepatitis A usually exhibits more severe inflammation, such as a higher fever and higher C-reactive protein levels, compared to acute hepatitis due to other hepatitis viruses [109–111]. Some cases of acute HAV infection present acute renal failure [112–114]. These results suggest that HAV infection activates human immune systems and induces cytokines [115–119]. Innate immunity also seems to be involved in the pathogenesis of hepatitis A [120,121]. Hypergammaglobulinemia and a high occurrence of autoantibodies are observed in HAV infection [122,123]. This may support the immunological basis of its pathogenesis. Moreover, the higher gammaglobulinemia in fulminant HAV suggests the existence of a more aggressive immunological reaction in severe hepatitis A [123].

Severe systemic inflammation can affect the functions of somatic cells in tissue and modify the clinical manifestation of cirrhosis and ACLF [124,125]. Patients with acute liver failure or ACLF are susceptible to infection, and early transplant-free survival is poor [126–129]. In liver transplantation for patients with ACLF, the role of the timing, bridging, and management of liver transplantation is important [130,131].

10.5. Recent Outbreak of HAV Infection in MSM

It has recently been reported that HAV susceptibility parallels the high COVID-19 mortality [132]. The 2019 coronavirus disease (COVID-19) has been observed in Japan, where the HAV susceptibility of the general population is high [34,35]. An HAV vaccination program is urgently required for individuals with or without HIV infection in this area. HAV infection is an imported infection, like novel severe acute respiratory syndrome coronavirus 2 (SARS-CoV-2) infection [133]. In the era of COVID-19, attention should also be paid to dual infection with HAV and SARS-CoV-2.

An outbreak of HAV infection in MSM has been observed worldwide. An outbreak of acute HAV infection among HIV-coinfected MSM in Taiwan was observed from June 2015 to September 2017 [50,134,135]. Between July 2016 and February 2017, 48 male cases of HAV infection were found in the Netherlands [48]. A total of 17 of them were MSM. This strain is identical to a strain causing a large outbreak among MSM in Taiwan [48]. In the United States, HAV infections also increased among MSM from 2016 to 2018 [54,136,137]. Since 2017, HAV infection has increased among MSM in Japan [34,37,52]. RIVM-HAV16-090-like hepatitis A virus strains, which were >99.6% identical to the 66 reported strains isolated from Taiwan and European countries from 2015 to 2017, were also recovered from Japanese MSM [52]. A recent outbreak of HAV infection was also reported in various countries, such as Brazil, Spain, and Italy [53,138–140].

11. Possible Molecular Mechanism of the Development of ACLF in Patients with HAV Infection

The molecular mechanism of the development of ACLF in patients with HAV infection is not fully understood. The possible mechanisms of the development of liver failure in the presence of coinfection with HCV and HAV are as follows. HAV is a virus that is generally sensitive to interferon [100–102]. In comparison with HCV, HAV induces a limited production of type I interferon when HAV infects chimpanzees [141]. Compared with HBV and HCV, HAV weakly induced the activation of NF-κB signaling pathways in human hepatocytes [142,143]. While HAV VP3 activates cell growth signaling [143], HAV VP1/2A reduces cell viabilities in HCV sub-genomic replicon cells [144].

HAV is usually a non-cytopathic virus, and HAV inhibits double-stranded (dsRNA)-induced interferon-beta gene expression by influencing the interferon-beta enhanceosome, as well as dsRNA-induced apoptosis [145]. Compared with HBV and HCV, HAV could evade mitochondrial antiviral signaling protein (MAVS)-mediated type I interferon responses [146]. HAV 3ABC is capable of MAVS cleavage, like HCV NS3/4A, which cleaves MAVS and disrupts interferon signaling [147]. HAV 3C inhibits HAV IRES-dependent translation and cleaves the polypyrimidine tract-binding protein [148]. HCV induces interferon-beta signaling pathways in human hepatocytes [149]. Controlling the effects of interferon signaling may determine the prognosis of patients coinfected with HCV and HAV (Figure 2).

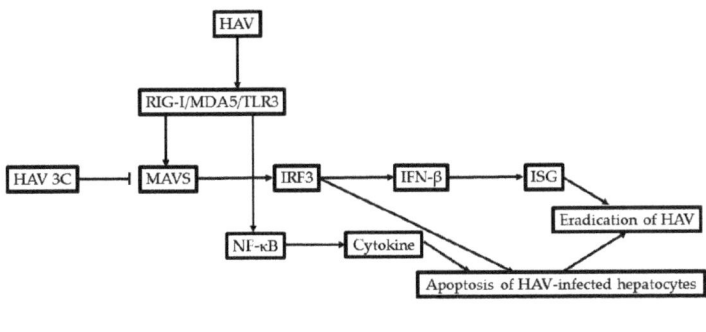

Figure 2. Possible molecular mechanism of the development of acute-on-chronic liver failure (ACLF) in patients coinfected with hepatitis A virus (HAV) and HCV. (**a**) Only HAV infection; (**b**) coinfection HAV and HCV. RIG-I, retinoic acid-inducible gene-I; MDA-5, melanoma differentiation associated gene 5; TLR3, toll-like receptor 3; MAVS, mitochondrial antiviral signaling protein; IRF3, interferon regulatory factor 3; IFN, interferon; ISG, interferon-stimulated gene; NF-κB, nuclear factor kappa B subunit 1.

HBV is a stealth virus which efficiently infects humans without alerting the innate immune system, although HCV strongly induces but cunningly evades the innate immune response [150]. The high glucose and fat deposition of hepatocytes seem to induce a chaperon-mediated autophagy (CMA) [151]. CMA targets interferon-alpha receptor chain-1 for degradation, dampens hepatic innate immunity, and disrupts interferon signaling pathways [151]. CMA is also observed in patients with ALD or MAFLD [152,153]. Altering interferon signaling may contribute to ALF-associated acute HAV infection. However, further studies are needed. Among HIV-positive patients with acute HAV infection, lower peaks in total bilirubin, AST, and ALT levels were observed in comparison with HIV-negative patients with acute HAV infection [154], suggesting that weaker immune responses occur in HIV-positive patients. These immune responses could enhance HAV replication and modify the pathogenesis in HIV-positive patients with acute hepatitis A [155].

12. Conclusions

We reviewed the literature concerning HAV infection in patients with chronic liver diseases. In patients with chronic liver diseases, HAV infection can occasionally lead to a critical condition, such as acute liver failure. There seems to be no etiological association between liver failure and HAV infection, but there is a significant correlation between the severity of liver disease and the degree to which the liver has already been damaged. While there are effective HAV vaccines currently in existence, antivirals against HAV should be further explored. The latter is urgent given that the lives of patients with HAV infection and a chronic liver disease of another etiology may be at immediate risk.

Author Contributions: Conceptualization, T.K., R.S. and R.M.; formal analysis, T.K.; investigation, T.K.; resources, T.K.; writing—original draft preparation, T.K.; writing—review and editing, T.K., R.S. and R.M.; supervision, H.T., T.M., N.M., K.N. and M.M.; funding acquisition, T.K. All authors have read and agreed to the published version of the manuscript.

Funding: This research was supported by the Japan Agency for Medical Research and Development (AMED), under grant number JP20fk0210075.

Conflicts of Interest: The authors declare no conflict of interest. The funders had no role in the design of the study; in the collection, analyses, or interpretation of data; in the writing of the manuscript, or in the decision to publish the results.

Abbreviations

HAV	Hepatitis A virus
HBV	Hepatitis B virus
HCV	Hepatitis C virus
MAFLD	Metabolic associated fatty liver disease
ACLF	Acute-on-chronic liver failure
NASH	Nonalcoholic steatohepatitis
NAFLD	Nonalcoholic fatty liver disease
HIV	Human immunodeficiency virus
LOHF	Late-onset hepatic failure
ER	Endoplasmic reticulum
IgG	Immunoglobulin
GRP78	Glucose-regulated protein 78
ALD	Alcoholic liver disease
CMA	Chaperon-mediated autophagy

References

1. Radha Krishna, Y.; Saraswat, V.A.; Das, K.; Himanshu, G.; Yachha, S.K.; Aggarwal, R.; Choudhuri, G. Clinical features and predictors of outcome in acute hepatitis A and hepatitis E virus hepatitis on cirrhosis. *Liver Int.* **2009**, *29*, 392–398. [CrossRef] [PubMed]
2. Sarin, S.K.; Choudhury, A.; Sharma, M.K.; Maiwall, R.; Al Mahtab, M.; Rahman, S.; Saigal, S.; Saraf, N.; Soin, A.S.; Devarbhavi, H.; et al. Acute-on-chronic liver failure: Consensus recommendations of the Asian Pacific association for the study of the liver (APASL): An update. *Hepatol. Int.* **2019**, *13*, 353–390. [CrossRef] [PubMed]
3. Kanda, T.; Yokosuka, O.; Hiraide, A.; Kojima, H.; Honda, A.; Fukai, K.; Imazeki, F.; Nagao, K.; Saisho, H. Prevalence of obesity in patients with acute hepatitis; is severe obesity a risk factor for fulminant hepatitis in Japan? *Hepatogastroenterology* **2005**, *52*, 180–182. [PubMed]
4. Nakao, M.; Nakayama, N.; Uchida, Y.; Tomiya, T.; Ido, A.; Sakaida, I.; Yokosuka, O.; Takikawa, Y.; Inoue, K.; Genda, T.; et al. Nationwide survey for acute liver failure and late-onset hepatic failure in Japan. *J. Gastroenterol.* **2018**, *53*, 752–769. [CrossRef] [PubMed]
5. Keeffe, E.B. Is hepatitis A more severe in patients with chronic hepatitis B and other chronic liver diseases? *Am. J. Gastroenterol.* **1995**, *90*, 201–205. [PubMed]
6. Sainokami, S.; Abe, K.; Ishikawa, K.; Suzuki, K. Influence of load of hepatitis A virus on disease severity and its relationship with clinical manifestations in patients with hepatitis A. *J. Gastroenterol. Hepatol.* **2005**, *20*, 1165–1175. [CrossRef]

7. Fujiwara, K.; Nakayama, N.; Kato, N.; Yokosuka, O.; Tsubouchi, H.; Takikawa, H.; Mochida, S.; Intractable Hepato-Biliary Diseases Study Group of Japan. Infectious complications and timing for liver transplantation in autoimmune acute liver failure in Japan: A subanalysis based on nationwide surveys between 2010 and 2015. *J. Gastroenterol.* **2020**. [CrossRef]
8. Tominaga, A.; Kanda, T.; Akiike, T.; Komoda, H.; Ito, K.; Abe, A.; Aruga, A.; Kaneda, S.; Saito, M.; Kiyohara, T.; et al. Hepatitis A outbreak associated with a revolving sushi bar in Chiba, Japan: Application of molecular epidemiology. *Hepatol. Res.* **2012**, *42*, 828–834. [CrossRef]
9. Vento, S.; Garofano, T.; Renzini, C.; Cainelli, F.; Casali, F.; Ghironzi, G.; Ferraro, T.; Concia, E. Fulminant hepatitis associated with hepatitis A virus superinfection in patients with chronic hepatitis C. *N. Engl. J. Med.* **1998**, *338*, 286–290. [CrossRef]
10. Mele, A.; Tosti, M.E.; Stroffolini, T. Hepatitis associated with hepatitis A superinfection in patients with chronic hepatitis C. *N. Engl. J. Med.* **1998**, *338*, 1771. [CrossRef]
11. Kanda, T.; Nakamoto, S.; Wu, S.; Nakamura, M.; Jiang, X.; Haga, Y.; Sasaki, R.; Yokosuka, O. Direct-acting Antivirals and Host-targeting Agents against the Hepatitis A Virus. *J. Clin. Transl. Hepatol.* **2015**, *3*, 205–210. [CrossRef] [PubMed]
12. Jagadisan, B.; Srivastava, A.; Yachha, S.K.; Poddar, U. Acute on chronic liver disease in children from the developing world: Recognition and prognosis. *J. Pediatr. Gastroenterol. Nutr.* **2012**, *54*, 77–82. [CrossRef] [PubMed]
13. Singal, A.K.; Kamath, P.S. Acute on chronic liver failure in non-alcoholic fatty liver and alcohol associated liver disease. *Transl. Gastroenterol. Hepatol.* **2019**, *4*, 74. [CrossRef] [PubMed]
14. Sarin, S.K.; Kumar, A.; Almeida, J.A.; Chawla, Y.K.; Fan, S.T.; Garg, H.; de Silva, H.J.; Hamid, S.S.; Jalan, R.; Komolmit, P.; et al. Acute-on-chronic liver failure: Consensus recommendations of the Asian Pacific Association for the study of the liver (APASL). *Hepatol. Int.* **2009**, *3*, 269–282. [CrossRef] [PubMed]
15. Lal, J.; Thapa, B.R.; Rawal, P.; Ratho, R.K.; Singh, K. Predictors of outcome in acute-on-chronic liver failure in children. *Hepatol. Int.* **2011**, *5*, 693–697. [CrossRef]
16. Kumar, A.; Saraswat, V.A. Hepatitis E and Acute-on-Chronic Liver Failure. *J. Clin. Exp. Hepatol.* **2013**, *3*, 225–230. [CrossRef]
17. Agrawal, S.; Rana, B.S.; Mitra, S.; Duseja, A.; Das, A.; Dhiman, R.K.; Chawla, Y. A Case of Acute-on-Chronic Liver Failure (ACLF) Due to An Uncommon Acute and Chronic Event. *J. Clin. Exp. Hepatol.* **2018**, *8*, 95–97. [CrossRef]
18. Axley, P.; Ahmed, Z.; Arora, S.; Haas, A.; Kuo, Y.F.; Kamath, P.S.; Singal, A.K. NASH Is the Most Rapidly Growing Etiology for Acute-on-Chronic Liver Failure-Related Hospitalization and Disease Burden in the United States: A Population-Based Study. *Liver Transpl.* **2019**, *25*, 695–705. [CrossRef]
19. Kahraman, A.; Miller, M.; Gieseler, R.K.; Gerken, G.; Scolaro, M.J.; Canbay, A. Non-alcoholic fatty liver disease in HIV-positive patients predisposes for acute-on-chronic liver failure: Two cases. *Eur. J. Gastroenterol. Hepatol.* **2006**, *18*, 101–105. [CrossRef]
20. Kanda, T.; Yokosuka, O.; Suzuki, Y. Prolonged hepatitis caused by cytomegalovirus and non-alcoholic steatohepatitis in 16-year-old obese boy. *Eur. J. Pediatr.* **2005**, *164*, 212–215. [CrossRef]
21. Lefilliatre, P.; Villeneuve, J.P. Fulminant hepatitis A in patients with chronic liver disease. *Can. J. Public Health* **2000**, *91*, 168–170. [CrossRef] [PubMed]
22. Spada, E.; Genovese, D.; Tosti, M.E.; Mariano, A.; Cuccuini, M.; Proietti, L.; Giuli, C.D.; Lavagna, A.; Crapa, G.E.; Morace, G.; et al. An outbreak of hepatitis A virus infection with a high case-fatality rate among injecting drug users. *J. Hepatol.* **2005**, *43*, 958–964. [CrossRef] [PubMed]
23. Eslam, M.; Sanyal, A.J.; George, J. International Consensus Panel. MAFLD: A Consensus-Driven Proposed Nomenclature for Metabolic Associated Fatty Liver Disease. *Gastroenterology* **2020**, *158*, 1999–2014.e1. [CrossRef] [PubMed]
24. Nakao, M.; Nakayama, N.; Uchida, Y.; Tomiya, T.; Oketani, M.; Ido, A.; Tsubouchi, H.; Takikawa, H.; Mochida, S. Deteriorated outcome of recent patients with acute liver failure and late-onset hepatic failure caused by infection with hepatitis A virus: A subanalysis of patients seen between 1998 and 2015 and enrolled in nationwide surveys in Japan. *Hepatol. Res.* **2019**, *49*, 844–852. [CrossRef] [PubMed]
25. Singh, K.K.; Panda, S.K.; Shalimar Acharya, S.K. Patients with Diabetes Mellitus are Prone to Develop Severe Hepatitis and Liver Failure due to Hepatitis Virus Infection. *J. Clin. Exp. Hepatol.* **2013**, *3*, 275–280. [CrossRef] [PubMed]

26. Win, N.N.; Kanda, T.; Nakamura, M.; Nakamoto, S.; Okamoto, H.; Yokosuka, O.; Shirasawa, H. Free fatty acids or high-concentration glucose enhances hepatitis A virus replication in association with a reduction in glucose-regulated protein 78 expression. *Biochem. Biophys. Res. Commun.* **2017**, *483*, 694–699. [CrossRef]
27. Jiang, X.; Kanda, T.; Nakamoto, S.; Haga, Y.; Sasaki, R.; Nakamura, M.; Wu, S.; Mikata, R.; Yokosuka, O. Knockdown of glucose-regulated protein 78 enhances poly(ADP-ribose) polymerase cleavage in human pancreatic cancer cells exposed to endoplasmic reticulum stress. *Oncol. Rep.* **2014**, *32*, 2343–2348. [CrossRef]
28. Jiang, X.; Kanda, T.; Haga, Y.; Sasaki, R.; Nakamura, M.; Wu, S.; Nakamoto, S.; Shirasawa, H.; Okamoto, H.; Yokosuka, O. Glucose-regulated protein 78 is an antiviral against hepatitis A virus replication. *Exp. Ther. Med.* **2017**, *13*, 3305–3308. [CrossRef]
29. O'Grady, J.G. Fulminant hepatitis in patients with chronic liver disease. *J. Viral Hepat.* **2000**, *7*, 9–10. [CrossRef]
30. Feller, A.; Uchida, T.; Rakela, J. Acute viral hepatitis superimposed on alcoholic liver cirrhosis: Clinical and histopathologic features. *Liver* **1985**, *5*, 239–246. [CrossRef]
31. Duseja, A.; Chawla, Y.K.; Dhiman, R.K.; Kumar, A.; Choudhary, N.; Taneja, S. Non-hepatic insults are common acute precipitants in patients with acute on chronic liver failure (ACLF). *Dig. Dis. Sci.* **2010**, *55*, 3188–3192. [CrossRef] [PubMed]
32. Kiyosawa, K.; Oofusa, H.; Saitoh, H.; Sodeyama, T.; Tanaka, E.; Furuta, S.; Itoh, S.; Ogata, H.; Kobuchi, H.; Kameko, M.; et al. Seroepidemiology of hepatitis A, B, and D viruses and human T-lymphocyte tropic viruses in Japanese drug abusers. *J. Med. Virol.* **1989**, *29*, 160–163. [CrossRef] [PubMed]
33. Hayashi, K.; Fukuda, Y.; Nakano, I.; Katano, Y.; Nagano, K.; Yokozaki, S.; Hayakawa, T.; Toyoda, H.; Takamatsu, J. Infection of hepatitis A virus in Japanese haemophiliacs. *J. Infect.* **2001**, *42*, 57–60. [CrossRef] [PubMed]
34. Koibuchi, T.; Koga, M.; Kikuchi, T.; Horikomi, T.; Kawamura, Y.; Lim, L.A.; Adachi, E.; Tsutsumi, T.; Yotsuyanagi, H. Prevalence of Hepatitis a Immunity and Decision-tree Analysis Among Men Who Have Sex With Men and Are Living With Human Immunodeficiency Virus in Tokyo. *Clin. Infect. Dis.* **2020**, *71*, 473–479. [CrossRef]
35. Yan, J.; Kanda, T.; Wu, S.; Imazeki, F.; Yokosuka, O. Hepatitis A, B, C and E virus markers in Chinese residing in Tokyo, Japan. *Hepatol. Res.* **2012**, *42*, 974–981. [CrossRef]
36. Yamamoto, C.; Ko, K.; Nagashima, S.; Harakawa, T.; Fujii, T.; Ohisa, M.; Katayama, K.; Takahashi, K.; Okamoto, H.; Tanaka, J. Very low prevalence of anti-HAV in Japan: High potential for future outbreak. *Sci. Rep.* **2019**, *9*, 1493. [CrossRef]
37. Koga, M.; Lim, L.A.; Ogishi, M.; Satoh, H.; Kikuchi, T.; Adachi, E.; Sugiyama, R.; Kiyohara, T.; Suzuki, R.; Muramatsu, M.; et al. Comparison of the Clinical Features of Hepatitis A in People Living with HIV between Pandemics in 1999-2000 and 2017-2018 in the Metropolitan Area of Japan. *Jpn. J. Infect. Dis.* **2020**, *73*, 89–95. [CrossRef]
38. Akao, T.; Onji, M.; Kawasaki, K.; Uehara, T.; Kuwabara, Y.; Nishimoto, T.; Yamamoto, S.; Miyaike, J.; Oomoto, M.; Miyake, T. Surveillance of Hepatitis Viruses in Several Small Islands of Japan by Ship: A Public Health Approach for Elimination of Hepatitis Viruses by 2030. *Euroasian J. Hepatogastroenterol.* **2019**, *9*, 57–62. [CrossRef]
39. Franco, E.; Giambi, C.; Ialacci, R.; Coppola, R.C.; Zanetti, A.R. Risk groups for hepatitis A virus infection. *Vaccine* **2003**, *21*, 2224–2233. [CrossRef]
40. Puoti, M.; Moioli, M.C.; Travi, G.; Rossotti, R. The burden of liver disease in human immunodeficiency virus-infected patients. *Semin. Liver Dis.* **2012**, *32*, 103–113. [CrossRef]
41. O'Riordan, M.; Goh, L.; Lamba, H. Increasing hepatitis A IgG prevalence rate in men who have sex with men attending a sexual health clinic in London: Implications for immunization policy. *Int. J. STD AIDS* **2007**, *18*, 707–710. [CrossRef] [PubMed]
42. Sadlier, C.; O'Rourke, A.; Carr, A.; Bergin, C. Seroepidemiology of hepatitis A, hepatitis B and varicella virus in people living with HIV in Ireland. *J. Infect. Public Health* **2017**, *10*, 888–890. [CrossRef] [PubMed]
43. Cohall, A.; Zucker, J.; Krieger, R.; Scott, C.; Guido, C.; Hakala, S.; Carnevale, C. Missed Opportunities for Hepatitis A Vaccination Among MSM Initiating PrEP. *J. Community Health* **2020**, *45*, 506–509. [CrossRef] [PubMed]
44. Costa-Mattioli, M.; Allavena, C.; Poirier, A.S.; Billaudel, S.; Raffi, F.; Ferré, V. Prolonged hepatitis A infection in an HIV-1 seropositive patient. *J. Med. Virol.* **2002**, *68*, 7–11. [CrossRef] [PubMed]

45. Maki, Y.; Kimizuka, Y.; Sasaki, H.; Yamamoto, T.; Hamakawa, Y.; Tagami, Y.; Miyata, J.; Hayashi, N.; Fujikura, Y.; Kawana, A. Hepatitis A virus-associated fulminant hepatitis with human immunodeficiency virus coinfection. *J. Infect. Chemother.* **2020**, *26*, 282–285. [CrossRef]
46. Kanda, T.; Sasaki, R.; Masuzaki, R.; Matsumoto, N.; Ogawa, M.; Moriyama, M. Cell Culture Systems and Drug Targets for Hepatitis A Virus Infection. *Viruses* **2020**, *12*, 533. [CrossRef]
47. Beebeejaun, K.; Degala, S.; Balogun, K.; Simms, I.; Woodhall, S.C.; Heinsbroek, E.; Crook, P.D.; Kar-Purkayastha, I.; Treacy, J.; Wedgwood, K.; et al. Outbreak of hepatitis A associated with men who have sex with men (MSM), England, July 2016 to January 2017. *Euro. Surveill.* **2017**, *22*, 30454. [CrossRef]
48. Freidl, G.S.; Sonder, G.J.; Bovée, L.P.; Friesema, I.H.; van Rijckevorsel, G.G.; Ruijs, W.L.; van Schie, F.; Siedenburg, E.C.; Yang, J.Y.; Vennema, H. Hepatitis A outbreak among men who have sex with men (MSM) predominantly linked with the EuroPride, the Netherlands, July 2016 to February 2017. *Euro. Surveill.* **2017**, *22*, 30468. [CrossRef]
49. Comelli, A.; Izzo, I.; Casari, S.; Spinetti, A.; Bergamasco, A.; Castelli, F. Hepatitis A outbreak in men who have sex with men (MSM) in Brescia (Northern Italy), July 2016–July 2017. *Infez. Med.* **2018**, *26*, 46–51.
50. Cheng, C.Y.; Wu, H.H.; Zou, H.; Lo, Y.C. Epidemiological characteristics and associated factors of acute hepatitis A outbreak among HIV-coinfected men who have sex with men in Taiwan, June 2015–December 2016. *J. Viral. Hepat.* **2018**, *25*, 1208–1215. [CrossRef]
51. Boucher, A.; Meybeck, A.; Alidjinou, K.; Huleux, T.; Viget, N.; Baclet, V.; Valette, M.; Alcaraz, I.; Sauser, E.; Bocket, L.; et al. Clinical and virological features of acute hepatitis A during an ongoing outbreak among men who have sex with men in the North of France. *Sex. Transm. Infect.* **2019**, *95*, 75–77. [CrossRef]
52. Watanabe, S.; Morimoto, N.; Miura, K.; Takaoka, Y.; Nomoto, H.; Tsukui, M.; Isoda, N.; Ohnishi, H.; Nagashima, S.; Takahashi, M.; et al. Full-genome characterization of the RIVM-HAV16-090-like hepatitis A virus strains recovered from Japanese men who have sex with men, with sporadic acute hepatitis A. *Hepatol. Res.* **2019**, *49*, 521–530. [CrossRef] [PubMed]
53. Lombardi, A.; Rossotti, R.; Moioli, M.C.; Merli, M.; Valsecchi, P.; Zuccaro, V.; Vecchia, M.; Grecchi, C.; Patruno, S.F.A.; Sacchi, P.; et al. The impact of HIV infection and men who have sex with men status on hepatitis A infection: The experience of two tertiary centres in Northern Italy during the 2017 outbreak and in the 2009–2016 period. *J. Viral Hepat.* **2019**, *26*, 761–765. [CrossRef] [PubMed]
54. Foster, M.A.; Hofmeister, M.G.; Kupronis, B.A.; Lin, Y.; Xia, G.L.; Yin, S.; Teshale, E. Increase in Hepatitis A Virus Infections—United States, 2013–2018. *MMWR Morb. Mortal. Wkly. Rep.* **2019**, *68*, 413–415. [CrossRef] [PubMed]
55. Raczyńska, A.; Wickramasuriya, N.N.; Kalinowska-Nowak, A.; Garlicki, A.; Bociaga-Jasik, M. Acute Hepatitis A Outbreak Among Men Who Have Sex With Men in Krakow, Poland; February 2017-February 2018. *Am. J. Mens. Health* **2019**, *13*, 1557988319895141. [CrossRef]
56. Tsai, P.H.; Tsai, M.S.; Chiang, Y.H.; Shih, C.Y.; Liu, C.Y.; Chuang, Y.C.; Yang, C.J. Effectiveness of hepatitis A vaccination among people living with HIV in Taiwan: Is one dose enough? *J. Microbiol. Immunol. Infect.* **2020**. [CrossRef]
57. Tassopoulos, N.; Papaevangelou, G.; Roumeliotou-Karayannis, A.; Kalafatas, P.; Engle, R.; Gerin, J.; Purcell, R.H. Double infections with hepatitis A and B viruses. *Liver* **1985**, *5*, 348–353. [CrossRef]
58. Cooksley, W.G. What did we learn from the Shanghai hepatitis A epidemic? *J. Viral Hepat.* **2000**, *7*, 1–3. [CrossRef]
59. Sagnelli, E.; Coppola, N.; Pisaturo, M.; Pisapia, R.; Onofrio, M.; Sagnelli, C.; Catuogno, A.; Scolastico, C.; Piccinino, F.; Filippini, P. Clinical and virological improvement of hepatitis B virus-related or hepatitis C virus-related chronic hepatitis with concomitant hepatitis A virus infection. *Clin. Infect. Dis.* **2006**, *42*, 1536–1543. [CrossRef]
60. Zhang, X.; Ke, W.; Xie, J.; Zhao, Z.; Xie, D.; Gao, Z. Comparison of effects of hepatitis E or A viral superinfection in patients with chronic hepatitis B. *Hepatol. Int.* **2010**, *4*, 615–620. [CrossRef]
61. Fu, J.; Gao, D.; Huang, W.; Li, Z.; Jia, B. Clinical analysis of patients suffering from chronic hepatitis B superinfected with other hepadnaviruses. *J. Med. Virol.* **2016**, *88*, 1003–1009. [CrossRef] [PubMed]
62. Beisei, C.; Addo, M.M.; Schulze Zur Wiesch, J. Seroconversion of HBsAG coincides with hepatitis A super-infection: A case report. *World J. Clin. Cases* **2020**, *8*, 1651–1655. [CrossRef] [PubMed]

63. Pramoolsinsap, C.; Poovorawan, Y.; Hirsch, P.; Busagorn, N.; Attamasirikul, K. Acute, hepatitis-A super-infection in HBV carriers, or chronic liver disease related to HBV or HCV. *Ann. Trop. Med. Parasitol.* **1999**, *93*, 745–751. [CrossRef] [PubMed]
64. Sung, J.J.Y. Epidemiology of hepatitis A in Asia and experience with the HAV vaccine in Hong Kong. *J. Viral Hepat.* **2000**, *7* (Suppl. 1), 27–28. [CrossRef] [PubMed]
65. Tsang, S.W.; Sung, J.J. Inactivated hepatitis A vaccine in Chinese patients with chronic hepatitis B infection. *Aliment. Pharmacol. Ther.* **1999**, *13*, 1445–1449. [CrossRef] [PubMed]
66. Locarnini, S. A virological perspective on the need for vaccination. *J. Viral Hepat.* **2000**, *7*, 5–6. [CrossRef]
67. Kurata, R.; Kodama, Y.; Takamura, N.; Gomi, H. Hepatitis A in a human immunodeficiency virus-infected patient: Impending risk during the Tokyo Olympic Games in 2020. *J. Infect. Chemother.* **2020**. [CrossRef]
68. Joshi, N.; Rao, S.; Kumar, A.; Patil, S.; Rani, S. Hepatitis A vaccination in chronic liver disease: Is it really required in a tropical country like India? *Indian J. Med. Microbiol.* **2007**, *25*, 137–139. [CrossRef]
69. Anand, A.C.; Nagpal, A.K.; Seth, A.K.; Dhot, P.S. Should one vaccinate patients with chronic liver disease for hepatitis A virus in India? *J. Assoc. Physicians India* **2004**, *52*, 785–787.
70. Van Nunen, A.B.; Pontesilli, O.; Uytdehaag, F.; Osterhaus, A.D.; de Man, R.A. Suppression of hepatitis B virus replication mediated by hepatitis A-induced cytokine production. *Liver* **2001**, *21*, 45–49. [CrossRef]
71. Berthillon, P.; Crance, J.M.; Leveque, F.; Jouan, A.; Petit, M.A.; Deloince, R.; Trepo, C. Inhibition of the expression of hepatitis A and B viruses (HAV and HBV) proteins by interferon in a human hepatocarcinoma cell line (PLC/PRF/5). *J. Hepatol.* **1996**, *25*, 15–19. [CrossRef]
72. Ishii, T.; Tamura, A.; Shibata, T.; Kuroda, K.; Kanda, T.; Sugiyama, M.; Mizokami, M.; Moriyama, M. Analysis of HBV Genomes Integrated into the Genomes of Human Hepatoma PLC/PRF/5 Cells by HBV Sequence Capture-Based Next-Generation Sequencing. *Genes* **2020**, *11*, 661. [CrossRef] [PubMed]
73. Win, N.N.; Kanda, T.; Ogawa, M.; Nakamoto, S.; Haga, Y.; Sasaki, R.; Nakamura, M.; Wu, S.; Matsumoto, N.; Matsuoka, S.; et al. Superinfection of hepatitis A virus in hepatocytes infected with hepatitis B virus. *Int. J. Med. Sci.* **2019**, *16*, 1366–1370. [CrossRef] [PubMed]
74. Kanda, T.; Yokosuka, O.; Imazeki, F.; Saisho, H. Acute hepatitis C virus infection, 1986-2001: A rare cause of fulminant hepatitis in Chiba, Japan. *Hepatogastroenterology* **2004**, *51*, 556–558.
75. Villamil, F.G.; Hu, K.Q.; Yu, C.H.; Lee, C.H.; Rojter, S.E.; Podesta, L.G.; Makowka, L.; Geller, S.A.; Vierling, J.M. Detection of hepatitis C virus with RNA polymerase chain reaction in fulminant hepatic failure. *Hepatology* **1995**, *22*, 1379–1386.
76. Vento, S. Fulminant hepatitis associated with hepatitis A virus superinfection in patients with chronic hepatitis C. *J. Viral Hepat.* **2000**, *7*, 7–8. [CrossRef]
77. Deterding, K.; Tegtmeyer, B.; Cornberg, M.; Hadem, J.; Potthoff, A.; Böker, K.H.; Tillmann, H.L.; Manns, M.P.; Wedemeyer, H. Hepatitis A virus infection suppresses hepatitis C virus replication and may lead to clearance of HCV. *J. Hepatol.* **2006**, *45*, 770–778. [CrossRef]
78. Cacopardo, B.; Nunnari, G.; Nigro, L. Clearance of HCV RNA following acute hepatitis A superinfection. *Dig. Liver Dis.* **2009**, *41*, 371–374. [CrossRef]
79. Esser-Nobis, K.; Harak, C.; Schult, P.; Kusov, Y.; Lohmann, V. Novel perspectives for hepatitis A virus therapy revealed by comparative analysis of hepatitis C virus and hepatitis A virus RNA replication. *Hepatology* **2015**, *62*, 397–408. [CrossRef]
80. Sagnelli, E.; Sagnelli, C.; Pisaturo, M.; Coppola, N. Hepatic flares in chronic hepatitis C: Spontaneous exacerbation vs hepatotropic viruses superinfection. *World J. Gastroenterol.* **2014**, *20*, 6707–6715. [CrossRef]
81. Koff, R.S. Risks associated with hepatitis A and B in patients with hepatitis C. *J. Clin. Gastroenterol.* **2001**, *33*, 20–26. [CrossRef] [PubMed]
82. Devalle, S.; de Paula, V.S.; de Oliveira, J.M.; Niel, C.; Gaspar, A.M. Hepatitis A virus infection in hepatitis C Brazilian patients. *J. Infect.* **2003**, *47*, 125–128. [CrossRef]
83. Shim, M.; Khaykis, I.; Park, J.; Bini, E.J. Susceptibility to hepatitis A in patients with chronic liver disease due to hepatitis C virus infection: Missed opportunities for vaccination. *Hepatology* **2005**, *42*, 688–695. [CrossRef]
84. Ramsay, D.B.; Friedman, M.; Borum, M.L. Does the race or gender of hepatitis C infected patients influence physicians' assessment of hepatitis A and hepatitis B serologic status? *South Med. J.* **2007**, *100*, 683–685. [CrossRef] [PubMed]

85. Villar, L.M.; de Melo, M.M.; Calado, I.A.; de Almeida, A.J.; Lampe, E.; Gaspar, A.M. Should Brazilian patients with chronic hepatitis C virus infection be vaccinated against hepatitis A virus? *J. Gastroenterol. Hepatol.* **2009**, *24*, 238–242. [CrossRef] [PubMed]
86. Buxton, J.A.; Kim, J.H. Hepatitis A and hepatitis B vaccination responses in persons with chronic hepatitis C infections: A review of the evidence and current recommendations. *Can. J. Infect. Dis. Med. Microbiol.* **2008**, *19*, 197–202. [CrossRef] [PubMed]
87. Kramer, J.R.; Hachem, C.Y.; Kanwal, F.; Mei, M.; El-Serag, H.B. Meeting vaccination quality measures for hepatitis A and B virus in patients with chronic hepatitis C infection. *Hepatology* **2011**, *53*, 42–52. [CrossRef]
88. Rowe, I.A.; Parker, R.; Armstrong, M.J.; Houlihan, D.D.; Mutimer, D.J. Hepatitis A virus vaccination in persons with hepatitis C virus infection: Consequences of quality measure implementation. *Hepatology* **2012**, *56*, 501–506. [CrossRef]
89. Sarin, S.K.; Kedarisetty, C.K.; Abbas, Z.; Amarapurkar, D.; Bihari, C.; Chan, A.C.; Chawla, Y.K.; Dokmeci, A.K.; Garg, H.; Ghazinyan, H.; et al. Acute-on-chronic liver failure: Consensus recommendations of the Asian Pacific Association for the Study of the Liver (APASL) 2014. *Hepatol. Int.* **2014**, *8*, 453–471. [CrossRef]
90. Arroyo, V.; Moreau, R.; Jalan, R.; Ginès, P. EASL-CLIF Consortium CANONIC Study. Acute-on-chronic liver failure: A new syndrome that will re-classify cirrhosis. *J. Hepatol.* **2015**, *62*, S131–S143. [CrossRef]
91. O'Leary, J.G.; Reddy, K.R.; Garcia-Tsao, G.; Biggins, S.W.; Wong, F.; Fallon, M.B.; Subramanian, R.M.; Kamath, P.S.; Thuluvath, P.; Vargas, H.E.; et al. NACSELD acute-on-chronic liver failure (NACSELD-ACLF) score predicts 30-day survival in hospitalized patients with cirrhosis. *Hepatology* **2018**, *67*, 2367–2374. [CrossRef] [PubMed]
92. Zhang, L.; Yesupriya, A.; Hu, D.J.; Chang, M.H.; Dowling, N.F.; Ned, R.M.; Udhayakumar, V.; Lindegren, M.L.; Khudyakov, Y. Variants in ABCB1, TGFB1, and XRCC1 genes and susceptibility to viral hepatitis A infection in Mexican Americans. *Hepatology* **2012**, *55*, 1008–1018. [CrossRef] [PubMed]
93. Kashyap, P.; Deka, M.; Medhi, S.; Dutta, S.; Kashyap, K.; Kumari, N. Association of Toll-like receptor 4 with hepatitis A virus infection in Assam. *Acta. Virol.* **2018**, *62*, 58–62. [CrossRef] [PubMed]
94. Rubicz, R.; Yolken, R.; Drigalenko, E.; Carless, M.A.; Dyer, T.D.; Kent, J., Jr.; Curran, J.E.; Johnson, M.P.; Cole, S.A.; Fowler, S.P.; et al. Genome-wide genetic investigation of serological measures of common infections. *Eur. J. Hum. Genet.* **2015**, *23*, 1544–1548. [CrossRef]
95. Hundekar, S.; Thorat, N.; Gurav, Y.; Lole, K. Viral excretion and antibody titers in children infected with hepatitis A virus from an orphanage in western India. *J. Clin. Virol.* **2015**, *73*, 27–31. [CrossRef] [PubMed]
96. Brouwer, A.F.; Zelner, J.L.; Eisenberg, M.C.; Kimmins, L.; Ladisky, M.; Collins, J.; Eisenberg, J.N.S. The Impact of Vaccination Efforts on the Spatiotemporal Patterns of the Hepatitis A Outbreak in Michigan, 2016-2018. *Epidemiology* **2020**, *31*, 628–635. [CrossRef] [PubMed]
97. Win, N.N.; Kanda, T.; Nakamoto, S.; Moriyama, M.; Jiang, X.; Suganami, A.; Tamura, Y.; Okamoto, H.; Shirasawa, H. Inhibitory effect of Japanese rice-koji miso extracts on hepatitis A virus replication in association with the elevation of glucose-regulated protein 78 expression. *Int. J. Med. Sci.* **2018**, *15*, 1153–1159. [CrossRef]
98. Ogawa, M.; Kanda, T.; Suganami, A.; Nakamoto, S.; Win, N.N.; Tamura, Y.; Nakamura, M.; Matsuoka, S.; Yokosuka, O.; Kato, N.; et al. Antiviral activity of zinc sulfate against hepatitis A virus replication. *Future Virol.* **2019**, *14*, 399–406. [CrossRef]
99. Cao, L.; Liu, P.; Yang, P.; Gao, Q.; Li, H.; Sun, Y.; Zhu, L.; Lin, J.; Su, D.; Rao, Z.; et al. Structural basis for neutralization of hepatitis A virus informs a rational design of highly potent inhibitors. *PLoS Biol.* **2019**, *17*, e3000229. [CrossRef]
100. Yang, L.; Kiyohara, T.; Kanda, T.; Imazeki, F.; Fujiwara, K.; Gauss-Müller, V.; Ishii, K.; Wakita, T.; Yokosuka, O. Inhibitory effects on HAV IRES-mediated translation and replication by a combination of amantadine and interferon-alpha. *Virol. J.* **2010**, *7*, 212. [CrossRef]
101. Kanda, T.; Wu, S.; Kiyohara, T.; Nakamoto, S.; Jiang, X.; Miyamura, T.; Imazeki, F.; Ishii, K.; Wakita, T.; Yokosuka, O. Interleukin-29 suppresses hepatitis A and C viral internal ribosomal entry site-mediated translation. *Viral Immunol.* **2012**, *25*, 379–386. [CrossRef] [PubMed]
102. Kanda, T.; Yokosuka, O.; Imazeki, F.; Fujiwara, K.; Nagao, K.; Saisho, H. Amantadine inhibits hepatitis A virus internal ribosomal entry site-mediated translation in human hepatoma cells. *Biochem. Biophys. Res. Commun.* **2005**, *331*, 621–629. [CrossRef] [PubMed]

103. Kanda, T.; Imazeki, F.; Nakamoto, S.; Okitsu, K.; Fujiwara, K.; Yokosuka, O. Internal ribosomal entry-site activities of clinical isolate-derived hepatitis A virus and inhibitory effects of amantadine. *Hepatol. Res.* **2010**, *40*, 415–423. [CrossRef] [PubMed]
104. Kanda, T.; Sasaki, R.; Nakamoto, S.; Haga, Y.; Nakamura, M.; Shirasawa, H.; Okamoto, H.; Yokosuka, O. The sirtuin inhibitor sirtinol inhibits hepatitis A virus (HAV) replication by inhibiting HAV internal ribosomal entry site activity. *Biochem. Biophys. Res. Commun.* **2015**, *466*, 567–571. [CrossRef]
105. Jiang, X.; Kanda, T.; Nakamoto, S.; Saito, K.; Nakamura, M.; Wu, S.; Haga, Y.; Sasaki, R.; Sakamoto, N.; Shirasawa, H.; et al. The JAK2 inhibitor AZD1480 inhibits hepatitis A virus replication in Huh7 cells. *Biochem. Biophys. Res. Commun.* **2015**, *458*, 908–912. [CrossRef]
106. Kaplan, G.; Totsuka, A.; Thompson, P.; Akatsuka, T.; Moritsugu, Y.; Feinstone, S.M. Identification of a surface glycoprotein on African green monkey kidney cells as a receptor for hepatitis A virus. *EMBO J.* **1996**, *15*, 4282–4296. [CrossRef]
107. Rivera-Serrano, E.E.; González-López, O.; Das, A.; Lemon, S.M. Cellular entry and uncoating of naked and quasi-enveloped human hepatoviruses. *Elife* **2019**, *8*, e43983. [CrossRef]
108. Das, A.; Barrientos, R.; Shiota, T.; Madigan, V.; Misumi, I.; McKnight, K.L.; Sun, L.; Li, Z.; Meganck, R.M.; Li, Y.; et al. Gangliosides are essential endosomal receptors for quasi-enveloped and naked hepatitis A virus. *Nat. Microbiol.* **2020**. [CrossRef]
109. Miura, Y.; Kanda, T.; Yasui, S.; Takahashi, K.; Haga, Y.; Sasaki, R.; Nakamura, M.; Wu, S.; Nakamoto, S.; Arai, M.; et al. Hepatitis A virus genotype IA-infected patient with marked elevation of aspartate aminotransferase levels. *Clin. J. Gastroenterol.* **2017**, *10*, 52–56. [CrossRef]
110. Tsukada, R.; Ono, S.; Kobayashi, H.; Wada, Y.; Nishizawa, K.; Fujii, M.; Takeuchi, M.; Kuroiwa, K.; Kobayashi, Y.; Ishii, K.; et al. A Cluster of Hepatitis A Infections Presumed to be Related to Asari Clams and Investigation of the Spread of Viral Contamination from Asari Clams. *Jpn. J. Infect. Dis.* **2019**, *72*, 44–48. [CrossRef]
111. Kogiso, T.; Sagawa, T.; Oda, M.; Yoshiko, S.; Kodama, K.; Taniai, M.; Tokushige, K. Characteristics of acute hepatitis A virus infection before and after 2001: A hospital-based study in Tokyo, Japan. *J. Gastroenterol. Hepatol.* **2019**, *34*, 1836–1842. [CrossRef] [PubMed]
112. Yoshida, Y.; Okada, Y.; Suzuki, A.; Kakisaka, K.; Miyamoto, Y.; Miyasaka, A.; Takikawa, Y.; Nishizawa, T.; Okamoto, H. Fatal acute hepatic failure in a family infected with the hepatitis A virus subgenotype IB: A case report. *Medicine* **2017**, *96*, e7847. [CrossRef] [PubMed]
113. Bajpai, M.; Kakkar, B.; Patale, D. Role of high-volume plasma exchange in a case of a G6PD deficient patient presenting with HAV related acute liver failure and concomitant acute renal failure. *Transfus. Apher. Sci.* **2019**, *58*, 102677. [CrossRef] [PubMed]
114. Kim, J.D.; Cho, E.J.; Ahn, C.; Park, S.K.; Choi, J.Y.; Lee, H.C.; Kim, D.Y.; Choi, M.S.; Wang, H.J.; Kim, I.H.; et al. A Model to Predict 1-Month Risk of Transplant or Death in Hepatitis A-Related Acute Liver Failure. *Hepatology* **2019**, *70*, 621–629. [CrossRef] [PubMed]
115. Sung, P.S.; Hong, S.H.; Lee, J.; Park, S.H.; Yoon, S.K.; Chung, W.J.; Shin, E.C. CXCL10 is produced in hepatitis A virus-infected cells in an IRF3-dependent but IFN-independent manner. *Sci. Rep.* **2017**, *7*, 6387. [CrossRef]
116. Trujillo-Ochoa, J.L.; Corral-Jara, K.F.; Charles-Niño, C.L.; Panduro, A.; Fierro, N.A. Conjugated Bilirubin Upregulates TIM-3 Expression on CD4(+)CD25(+) T Cells: Anti-Inflammatory Implications for Hepatitis A Virus Infection. *Viral Immunol.* **2018**, *31*, 223–232. [CrossRef]
117. Choi, Y.S.; Jung, M.K.; Lee, J.; Choi, S.J.; Choi, S.H.; Lee, H.W.; Lee, J.J.; Kim, H.J.; Ahn, S.H.; Lee, D.H.; et al. Tumor Necrosis Factor-producing T-regulatory Cells Are Associated With Severe Liver Injury in Patients With Acute Hepatitis A. *Gastroenterology* **2018**, *154*, 1047–1060. [CrossRef]
118. Belkaya, S.; Michailidis, E.; Korol, C.B.; Kabbani, M.; Cobat, A.; Bastard, P.; Lee, Y.S.; Hernandez, N.; Drutman, S.; de Jong, Y.P.; et al. Inherited IL-18BP deficiency in human fulminant viral hepatitis. *J. Exp. Med.* **2019**, *216*, 1777–1790. [CrossRef]
119. Jouanguy, E. Human genetic basis of fulminant viral hepatitis. *Hum. Genet.* **2020**, *139*, 877–884. [CrossRef]
120. Kim, J.; Chang, D.Y.; Lee, H.W.; Lee, H.; Kim, J.H.; Sung, P.S.; Kim, K.H.; Hong, S.H.; Kang, W.; Lee, J.; et al. Innate-like Cytotoxic Function of Bystander-Activated CD8(+) T Cells Is Associated with Liver Injury in Acute Hepatitis A. *Immunity* **2018**, *48*, 161–173.e5. [CrossRef]
121. Feng, Z.; Lemon, S.M. Innate Immunity to Enteric Hepatitis Viruses. *Cold Spring Harb. Perspect. Med.* **2019**, *9*, a033464. [CrossRef] [PubMed]

122. Mikata, R.; Yokosuka, O.; Imazeki, F.; Fukai, K.; Kanda, T.; Saisho, H. Prolonged acute hepatitis A mimicking autoimmune hepatitis. *World J. Gastroenterol.* **2005**, *11*, 3791–3793. [CrossRef] [PubMed]
123. Abdel-Ghaffar, T.Y.; Sira, M.M.; Sira, A.M.; Salem, T.A.; El-Sharawy, A.A.; El Naghi, S. Serological markers of autoimmunity in children with hepatitis A: Relation to acute and fulminant presentation. *Eur. J. Gastroenterol. Hepatol.* **2015**, *27*, 1161–1169. [CrossRef]
124. Albillos, A.; Lario, M.; Álvarez-Mon, M. Cirrhosis-associated immune dysfunction: Distinctive features and clinical relevance. *J. Hepatol.* **2014**, *61*, 1385–1396. [CrossRef] [PubMed]
125. Ji, D.; Zhang, D.; Yang, T.; Mu, J.; Zhao, P.; Xu, J.; Li, C.; Cheng, G.; Wang, Y.; Chen, Z.; et al. Effect of COVID-19 on patients with compensated chronic liver diseases. *Hepatol. Int.* **2020**, 1–10. [CrossRef]
126. Arai, M.; Imazeki, F.; Yonemitsu, Y.; Kanda, T.; Fujiwara, K.; Fukai, K.; Watanabe, A.; Sato, T.; Oda, S.; Yokosuka, O. Opportunistic infection in the patients with acute liver failure: A report of three cases with one fatality. *Clin. J. Gastroenterol.* **2009**, *2*, 420–424. [CrossRef] [PubMed]
127. Arai, M.; Kanda, T.; Yasui, S.; Fujiwara, K.; Imazeki, F.; Watanabe, A.; Sato, T.; Oda, S.; Yokosuka, O. Opportunistic infection in patients with acute liver failure. *Hepatol. Int.* **2014**, *8*, 233–239. [CrossRef]
128. Yasui, S.; Fujiwara, K.; Haga, Y.; Nakamura, M.; Mikata, R.; Arai, M.; Kanda, T.; Oda, S.; Yokosuka, O. Infectious complications, steroid use and timing for emergency liver transplantation in acute liver failure: Analysis in a Japanese center. *J. Hepato-Biliary-Pancreat Sci.* **2016**, *23*, 756–762. [CrossRef]
129. Doycheva, I.; Thuluvath, P.J. Acute-on-chronic liver failure in liver transplant candidates with non-alcoholic steatohepatitis. *Transl. Gastroenterol. Hepatol.* **2020**, *5*, 38. [CrossRef]
130. Trebicka, J.; Sundaram, V.; Moreau, R.; Jalan, R.; Arroyo, V. Liver Transplantation for Acute-on-Chronic Liver Failure: Science or Fiction? *Liver Transpl.* **2020**, *26*, 906–915. [CrossRef]
131. Sundaram, V.; Mahmud, N.; Perricone, G.; Katarey, D.; Wong, R.J.; Karvellas, C.J.; Fortune, B.E.; Rahimi, R.S.; Maddur, H.; Jou, J.H.; et al. Long-term outcomes of patients undergoing liver transplantation for acute-on-chronic liver failure. *Liver Transpl.* **2020**. [CrossRef] [PubMed]
132. Meyer, A.; Regunath, H.; Rojas Moreno, C.; Salzer, W.; Christensen, G. Imported Infections in Rural Mid-West United States—A Report from a Tertiary Care Center. *Mo. Med.* **2020**, *117*, 89–94. [PubMed]
133. SarialIoĞlu, F.; Belen, F.B.; Hayran, K.M. Hepatitis A susceptibility parallels high COVID-19 mortality. *Turk. J. Med. Sci.* **2020**. [CrossRef]
134. Chen, G.J.; Lin, K.Y.; Sun, H.Y.; Sheng, W.H.; Hsieh, S.M.; Huang, Y.C.; Cheng, A.; Liu, W.C.; Hung, C.C.; Chang, S.C. Incidence of acute hepatitis A among HIV-positive patients during an outbreak among MSM in Taiwan: Impact of HAV vaccination. *Liver Int.* **2018**, *38*, 594–601. [CrossRef]
135. Chen, W.C.; Chiang, P.H.; Liao, Y.H.; Huang, L.C.; Hsieh, Y.J.; Chiu, C.M.; Lo, Y.C.; Yang, C.H.; Yang, J.Y. Outbreak of hepatitis A virus infection in Taiwan, June 2015 to September 2017. *Euro. Surveill.* **2019**, *24*, 1800133. [CrossRef]
136. Campos-Outcalt, D. CDC provides advice on recent hepatitis A outbreaks. *J. Fam. Pract.* **2018**, *67*, 30–32.
137. Latash, J.; Dorsinville, M.; Del Rosso, P.; Antwi, M.; Reddy, V.; Waechter, H.; Lawler, J.; Boss, H.; Kurpiel, P.; Backenson, P.B.; et al. Notes from the Field: Increase in Reported Hepatitis A Infections Among Men Who Have Sex with Men - New York City, January-August 2017. *MMWR Morb. Mortal. Wkly. Rep.* **2017**, *66*, 999–1000. [CrossRef]
138. Fraile, M.; Barreiro Alonso, E.; de la Vega, J.; Rodríguez, M.; García-López, R.; Rodríguez, M. Acute hepatitis due to hepatitis A virus during the 2017 epidemic expansion in Asturias. Spain. *Med. Clin.* **2019**, *152*, 391–394. [CrossRef]
139. Mello, V.M.; Lago, B.V.; Sousa, P.S.F.; Mello, F.C.A.; Souza, C.B.; Pinto, L.C.M.; Ginuino, C.F.; Fernandes, C.A.S.; Aguiar, S.F.; Villar, L.M.; et al. Hepatitis A Strain Linked to the European Outbreaks During Gay Events between 2016 and 2017, Identified in a Brazilian Homosexual Couple in 2017. *Viruses* **2019**, *11*, 281. [CrossRef]
140. Minosse, C.; Messina, F.; Garbuglia, A.R.; Meschi, S.; Scognamiglio, P.; Capobianchi, M.R.; Ippolito, G.; Lanini, S. Origin of HAV strains responsible for 2016-2017 outbreak among MSM: Viral phylodynamics in Lazio region. *PLoS ONE* **2020**, *15*, e0234010. [CrossRef]
141. Lanford, R.E.; Feng, Z.; Chavez, D.; Guerra, B.; Brasky, K.M.; Zhou, Y.; Yamane, D.; Perelson, A.S.; Walker, C.M.; Lemon, S.M. Acute hepatitis A virus infection is associated with a limited type I interferon response and persistence of intrahepatic viral RNA. *Proc. Natl. Acad. Sci. USA* **2011**, *108*, 11223–11228. [CrossRef]

142. Kato, N.; Yoshida, H.; Ono-Nita, S.K.; Kato, J.; Goto, T.; Otsuka, M.; Lan, K.; Matsushima, K.; Shiratori, Y.; Omata, M. Activation of intracellular signaling by hepatitis B and C viruses: C-viral core is the most potent signal inducer. *Hepatology* **2000**, *32*, 405–412. [CrossRef]
143. Kanda, T.; Yokosuka, O.; Kato, N.; Imazeki, F.; Fujiwara, K.; Kawai, S.; Saisho, H.; Omata, M. Hepatitis A virus VP3 may activate serum response element associated transcription. *Scand. J. Gastroenterol.* **2003**, *38*, 307–313. [CrossRef] [PubMed]
144. Kanda, T.; Yokosuka, O.; Imazeki, F.; Saisho, H. Hepatitis A protein VP1-2A reduced cell viability in Huh-7 cells with hepatitis C virus subgenomic RNA replication. *J. Gastroenterol. Hepatol.* **2006**, *21*, 625–626. [CrossRef] [PubMed]
145. Brack, K.; Berk, I.; Magulski, T.; Lederer, J.; Dotzauer, A.; Vallbracht, A. Hepatitis A virus inhibits cellular antiviral defense mechanisms induced by double-stranded RNA. *J. Virol.* **2002**, *76*, 11920–11930. [CrossRef]
146. Hirai-Yuki, A.; Hensley, L.; McGivern, D.R.; González-López, O.; Das, A.; Feng, H.; Sun, L.; Wilson, J.E.; Hu, F.; Feng, Z.; et al. MAVS-dependent host species range and pathogenicity of human hepatitis A virus. *Science* **2016**, *353*, 1541–1545. [CrossRef] [PubMed]
147. Yang, Y.; Liang, Y.; Qu, L.; Chen, Z.; Yi, M.; Li, K.; Lemon, S.M. Disruption of innate immunity due to mitochondrial targeting of a picornaviral protease precursor. *Proc. Natl. Acad. Sci. USA* **2007**, *104*, 7253–7258. [CrossRef] [PubMed]
148. Kanda, T.; Gauss-Müller, V.; Cordes, S.; Tamura, R.; Okitsu, K.; Shuang, W.; Nakamoto, S.; Fujiwara, K.; Imazeki, F.; Yokosuka, O. Hepatitis A virus (HAV) proteinase 3C inhibits HAV IRES-dependent translation and cleaves the polypyrimidine tract-binding protein. *J. Viral Hepat.* **2010**, *17*, 618–623. [CrossRef]
149. Kanda, T.; Steele, R.; Ray, R.; Ray, R.B. Hepatitis C virus infection induces the beta interferon signaling pathway in immortalized human hepatocytes. *J. Virol.* **2007**, *81*, 12375–12381. [CrossRef]
150. Wieland, S.F.; Chisari, F.V. Stealth and cunning: Hepatitis B and hepatitis C viruses. *J. Virol.* **2005**, *79*, 9369–9380. [CrossRef]
151. Dash, S.; Aydin, Y.; Moroz, K. Chaperone-Mediated Autophagy in the Liver: Good or Bad? *Cells* **2019**, *8*, 1308. [CrossRef] [PubMed]
152. You, Y.; Li, W.Z.; Zhang, S.; Hu, B.; Li, Y.X.; Li, H.D.; Tang, H.H.; Li, Q.W.; Guan, Y.Y.; Liu, L.X.; et al. SNX10 mediates alcohol-induced liver injury and steatosis by regulating the activation of chaperone-mediated autophagy. *J. Hepatol.* **2018**, *69*, 129–141. [CrossRef] [PubMed]
153. Angelini, G.; Castagneto Gissey, L.; Del Corpo, G.; Giordano, C.; Cerbelli, B.; Severino, A.; Manco, M.; Basso, N.; Birkenfeld, A.L.; Bornstein, S.R.; et al. New insight into the mechanisms of ectopic fat deposition improvement after bariatric surgery. *Sci. Rep.* **2019**, *9*, 17315. [CrossRef]
154. Ida, S.; Tachikawa, N.; Nakajima, A.; Daikoku, M.; Yano, M.; Kikuchi, Y.; Yasuoka, A.; Kimura, S.; Oka, S. Influence of human immunodeficiency virus type 1 infection on acute hepatitis A virus infection. *Clin. Infect. Dis.* **2002**, *34*, 379–385. [CrossRef]
155. Lin, K.Y.; Chen, G.J.; Lee, Y.L.; Huang, Y.C.; Cheng, A.; Sun, H.Y.; Chang, S.Y.; Liu, C.E.; Hung, C.C. Hepatitis A virus infection and hepatitis A vaccination in human immunodeficiency virus-positive patients: A review. *World J. Gastroenterol.* **2017**, *23*, 3589–3606. [CrossRef] [PubMed]

© 2020 by the authors. Licensee MDPI, Basel, Switzerland. This article is an open access article distributed under the terms and conditions of the Creative Commons Attribution (CC BY) license (http://creativecommons.org/licenses/by/4.0/).

Article

Clusters of Circulating let-7 Family Tumor Suppressors Are Associated with Clinical Characteristics of Chronic Hepatitis C

Yi-Shan Tsai [1], Ming-Lun Yeh [1,2], Pei-Chien Tsai [1,3], Ching-I Huang [1], Chung-Feng Huang [1,2,3,4], Meng-Hsuan Hsieh [1,2,3,4], Ta-Wei Liu [1], Yi-Hung Lin [1], Po-Cheng Liang [1], Zu-Yau Lin [1,2], Shinn-Cherng Chen [1,2], Jee-Fu Huang [1,2], Wan-Long Chuang [1,2,5], Chia-Yen Dai [1,2,3,4,5,6,7,*,†] and Ming-Lung Yu [1,2,3,5,6,†]

1. Hepatobiliary Division, Department of Internal Medicine and Hepatitis Center, Kaohsiung Medical University Hospital, Kaohsiung Medical University, Kaohsiung 807, Taiwan; 1016ys@gmail.com (Y.-S.T.); yeh_ming_lun@yahoo.com.tw (M.-L.Y.); pctsai1225@gmail.com (P.-C.T.); tom65222@gmail.com (C.-I.H.); fengcheerup@gmail.com (C.-F.H.); hsmonyan@gmail.com (M.-H.H.); davyliu@gmail.com (T.-W.L.); 990076@kmuh.org.tw (Y.-H.L.); pocheng.liang@gmail.com (P.-C.L.); zuyali@kmu.edu.tw (Z.-Y.L.); chshch@kmu.edu.tw (S.-C.C.); jf71218@gmail.com (J.-F.H.); waloch@kmu.edu.tw (W.-L.C.); fish6069@gmail.com (M.-L.Y.)
2. Health Management Center, Kaohsiung Medical University Hospital, Kaohsiung Medical University, Kaohsiung 807, Taiwan
3. Department of Occupational Medicine, Kaohsiung Medical University Hospital, Kaohsiung Medical University, Kaohsiung 807, Taiwan
4. Faculty of Internal Medicine, College of Medicine, Graduate Institute of Clinical Medicine, Kaohsiung Medical University, Kaohsiung 807, Taiwan
5. Lipid Science and Aging Research Center (LSARC), Kaohsiung Medical University, Kaohsiung 807, Taiwan
6. Center for Infectious Disease and Cancer Research, Kaohsiung Medical University, Kaohsiung 807, Taiwan
7. Department of Biological Science and Technology, College of Biological Science and Technology, National Chiao Tung University, Hsin-Chu 300, Taiwan
* Correspondence: daichiayen@gmail.com; Tel.: +886-7-312-1101 (ext. 7475); Fax: +886-7-323-4553
† These authors contributed equally to this work.

Received: 10 June 2020; Accepted: 10 July 2020; Published: 13 July 2020

Abstract: Hepatitis C virus (HCV) infections can cause permanent liver-related diseases, including hepatocellular carcinoma (HCC). Low mortality and incidence of HCC have been observed in patients with chronic hepatitis C undergoing direct-acting antiviral therapy. Tumor suppressive let-7 family members are down-regulated in HCC. The present study, therefore, aimed to investigate whether expression levels for the full spectrum of let-7 family members (let-7a, 7b, 7c, 7d, 7e, 7f, 7g, 7i, and miR-98) in the circulatory system are useful as surveillance biomarkers for liver-related diseases to monitor treatment efficacy during HCV infection. To this end, we measured the levels of mature circulating let-7 family members using quantitative reverse transcription-PCR in 236 patients with HCV infection, and 147 age- and sex-matched controls. Using hierarchical cluster analysis and principal component analysis, three clusters were obtained after measuring expression levels of let-7 family members in the patients and controls. Cluster 1 included let-7a/d/e/g, Cluster 2 comprised let-7b and let-7i, and Cluster 3 comprised let-7c/f/miR-98. Let-7b/c/g represented the three clusters and showed the best survival response to liver cancer when analyzed with respect to patient data. Therefore, considering the circulating levels of let7 b/c/g as representatives of the let-7 family may facilitate effective monitoring of liver-related disease.

Keywords: chronic hepatitis C; let-7 family; hepatitis C virus; miRNA; biomarker; hepatocellular carcinoma

1. Introduction

Chronic hepatitis C (CHC) virus infection can cause serious liver disorders. It can also increase the risk of hepatocellular carcinoma (HCC) and the progression of severe hepatic and extrahepatic diseases [1]. Compared to non-virological response (NVR), the sustained virological response (SVR) resulting from treatment with pegylated interferon-α (PegIFNα) and ribavirin (RBV) is associated with a lower risk of HCC development [2]. However, patients with significant hepatic fibrosis remain at high risk for HCC, even when they achieve SVR with antiviral therapy [3,4]. Since 2013, the development of direct-acting antivirals (DAAs) has increased SVR rates by 95% above those of interferon (IFN)-based treatments in patients with chronic HCV infection regardless of viral genotype [5]. However, there is no evidence that HCC occurrence or recurrence differs between patients receiving DAA or IFN therapy [6]. Furthermore, the annual post-SVR HCC incidence (approximately 1%) remains higher than that for cancers of other organs. Therefore, it is necessary to establish a clinical strategy for monitoring cancer risk in post-SVR patients [7,8].

Mature microRNAs (miRNAs) are short, single-stranded RNA molecules (approximately 22 nucleotides in length) that post-transcriptionally silence gene expression and play important roles in a broad variety of biological processes, including intrinsic antiviral immunity. Chen et al. systematically characterized serum/plasma miRNAs and found that they were stable, reproducible, and consistent among individuals of the same species. These miRNAs also represent promising, non-invasive biomarkers for diagnosing cancer and other diseases [9]. Furthermore, it has been suggested that miRNAs can be used as a prediction model for the treatment outcome of HCV virus genotype 1 infection [10].

Previous studies have shown that the miRNA let-7b exhibits a significant anti-HCV effect [11], and that IFNα rapidly modulates the expression of let-7s with anti-HCV activity by targeting *IGF2BP* [12]. In our previous study, we demonstrated the effects of let-7g on HCV infection in vitro in clinical tissue and serum samples. We found that IFN/RBV treatment induces let-7g expression. Furthermore, overexpression of let-7g reduces the expression of the HCV gene and core protein level, thereby inhibiting viral replication. Let-7g and IFN/RBV treatment also synergistically inhibits HCV replication and represses Lin28A/B [13].

The let-7 family, comprised of ten members (let-7a, 7b, 7c, 7d, 7e, 7f, 7g, 7i, miR-98, and miR-202), target the 3′ untranslated regions (UTRs) of genes essential for development and are conserved from *Caenorhabditis elegans* to humans [14]. Next-generation sequencing and microarray studies have revealed that various HCC-specific miRNA signatures in the liver tissue showed lower let-7 (a/b/c/d/e/f/g) expression levels compared to healthy liver tissues [15]. Matsuura et al. performed a longitudinal miRNA microarray study on plasma and extracellular vesicles (EVs) in patients with CHC and found that the plasma levels of circulating let-7(a/c/d) were higher than those in EVs, and were inversely correlated with the severity of hepatic fibrosis [16].

Despite these studies, the roles of mature let-7 family members (let-7a, 7b, 7c, 7d, 7e, 7f, 7g, 7i, and miR-98) in the circulating plasma of patients with CHC and their clinical relevance remain unclear. Moreover, due to the large number of let-7 family members, and the difficulty associated with obtaining liver tissues from CHC patients and the control group, detection of all family members for the purposes of monitoring liver-related diseases is not feasible. Nevertheless, this study aimed to evaluate the association between circulating let-7 family members and the clinical characteristics of CHC patients. We also examined the potential for use of nine mature let-7 family members as non-invasive biomarkers for CHC patients, using cluster analysis and principal component analysis (PCA). An independent dataset was then employed to evaluate the clusters of the let-7 family in normal tissue (N), and tumors (T) from the Cancer Genome Atlas (TCGA) liver cancer samples. Here we demonstrate that assessing the levels of the circulating let-7 family members could represent a promising new method to monitor liver-related diseases.

2. Results

2.1. Clinical Characteristics of Patients

The characteristics of the subjects enrolled in this study are listed in Table 1. Compared with the healthy control group, CHC patients had significantly higher aspartate transaminase (AST, $p < 0.0001$), alanine aminotransferase (ALT, $p < 0.0001$), gamma-glutamyl transferase (γGT, $p < 0.0001$), and fasting plasma glucose ($p < 0.0001$) levels. Alternatively, creatinine (Cr, $p < 0.0001$), white blood cell counts (WBC, $p < 0.0001$), platelet counts (PLT, $p < 0.0001$), hemoglobin ($p < 0.0001$), total triglycerides (TG, $p = 0.0002$), total cholesterol (CHLO, $p < 0.0001$), HDL cholesterol (HDL-C, $p < 0.0001$), and LDL cholesterol (LDL-C, $p < 0.0001$) were significantly lower in CHC subjects.

Table 1. Descriptive characteristics of baseline factors in study participants ($n = 383$) [1].

	Control Group ($n = 147$)	CHC Group ($n = 236$)	p Value
Age (years)	54.82 ± 9.96	55.11 ± 8.70	0.7705
Gender (F/M)	71/76	120/116	0.6276
BMI	25.09 ± 3.80	25.33 ± 3.57	0.5337
Total viral load [$\log_{10}$ (IU/mL) #]	N/A	5.62 ± 0.84	N/A
HCV genotype (type1/non-type1/missing)	N/A	(131/100/5)	N/A
HCC (−/+) %	N/A	(94.9/5.1)	N/A
LC (−/+) %	N/A	(86/14)	N/A
Cr	0.98 ± 0.18	0.83 ± 0.25	< 0.0001 *
AST (IU/L)	24.62 ± 9.13	90.13 ± 52.90	< 0.0001 *
ALT (IU/L)	26.48 ± 18.23	122.48 ± 69.00	< 0.0001 *
GGT (IU/L)	33.08 ± 23.50	68.46 ± 65.51	< 0.0001 *
WBC	6370.88 ± 1699.14	5430.42 ± 1623.39	< 0.0001 *
PLT (×10^3/μL)	252.85 ± 66.63	152.42 ± 61.06	< 0.0001 *
Hemoglobin (g/dL)	14.42 ± 1.44	14.02 ± 1.46	0.0085 *
TG (mg/dL)	133.42 ± 99.02	98.87 ± 56.52	0.0002 *
CHLO (mg/dL)	213.61 ± 39.74	169.11 ± 35.53	< 0.0001 *
HDL-C (mg/dL)	55.54 ± 14.26	45.47 ± 14.87	< 0.0001 *
LDL-C (mg/dL)	123.20 ± 33.33	99.54 ± 31.78	< 0.0001 *
AC_sugar (mg/dL)	92.26 ± 20.49	103.71 ± 32.25	< 0.0001 *
HbA1c (%)	5.88 ± 0.78	5.92 ± 1.07	0.7101

[1] BMI, body mass index; HCC, hepatocellular carcinoma; LC, liver cirrhosis; Cr, creatinine; AST, aspartate aminotransferase; ALT, alanine aminotransferase; γGT, gamma-glutamyl transferase; WBC, white blood cell count; PLT, platelet count; TG, triglyceride; CHLO, cholesterol; HDL-C, HDL cholesterol; LDL-C, LDL cholesterol; AC_Sugar, fasting plasma glucose; HbA1c, hemoglobin A1c. All values are expressed as the mean ± standard deviation (SD). The p value was calculated for the continuous variables using the Student's t-test or Mann–Whitney test, and the χ^2 test was used for the categorical variables, with α = 0.05. * = $p < 0.05$. # The HCV virus loads were determined by log-transformation.

2.2. Circulating Let-7 Family Member Profiling

To determine the expression of let-7 family members in the blood, a qRT-PCR was performed. The −ΔCt (cycle threshold) value of each miRNA was measured and normalized to that of cel-39, as it showed the most consistent Ct value among all donors (27.10 ± 0.82 and 27.18 ± 1.06 for healthy controls and CHC patients, respectively) (Table S1). After statistical analyses, the expression levels of the let-7 family members were significantly lower in patients with CHC compared to the control group (Table 2 and Figure 1). The distribution of individuals is provided in Figure S2.

Table 2. Circulating let-7 family expression at baseline ($Log_{10}2^{-\Delta Ct}$) [1].

	Control (n = 147)	CHC (n = 236)	p Value
let-7a	−1.04 ± 0.74	−1.91 ± 0.57	< 0.0001 *
let-7b	−0.42 ± 0.43	−1.56 ± 0.60	< 0.0001 *
let-7c	−2.04 ± 0.36	−2.17 ± 0.44	< 0.0014 *
let-7d	−1.09 ± 0.61	−1.92 ± 0.50	< 0.0001 *
let-7e	−0.95 ± 0.64	−1.68 ± 0.62	< 0.0001 *
let-7f	−1.59 ± 0.54	−2.18 ± 0.40	< 0.0001 *
let-7g	−1.28 ± 0.52	−1.88 ± 0.55	< 0.0001 *
let-7i	−0.78 ± 0.47	−1.82 ± 0.57	< 0.0001 *
miR-98	−1.77 ± 0.54	−2.29 ± 0.33	< 0.0001 *

[1] Data is presented as the mean ± SD. $\Delta Ct = C_{target} - CT_{cel39}$; * = $p < 0.05$ following statistical analysis using an ANOVA with Bonferroni correction ($\alpha = 0.0056$).

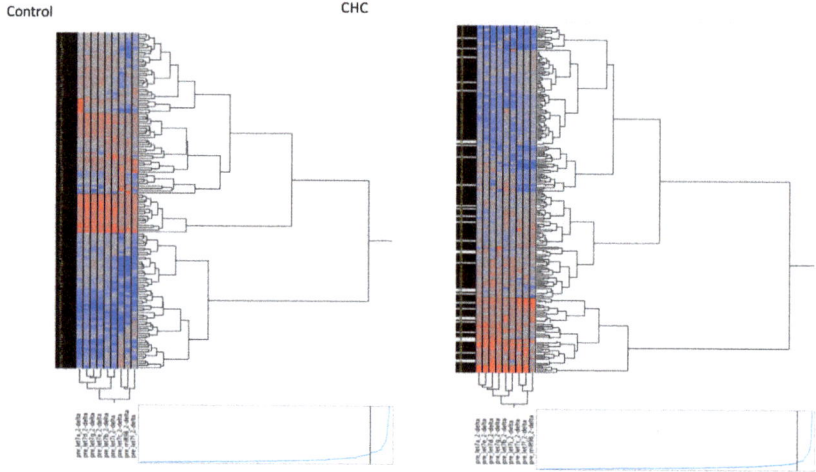

Figure 1. Hierarchical clustering plot (heatmap) of circulating let-7 family in the control group without hepatitis C virus (HCV) infection (n = 147) and HCV-infected patients (n = 236).

2.3. Three Clusters Distinguish the Let-7 Family Members

Due to let-7 family members (let-7a, 7b, 7c, 7d, 7e, 7f, 7g, 7i, and miR-98) with highly correlated (Table S2). To further investigate associations between the expression levels of let-7 family members in individuals from the control and HCV-infected groups, hierarchical clustering was performed using Ward's method. Three distinct clusters of let-7 family members were identified, in both the control and HCV-infected groups as represented in the hierarchical clustering plot (heatmap, Figure 1). Cluster 1 included let-7a, let-7d, let-7e, and let-7g. Cluster 2 was comprised of let-7b and let-7i, while Cluster 3 was made of let-7c, let-7f, and miR-98. We also performed a PCA to investigate the similarities between the expression levels of let-7 family members among the study participants and found that Cluster 3 (let-7c, f, and miR-98) was clearly distinct from clusters 1 and 2 in both patient groups (Figure S3).

2.4. Circulating Let-7 Family Expression Levels Correlate with Baseline Clinical Parameters

Correlation analyses between differentially expressed let-7 family members and clinical parameters were performed, including characteristics such as age, indicators of liver damage or injury (AST and ALT), platelet count, and HCV viral load (Table 3). The expression levels of Cluster 1 members (let-7a and let-7g) were significantly negatively correlated with AST ($r = -0.1898$ and -0.2038; $p = 0.0037$ and 0.0018, respectively). Meanwhile, the expression of Cluster 1 members (let-7a/d/e/g) were significantly positively correlated with PLT ($r = 0.2433, 0.2209, 0.2113$, and 0.1911; $p = 0.0002, 0.0007, 0.0012$, and 0.0034, respectively). However, no correlation was observed between any of the three let-7 clusters and ALT or HCV load. These results demonstrate that Cluster 1 (let-7a/d/e/g) was a better indicator of clinical characteristics than the other two let-7 clusters. Additionally, the circulating let-7 levels were not correlated with the HCV genotype (Table S3) or HCV viral load (Table S4).

Table 3. Correlation between circulating expression of let-7 family members and various clinical parameters ($n = 236$) [1].

		Age	AST	ALT	PLT	HCV RNA
Cluster1	let7a	−0.0986	−0.1898 *	−0.0772	0.2433 *	0.1118
	let7d	−0.0846	−0.1757	−0.0747	0.2209 *	0.0829
	let7e	−0.1431	−0.1504	−0.0546	0.2113 *	0.1211
	let7g	−0.1495	−0.2038 *	−0.1041	0.1911 *	0.1386
Cluster2	let7b	−0.0172	−0.0746	−0.0106	0.1384	0.1118
	let7i	−0.1141	−0.126	−0.0153	0.1365	0.0848
	let7c	−0.0456	−0.1298	−0.0448	0.0473	0.0753
Cluster3	let7f	−0.045	−0.1576	−0.0499	0.0728	0.1442
	miR98	−0.0195	−0.0915	−0.0373	0.0046	0.062

[1] Data represents correlation between miRNA expression and the values of each clinical parameter, as reported in Table 1. Correlation was determined using Pearson's test. AST, aspartate aminotransferase; ALT, alanine aminotransferase; PLT, platelet count; HCV, hepatitis C viral load. * = $p < 0.05$ following the Bonferroni correction ($\alpha = 0.0056$).

2.5. Let-7b/c/g Levels Are Associated with Clinical Progression

An independent dataset was used to further evaluate the let-7 clusters in normal tissue (N) and tumors (T) from TCGA liver cancer samples. A hierarchical clustering plot revealed three clusters, grouped into let7a-1/a-2/a-3/f-1/f-2/g/e, let-7b/c, and let7d/i (Figure 2). The expression levels of let-7a/b/c/g/i were significantly lower in tumors than in healthy tissue. Furthermore, the greatest reduction in let-7b/c/g expression was observed in tumors (red line, Figure 3). This observation was supported by OncomiR (www.oncomir.org.), which was used to explore the associations between TCGA-LIHC (liver hepatocellular carcinoma) survival data and the let-7 family expression levels. Kaplan–Meier survival analysis demonstrated that patients with high expression of let-7b/c/g had significantly increased overall survival compared to patients with low expression ($p = 0.03162$, Figure 4). Taken together, these data indicate that reduced expression of let-7b/c/g may be associated with liver tumor progression.

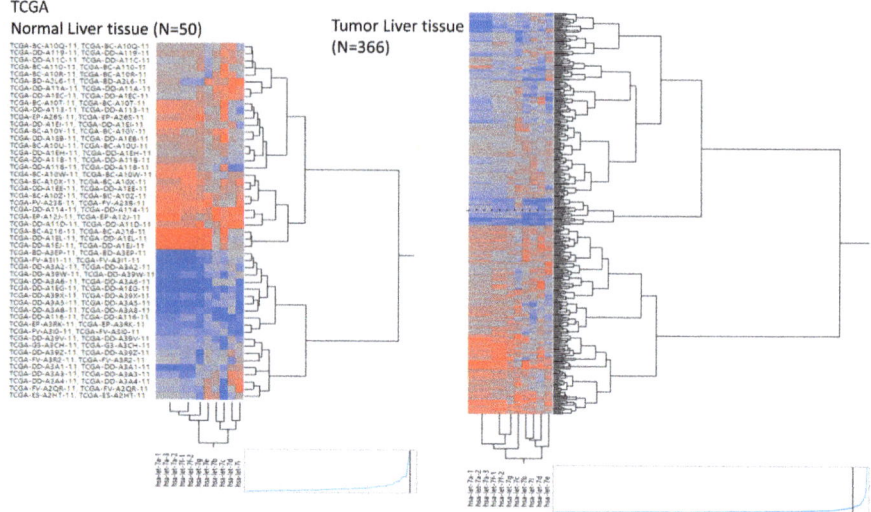

Figure 2. Hierarchical clustering plot (heatmap) of the let-7 miRNA family expression in healthy ($n = 50$) and tumor ($n = 366$) liver tissue samples obtained from TCGA-LIHC.

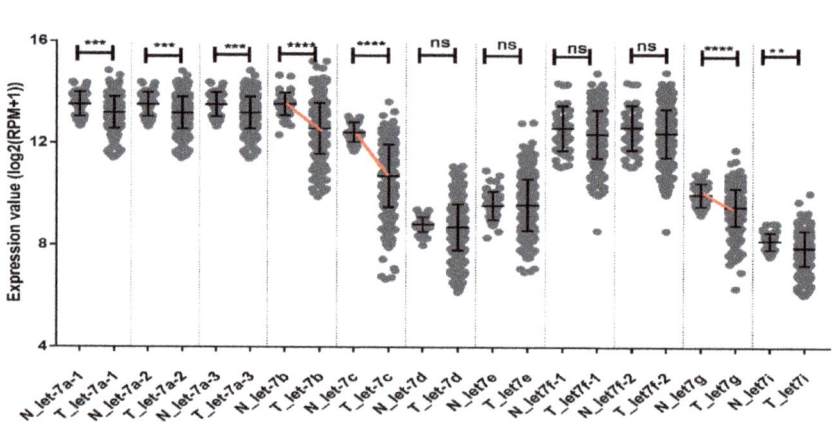

Figure 3. Dot plot showing the relationship between the expression of let-7 family members in normal ($n = 50$) and tumor ($n = 366$) tissues from liver cancer patients in the TCGA dataset. $\log_2$ (RPM +1) transformed values for let-7 family members are shown as the mean ± SD. Prominent declines in let-7b/c/g are indicated by red lines. Statistical significance was assessed using the Mann–Whitney test. The p values are represented as follows: ** = $p < 0.01$, *** = $p < 0.001$, **** = $p < 0.0001$.

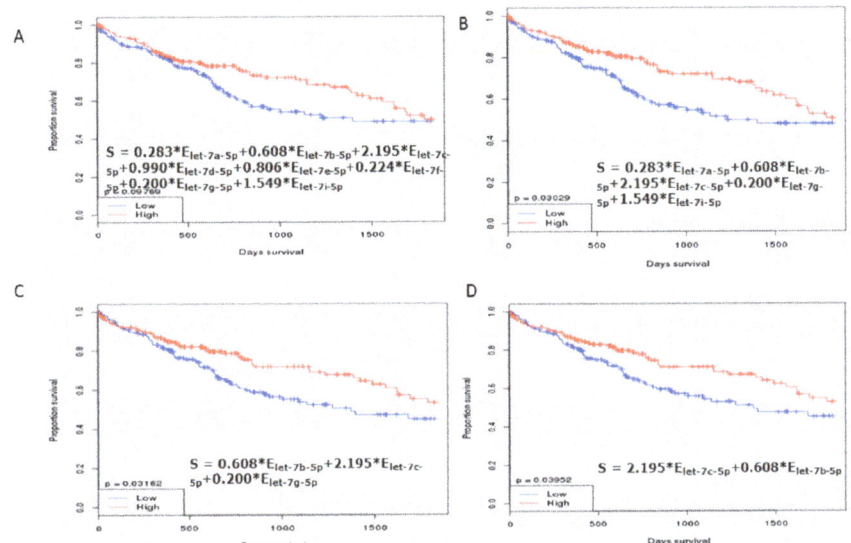

Figure 4. Kaplan–Meier (KM) survival analysis curve for let-7 family expression in TCGA-LIHC patients. The KM survival curves were examined according to (**A**) let-7 a/b/c/d/e/f/g/i expression level and (**B**) let-7 a/b/c/g/i expression levels. No differences in overall survival were observed. (**C**) let-7 b/c/g expression levels and (**D**) let-7 b/c expression levels show clear differences in overall survival. Statistical significance was obtained by log-rank tests, with $\alpha = 0.05$.

3. Discussion

Circulating mature miRNAs are small RNAs measuring approximately 22 nucleotides, and are known to be stable in the serum/plasma [9]. These nucleic acids represent novel non-invasive biomarkers for liver inflammation, liver fibrosis, liver cancer [17], and non-alcoholic fatty liver disease (NAFLD), [18]; they have also been shown to be useful for cancer detection [19]. Next-generation sequencing or microarray methods may be useful for identifying let-7 (a/b/c/d/e/f/g) members that are down-regulated in plasma or liver tissues to diagnose patients with hepatic fibrosis or hepatocellular carcinoma [15,16]. The ten mature let-7 family members are derived from 13 precursors located in nine different chromosomes with similar seed regions [20]. These let-7 family members target 3' UTRs of genes that are essential for development and have been conserved from *C. elegans* to humans [14]. However, the precise roles of circulating let-7 family members in humans remain uncharacterized. Here, we studied nine mature let-7 family members, including let-7a, 7b, 7c, 7d, 7e, 7f, 7g, 7i, and miR-98 (*Homo sapiens* [has]-miR-202 was excluded), in the circulating plasma of patients with CHC and healthy controls, using TaqMan quantitative RT-PCR assays. To the best of our knowledge, this is the first study to demonstrate that circulating let-7 family members can be classified into three similar clusters in control and CHC groups. The highest expression levels were found for Cluster 2 (let-7b and let-7i), while the lowest expression levels were found in Cluster 3 (let-7c/let-7f/miR-98). Moreover, the expression levels of circulating let-7 family members in patients with CHC were lower than those in the healthy population. Here we also identified the circulating let-7 b/c/g as representatives from each of the three let-7 clusters as the most effective markers for detecting liver-related diseases based on their strong association with clinical characteristics.

Our previous study showed that the expression level of let-7g in liver tissues was significantly lower in NVR patients than in SVR patients and that antiviral treatment with IFN/RBV could induce let-7g expression [13]. Moreover, the ectopic overexpression of let-7 family members was found to repress HCV core protein, and HCV loads in a cell model system [12,13]. However, in this study, the HCV load and HCV genotype were not found to be dependent factors and were negatively correlated with the expression levels of let-7 family members in the circulatory system. Therefore, let-7 family members might specifically target naked HCV RNA in liver tissue or cell models, but not HCV RNA within the envelope coat.

Previously Kirschner et al. reported specific miRNAs for which the profiling suggested an influence of hemolysis (miR-16, -451, -92a, let-7b, -103, -106a, 17, -21, -210, -27a, -31,-625-3p, -92a) as well as miRNAs (let-7a and let-7d) that appeared to be unaffected by hemolysis [21]. We, therefore, also measured the absorbance peak at 414 nm to detect the level of hemolysis and observed values of 0.192 ± 0.1478 (mean $\pm$ SD) for the control group, and 0.3143 ± 0.1723 (mean $\pm$ SD) for the CHC group ($p < 0.05$; Figure S4). Hemolysis was higher in CHC group. Therefore, the circulating let-7 (a/d/e/g) Cluster1 for the control group and CHC group might be unaffected by hemolysis.

Down-regulated let-7 miRNA expression in the circulatory system might result in an increase in interleukin-10 (IL-10) from CD4+ T-cells, providing the virus with an important survival advantage by manipulating the host immune response [22]. Early IL-10 elevation has been shown to strongly suppress the priming of naïve HCV–specific CD8+ T-cells, causing T-cell failure and viral persistence [23]. In addition, HCV induces the expression of toll-like receptor 4 (TLR4), enhancing the production of IFNβ and IL-6 [24]. Vespasiani-Gentilucci et al. confirmed that dominant TLR4 hyperexpression in patients with CHC was significantly correlated with the inflammatory score and degree of fibrosis, indicating that TLR4 plays an important role in the pathogenesis of HCV-related chronic liver diseases [25]. It has also been reported that let-7b can target TLR4 through 3' UTR post-transcriptional regulation and attenuates NF-κB activity [26]. Furthermore, expression levels of circulating let-7 (a/c/d) are inversely correlated with the severity of hepatic fibrosis [16], indicating that decreases in expression levels of let-7 family members might be involved in HCV infection and may cause inflammation, which is clinically and epidemiologically linked to cancer. NF-κB has been shown to have a causative role in inflammation. Iliopoulos et al. previously showed that transient activation of Src oncoproteins could trigger an NF-κB-mediated inflammatory response that directly activates Lin28 transcription and rapidly reduces the miRNA levels of let-7 family members [27].

The HCV core protein has been shown to have oncogenic potential [28]. Ali et al. demonstrated that the expression of an HCV sub-genomic replicon in cultured cells could cause them to acquire cancer stem cell-like signatures, including the enhanced expression of Lin28 and other proteins [29]. More importantly, Lin28b has been shown as sufficient to drive liver cancer and necessary for cancer maintenance in murine models. Many human cancers exhibit deregulated let-7 expression [14,30], the specificity of which is inhibited by Lin28A/B [31].

Interestingly, we also observed that let-7 (a/d/e/g) expression levels were positively correlated with PLT. Platelets are known therapeutic targets for preventing ischemic damage, enhancing liver regeneration, and inhibiting hepatitis progression [32]. These miRNAs are also inversely correlated with AST and ALT, which are markers of liver damage. Together, these results indicate that decreases in let-7 b/c/g levels might be involved in HCV infection and damage; moreover, the literature suggests these could promote inflammatory responses and tumorigenesis associated with HCV-related fibrosis or HCC.

In human genomic loci clusters, miRNA genes, including let-7 genes, are frequently located at fragile sites. Inflammatory status promoters increase the production of reactive oxygen species, leading to oxidative DNA damage by reducing DNA repair and increasing genomic instability of these fragile sites [33]. Genomic regions involved in cancers as tumor suppressor genes, such as *let-7g/miR-135−1*, are located in fragile sites of the ARP-DRR1 region in 3p21.1-21.2 [34]. Therefore, decreasing levels of let-7 family members may not only be an important marker for disease progression, but may also suggest fragile site instability and promotion of oncogenes.

Certain limitations were noted in this study. First, plasma samples are easily contaminated with peripheral blood mononuclear cells. Although previous studies have reported that let-7b/c/g levels in

PBMCs decline rapidly in HIV infection [22,35], HIV patients were excluded in the current study. Second, the relationship between expression levels of mature let-7 family members and inflammatory factors was unclear. Detailed analysis of other inflammatory mediators as intermediate variables is required. Such an analysis may provide additional information regarding the roles of other inflammatory mediators in the progression of HCV infection. Third, a large population-based follow-up study that includes additional circulating miRNAs is needed. This would allow for the investigation of baseline vs. post-antiviral treatment expression of the tumor suppressor let-7 b/c/g genes as potential early monitoring targets for patients who are at high risk for fibrosis, cirrhosis, and HCC.

4. Materials and Methods

4.1. Ethics Approval and Consent to Participate

This study was reviewed and approved by the IRB ethics committee (KMUHIRB-980176, KMUHIRB-20120097, and KMUHIRB-20140054 with the approval dates of 16 July 2009, 11 April 2012 and 7 November 2014, respectively). All protocols were approved by the ethical committee of the Kaohsiung Medical University Hospital, based on the International Conference on Harmonization for Good Clinical Practice. All participants provided written informed consent before enrollment.

4.2. Patient Cohort

We analyzed stored plasma extracted from the HCV patient database collected from one medical center and two regional core hospitals of the Kaohsiung Medical University between October 2009 and December 2016. The members of the age- and sex-matched control groups were enrolled from the same geographic communities. A total of 236 patients with HCV infection were enrolled in the HCV group. The following inclusion criteria were established before selection: i) Positive for anti-HCV antibodies for more than 6 months, and positive for HCV RNA by PCR assay; ii) negative for hepatitis B surface antigen (HBsAg) and no concomitant HIV; iii) negative for other types of hepatitis, including autoimmune hepatitis, primary biliary cirrhosis, sclerosing cholangitis, Wilson's disease, and α_1-antitrypsin deficiency; iv) daily ethanol consumption of <20 g (both females and males), as confirmed through an interview with the patient and a family member; and v) a high serum ALT level for 6 months preceding the study entry. The control group comprised 147 age- and sex-matched subjects without viral hepatitis who were selected based on the following inclusion criteria: i) Normal liver echogenicity, as determined by ultrasound sonography and ii) normal liver function test. The exclusion criteria for the control group included a current or past history of alcohol abuse (≥20 g ethanol per day), being pregnant, and seropositivity for HBsAg or anti-HCV antibody. All participants were advised to fast for 12 h overnight before the standard biochemistry tests, which included tests for Cr, AST, ALT, γGT, WBC, PLT, hemoglobin, TG, CHLO, HDL-C, LDL-C, AC_sugar, and HbA1c. Anthropometric data, including body weight and height, were obtained using standardized techniques. HBsAg was detected with commercially available enzyme-linked immunosorbent assay kits (Abbott Laboratories, North Chicago, IL, USA). HCV RNA and HCV genotype were assayed using a real-time PCR assay (RealTime HCV; Abbott Molecular, Des Plaines, IL, USA; detection limit, 12 IU/mL) [36].

4.3. MicroRNA Extraction from Plasma

A fixed volume of 200 µL of plasma was extracted using 1 mL Trizol LS reagent (Thermo Scientific, Wilmington, DE, USA), according to the manufacturer's protocol. Molecular biology-grade 1–bromo–3–chloropropane (BCP; 300 µL/1 mL TRIzol LS) was then added. After centrifuging for 15 min at 12,000× g and 4 °C, a fixed volume of the aqueous phase was transferred into a new tube, which was treated with 2 µL of 100-pmol/L synthetic *C. elegans* Cel-39 as a spike-in control, and 10 µg of RNase-free glycogen as a co-precipitant carrier. The aqueous sample was mixed thoroughly with 100% molecular-grade isopropanol and incubated on ice for 1 h. A gel-like pellet was obtained after centrifugation at 12,000× g for 15 min. The flow-through was discarded and the pellet was washed with 80% ethanol. The pellet was again centrifuged at 7500× g for 5 min at 4 °C, and the supernatant was discarded. The RNA (including the miRNA) was air dried, eluted in 15 µL of RNase-free H$_2$O and stored at −80 °C until further analysis. A total of 2 µL of each sample was used to measure the absorbance peak at 414 nm for the level of hemolysis on a NanoDrop™ 2000 (Thermo Fisher Scientific, Inc., Waltham, MA, USA) [37].

4.4. Quantification of Circulating miRNAs

The total RNA (20 ng) was used as a template for reverse transcription, which was performed using the TaqMan MicroRNA Reverse Transcription kit and the associated miRNA-specific stem-loop primers to convert miRNA to cDNA as step 1 (Thermo Scientific, Wilmington, DE, USA), according to the manufacturer's instructions. The *C. elegans* synthetic cel-miR-39-3p, a suitable and reproducible normalizer, was used as the spiked-in control [38]. The relative levels of individual miRNAs were amplified using the TaqMan® Universal PCR Master Mix II, without uracil N-glycosylase (UNG), on a 7900HT Sequence detection system. Specific amplification was performed using the following program: 95 °C for 10 min, and amplification followed by 40 cycles of 95 °C for 15 s and 60 °C for 1 min as step 2. Specific primers of mature miRNA sequences were used for the TaqMan R microRNA assays (assay ID): hsa-let-7a (000377), hsa-let-7b (002619), hsa-let-7c (000379), hsa-let-7d (002283), hsa-let-7e (002406), hsa-let-7f (000382), hsa-let-7g (002282), hsa-let-7i (002221), hsa-miR-98 (000577), and an internal control, cel-miR-39-3p (000200). The hsa-miR-202 (002362) primer was excluded as it was under-determined in 99% of the samples with different nucleotides of the mature let-7 family members (Figure S1). The relative expression level of each let-7 member was determined using the comparative C$_t$ method, which was defined as $2^{-\Delta Ct}$, where $\Delta C_t = C_t$ of the let-7 member − C_t of cel-39.

4.5. miRNA-seq and Clinical Data from UCSC Xena Platform

LIHC samples, including healthy ($n = 50$) and primary tumor tissues ($n = 366$) were obtained from the UCSC Xena platform. This platform provides interactive online visualization of cancer genomics datasets, such as TCGA, a public data resource [39]. Expression of the let-7 miRNA family mature strand was transformed according to RNA sequencing guidelines (Illumina Hiseq 2000) and presented as log$_2$ (RPM +1). Kaplan–Meier survival curves and log-rank methods for the let-7 family clusters in LIHC were performed using OncomiR to evaluate overall survival (OS) rate [40].

4.6. Statistical Analysis

Statistically significant differences between the expression levels of let-7 family members in the different groups were determined using the Mann–Whitney test with Bonferroni correction for multiple comparisons. Pearson's correlation analysis was used to assess the relationships between the let-7 family members and the different clinical parameters. Hierarchical clustering and PCA were performed to identify the distinguishable let-7 family members. All analyses were performed using JMP 12.0 (SAS Institute, Cary, NC, USA). Graphs were generated using the GraphPad Prism 5.0 software (San Diego, CA, USA).

Supplementary Materials: Supplementary materials can be found at http://www.mdpi.com/1422-0067/21/14/4945/s1.

Author Contributions: Investigation, Y.-S.T.; Formal analysis, Y.-S.T. and P.-C.T.; Patient sample collection, M.-L.Y. (Ming-Lun Yeh), C.-I.H., C.-F.H., M.-H.H., T.-W.L., Y.-H.L., P.-C.L., Z.-Y.L., S.-C.C., J.-F.H., C.-Y.D., M.-L.Y. (Ming-Lung Yu), and W.-L.C.; Writing—Original Draft Preparation; Y.-S.T., C.-Y.D., and M.-L.Y.; Writing—Review and Editing, C.-Y.D. and M.-L.Y. All authors have read and agree to the published version of the manuscript.

Funding: This work was supported by grants from the National Science Council of Taiwan (grant number MOST104-2314-B-037-075-MY3) and Kaohsiung Medical University Hospital (grant number KMUH106-6R06 and KMUH107-7R06). Taiwan Liver Research Foundation (TLRF) provides free liver disease surveillance and health educational lectures in local community.

Conflicts of Interest: The authors declare no conflict of interest. The sponsors had no role in the design, execution, interpretation, or writing of the study.

Abbreviations

AC_sugar	Fasting plasma glucose
ALT	Alanine aminotransferase
AST	Aspartate transaminase
BCP	1–bromo–3–chloropropane
BMI	Body mass index
CHLO	Total cholesterol
CHC	Chronic hepatitis C virus infection
Cr	Creatinine
CT	Cycle threshold
DAA	Direct-acting antiviral
EV	Extracellular vesicle
γGT	Gamma-glutamyl transferase
HCC	Hepatocellular carcinoma
HCV	Hepatitis C virus
HBsAg	Hepatitis B surface antigen
HDL-C	HDL cholesterol
HIV	Human immunodeficiency virus
Hsa	*Homo spaiens*
IFN	Interferon
KM	Kaplan–Meier
LC	Liver cirrhosis
LDL-C	LDL cholesterol
LIHC	Liver hepatocellular carcinoma
miRNA	MicroRNA
NAFLD	Non-alcoholic fatty liver disease
NVR	Non-virological response
OS	Overall survival
PCA	Principal component analysis
PegIFNα	Pegylated interferon-α
PLT	Platelet count
RBV	Ribavirin
SD	Standard deviation
SVR	Sustained virologic response
TCGA	The Cancer Genome Atlas
TG	Total triglycerides
TLR4	Toll-like receptor 4
WBC	White blood cell

References

1. Lee, M.H.; Yang, H.I.; Lu, S.N.; Jen, C.L.; You, S.L.; Wang, L.Y.; Wang, C.H.; Chen, W.J.; Chen, C.J.; Reveal-HCV Study Group. Chronic hepatitis C virus infection increases mortality from hepatic and extrahepatic diseases: A community-based long-term prospective study. *J. Infect. Dis.* **2012**, *206*, 469–477. [CrossRef] [PubMed]
2. Yu, M.L.; Lin, S.M.; Chuang, W.L.; Dai, C.Y.; Wang, J.H.; Lu, S.N.; Sheen, I.S.; Chang, W.Y.; Lee, C.M.; Liaw, Y.F. A sustained virological response to interferon or interferon/ribavirin reduces hepatocellular carcinoma and improves survival in chronic hepatitis C: A nationwide, multicentre study in Taiwan. *Antivir. Ther.* **2006**, *11*, 985–994. [PubMed]
3. Huang, C.F.; Yeh, M.L.; Huang, C.I.; Lin, Y.J.; Tsai, P.C.; Lin, Z.Y.; Chan, S.Y.; Chen, S.C.; Yang, H.I.; Huang, J.F.; et al. Risk of hepatitis C virus related hepatocellular carcinoma between subjects with spontaneous and treatment-induced viral clearance. *Oncotarget* **2017**, *8*, 43925–43933. [CrossRef] [PubMed]
4. Huang, C.F.; Yeh, M.L.; Tsai, P.C.; Hsieh, M.H.; Yang, H.L.; Hsieh, M.Y.; Yang, J.F.; Lin, Z.Y.; Chen, S.C.; Wang, L.Y.; et al. Baseline gamma-glutamyl transferase levels strongly correlate with hepatocellular carcinoma

development in non-cirrhotic patients with successful hepatitis C virus eradication. *J. Hepatol.* **2014**, *61*, 67–74. [CrossRef] [PubMed]
5. WHO. *Global Hepatitis Report*; World Health Organization: Geneva, Switzerland, 2017.
6. Waziry, R.; Hajarizadeh, B.; Grebely, J.; Amin, J.; Law, M.; Danta, M.; George, J.; Dore, G.J. Hepatocellular carcinoma risk following direct-acting antiviral HCV therapy: A systematic review, meta-analyses, and meta-regression. *J. Hepatol.* **2017**, *67*, 1204–1212. [CrossRef] [PubMed]
7. Hoshida, Y.; Fuchs, B.C.; Bardeesy, N.; Baumert, T.F.; Chung, R.T. Pathogenesis and prevention of hepatitis C virus-induced hepatocellular carcinoma. *J. Hepatol.* **2014**, *61*, S79–S90. [CrossRef]
8. Baumert, T.F.; Juhling, F.; Ono, A.; Hoshida, Y. Hepatitis C-related hepatocellular carcinoma in the era of new generation antivirals. *BMC Med.* **2017**, *15*, 52. [CrossRef]
9. Chen, X.; Ba, Y.; Ma, L.; Cai, X.; Yin, Y.; Wang, K.; Guo, J.; Zhang, Y.; Chen, J.; Guo, X.; et al. Characterization of microRNAs in serum: A novel class of biomarkers for diagnosis of cancer and other diseases. *Cell Res.* **2008**, *18*, 997–1006. [CrossRef]
10. Hsi, E.; Huang, C.F.; Dai, C.Y.; Juo, S.H.; Chou, W.W.; Huang, J.F.; Yeh, M.L.; Lin, Z.Y.; Chen, S.C.; Wang, L.Y.; et al. Peripheral blood mononuclear cells microRNA predicts treatment outcome of hepatitis C virus genotype 1 infection. *Antivir. Res.* **2014**, *105*, 135–142. [CrossRef]
11. Cheng, J.C.; Yeh, Y.J.; Tseng, C.P.; Hsu, S.D.; Chang, Y.L.; Sakamoto, N.; Huang, H.D. Let-7b is a novel regulator of hepatitis C virus replication. *Cell. Mol. Life Sci.* **2012**, *69*, 2621–2633. [CrossRef]
12. Cheng, M.; Si, Y.; Niu, Y.; Liu, X.; Li, X.; Zhao, J.; Jin, Q.; Yang, W. High-throughput profiling of alpha interferon- and interleukin-28B-regulated microRNAs and identification of let-7s with anti-hepatitis C virus activity by targeting IGF2BP1. *J. Virol.* **2013**, *87*, 9707–9718. [CrossRef] [PubMed]
13. Chou, W.W.; Huang, C.F.; Yeh, M.L.; Tsai, Y.S.; Hsieh, M.Y.; Huang, C.I.; Huang, J.F.; Tsai, P.C.; Hsi, E.; Juo, S.H.; et al. MicroRNA let-7g cooperates with interferon/ribavirin to repress hepatitis C virus replication. *J. Mol. Med.* **2016**, *94*, 311–320. [CrossRef] [PubMed]
14. Roush, S.; Slack, F.J. The let-7 family of microRNAs. *Trends Cell Biol.* **2008**, *18*, 505–516. [CrossRef]
15. Borel, F.; Konstantinova, P.; Jansen, P.L. Diagnostic and therapeutic potential of miRNA signatures in patients with hepatocellular carcinoma. *J. Hepatol.* **2012**, *56*, 1371–1383. [CrossRef] [PubMed]
16. Matsuura, K.; De Giorgi, V.; Schechterly, C.; Wang, R.Y.; Farci, P.; Tanaka, Y.; Alter, H.J. Circulating let-7 levels in plasma and extracellular vesicles correlate with hepatic fibrosis progression in chronic hepatitis C. *Hepatology* **2016**, *64*, 732–745. [CrossRef]
17. Roderburg, C.; Luedde, T. Circulating microRNAs as markers of liver inflammation, fibrosis and cancer. *J. Hepatol.* **2014**, *61*, 1434–1437. [CrossRef]
18. Pirola, C.J.; Fernandez Gianotti, T.; Castano, G.O.; Mallardi, P.; San Martino, J.; Mora Gonzalez Lopez Ledesma, M.; Flichman, D.; Mirshahi, F.; Sanyal, A.J.; Sookoian, S. Circulating microRNA signature in non-alcoholic fatty liver disease: From serum non-coding RNAs to liver histology and disease pathogenesis. *Gut* **2015**, *64*, 800–812. [CrossRef]
19. Mitchell, P.S.; Parkin, R.K.; Kroh, E.M.; Fritz, B.R.; Wyman, S.K.; Pogosova-Agadjanyan, E.L.; Peterson, A.; Noteboom, J.; O'Briant, K.C.; Allen, A.; et al. Circulating microRNAs as stable blood-based markers for cancer detection. *Proc. Natl. Acad. Sci. USA* **2008**, *105*, 10513–10518. [CrossRef]
20. Lewis, B.P.; Burge, C.B.; Bartel, D.P. Conserved seed pairing, often flanked by adenosines, indicates that thousands of human genes are microRNA targets. *Cell* **2005**, *120*, 15–20. [CrossRef] [PubMed]
21. Kirschner, M.B.; Edelman, J.J.; Kao, S.C.; Vallely, M.P.; van Zandwijk, N.; Reid, G. The Impact of Hemolysis on Cell-Free microRNA Biomarkers. *Front. Genet.* **2013**, *4*, 94. [CrossRef]
22. Swaminathan, S.; Suzuki, K.; Seddiki, N.; Kaplan, W.; Cowley, M.J.; Hood, C.L.; Clancy, J.L.; Murray, D.D.; Mendez, C.; Gelgor, L.; et al. Differential regulation of the Let-7 family of microRNAs in CD4+ T cells alters IL-10 expression. *J. Immunol.* **2012**, *188*, 6238–6246. [CrossRef] [PubMed]
23. Niesen, E.; Schmidt, J.; Flecken, T.; Thimme, R. Suppressive effect of interleukin 10 on priming of naive hepatitis C virus-specific CD8+ T cells. *J. Infect. Dis.* **2015**, *211*, 821–826. [CrossRef]
24. Machida, K.; Cheng, K.T.; Sung, V.M.; Levine, A.M.; Foung, S.; Lai, M.M. Hepatitis C virus induces toll-like receptor 4 expression, leading to enhanced production of beta interferon and interleukin-6. *J. Virol.* **2006**, *80*, 866–874. [CrossRef] [PubMed]

25. Vespasiani-Gentilucci, U.; Carotti, S.; Onetti-Muda, A.; Perrone, G.; Ginanni-Corradini, S.; Latasa, M.U.; Avila, M.A.; Carpino, G.; Picardi, A.; Morini, S. Toll-like receptor-4 expression by hepatic progenitor cells and biliary epithelial cells in HCV-related chronic liver disease. *Mod. Pathol.* **2012**, *25*, 576–589. [CrossRef] [PubMed]
26. Teng, G.G.; Wang, W.H.; Dai, Y.; Wang, S.J.; Chu, Y.X.; Li, J. Let-7b is involved in the inflammation and immune responses associated with Helicobacter pylori infection by targeting Toll-like receptor 4. *PLoS ONE* **2013**, *8*, e56709. [CrossRef] [PubMed]
27. Iliopoulos, D.; Hirsch, H.A.; Struhl, K. An epigenetic switch involving NF-kappaB, Lin28, Let-7 MicroRNA, and IL6 links inflammation to cell transformation. *Cell* **2009**, *139*, 693–706. [CrossRef]
28. Moriya, K.; Fujie, H.; Shintani, Y.; Yotsuyanagi, H.; Tsutsumi, T.; Ishibashi, K.; Matsuura, Y.; Kimura, S.; Miyamura, T.; Koike, K. The core protein of hepatitis C virus induces hepatocellular carcinoma in transgenic mice. *Nat. Med.* **1998**, *4*, 1065–1067. [CrossRef]
29. Ali, N.; Allam, H.; May, R.; Sureban, S.M.; Bronze, M.S.; Bader, T.; Umar, S.; Anant, S.; Houchen, C.W. Hepatitis C virus-induced cancer stem cell-like signatures in cell culture and murine tumor xenografts. *J. Virol.* **2011**, *85*, 12292–12303. [CrossRef] [PubMed]
30. Boyerinas, B.; Park, S.M.; Hau, A.; Murmann, A.E.; Peter, M.E. The role of let-7 in cell differentiation and cancer. *Endocr. Relat. Cancer* **2010**, *17*, F19–F36. [CrossRef] [PubMed]
31. Nam, Y.; Chen, C.; Gregory, R.I.; Chou, J.J.; Sliz, P. Molecular basis for interaction of let-7 microRNAs with Lin28. *Cell* **2011**, *147*, 1080–1091. [CrossRef]
32. Lisman, T.; Porte, R.J. The role of platelets in liver inflammation and regeneration. *Semin. Thromb. Hemost.* **2010**, *36*, 170–174. [CrossRef]
33. Barash, H.; Gross, E.R.; Edrei, Y.; Ella, E.; Israel, A.; Cohen, I.; Corchia, N.; Ben-Moshe, T.; Pappo, O.; Pikarsky, E.; et al. Accelerated carcinogenesis following liver regeneration is associated with chronic inflammation-induced double-strand DNA breaks. *Proc. Natl. Acad. Sci. USA* **2010**, *107*, 2207–2212. [CrossRef] [PubMed]
34. Calin, G.A.; Sevignani, C.; Dumitru, C.D.; Hyslop, T.; Noch, E.; Yendamuri, S.; Shimizu, M.; Rattan, S.; Bullrich, F.; Negrini, M.; et al. Human microRNA genes are frequently located at fragile sites and genomic regions involved in cancers. *Proc. Natl. Acad. Sci. USA* **2004**, *101*, 2999–3004. [CrossRef]
35. Witwer, K.W.; Watson, A.K.; Blankson, J.N.; Clements, J.E. Relationships of PBMC microRNA expression, plasma viral load, and CD4+ T-cell count in HIV-1-infected elite suppressors and viremic patients. *Retrovirology* **2012**, *9*, 5. [CrossRef] [PubMed]
36. Vermehren, J.; Yu, M.L.; Monto, A.; Yao, J.D.; Anderson, C.; Bertuzis, R.; Schneider, G.; Sarrazin, C. Multi-center evaluation of the Abbott RealTime HCV assay for monitoring patients undergoing antiviral therapy for chronic hepatitis C. *J. Clin. Virol.* **2011**, *52*, 133–137. [CrossRef]
37. Kirschner, M.B.; Kao, S.C.; Edelman, J.J.; Armstrong, N.J.; Vallely, M.P.; van Zandwijk, N.; Reid, G. Haemolysis during sample preparation alters microRNA content of plasma. *PLoS ONE* **2011**, *6*, e24145. [CrossRef] [PubMed]
38. Vigneron, N.; Meryet-Figuiere, M.; Guttin, A.; Issartel, J.P.; Lambert, B.; Briand, M.; Louis, M.H.; Vernon, M.; Lebailly, P.; Lecluse, Y.; et al. Towards a new standardized method for circulating miRNAs profiling in clinical studies: Interest of the exogenous normalization to improve miRNA signature accuracy. *Mol. Oncol.* **2016**, *10*, 981–992. [CrossRef]
39. Goldman, M.; Craft, B.; Brooks, A.; Zhu, J.; Haussler, D. The UCSC Xena Platform for cancer genomics data visualization and interpretation. *BioRxiv* **2020**, in press.
40. Wong, N.W.; Chen, Y.; Chen, S.; Wang, X. OncomiR: An online resource for exploring pan-cancer microRNA dysregulation. *Bioinformatics* **2018**, *34*, 713–715. [CrossRef]

© 2020 by the authors. Licensee MDPI, Basel, Switzerland. This article is an open access article distributed under the terms and conditions of the Creative Commons Attribution (CC BY) license (http://creativecommons.org/licenses/by/4.0/).

Article

Post-Treatment M2BPGi Level and the Rate of Autotaxin Reduction are Predictive of Hepatocellular Carcinoma Development after Antiviral Therapy in Patients with Chronic Hepatitis C

Kazuya Takemura [1], Etsuko Takizawa [1], Akihiro Tamori [2,*], Mika Nakamae [1,3], Hiroshi Kubota [1], Sawako Uchida-Kobayashi [2], Masaru Enomoto [2], Norifumi Kawada [2] and Masayuki Hino [1,3]

1 Department of Central Clinical Laboratory, Osaka City University Hospital, 1-5-7, Asahi-machi, Abeno-ku, Osaka-shi, Osaka 545-8586, Japan; takemura-kazuya-rn@alumni.osaka-u.ac.jp (K.T.); takichan@med.osaka-cu.ac.jp (E.T.); mika-a@med.osaka-cu.ac.jp (M.N.); m1352197@med.osaka-cu.ac.jp (H.K.); hinom@med.osaka-cu.ac.jp (M.H.)
2 Department of Hepatology, Graduate School of Medicine, Osaka City University, 1-4-3, Asahi-machi, Abeno-ku, Osaka-shi, Osaka 545-8585, Japan; sawako@med.osaka-cu.ac.jp (S.U.-K.); enomoto-m@med.osaka-cu.ac.jp (M.E.); kawadanori@med.osaka-cu.ac.jp (N.K.)
3 Department of Hematology, Graduate School of Medicine, Osaka City University, 1-4-3, Asahi-machi, Abeno-ku, Osaka-shi, Osaka 545-8585, Japan
* Correspondence: atamori@med.osaka-cu.ac.jp; Tel.: +81-6-6645-3905

Received: 20 May 2020; Accepted: 23 June 2020; Published: 25 June 2020

Abstract: Patients with chronic hepatitis C virus (HCV) develop hepatocellular carcinoma (HCC) regardless of achieving a sustained viral response (SVR). Because advanced liver fibrosis is a powerful risk factor for HCC, we analyzed the association between autotaxin (ATX), a liver fibrosis marker, and post-SVR HCC development within 3 years after antiviral treatment. We included 670 patients with HCV who received direct-acting antivirals, achieved SVR and were followed up for at least 6 months (270 of them were followed up for 3 years or more). We measured serum ATX levels before treatment and 12/24 weeks after treatment. The diagnosis of HCC was based on imaging modalities, such as dynamic computed tomography and dynamic magnetic resonance imaging and/or liver biopsy. The present study revealed that high levels of serum ATX predicted post-SVR HCC development (area under the receiver operating characteristic: 0.70–0.76). However, Wisteria floribunda agglutinin positive Mac-2 binding protein (M2BPGi), another liver fibrosis marker, was a more useful predictive marker especially post-treatment according to a multivariate analysis. Patients with a high rate of ATX reduction before and after antiviral treatment did not develop HCC regardless of high pretreatment ATX levels. In conclusion, post-treatment M2BPGi level and the combination of pretreatment ATX levels and rate of ATX reduction were useful predictive markers for post-SVR HCC development in patients with chronic HCV infection.

Keywords: autotaxin; direct-acting antivirals; hepatocellular carcinoma; hepatitis C virus; sustained viral response; Wisteria floribunda agglutinin positive Mac-2 binding protein

1. Introduction

Globally, it is estimated that 71.1 million individuals are chronically infected with hepatitis C virus (HCV), of whom 10–20% will develop liver complications, including decompensated cirrhosis and hepatocellular carcinoma (HCC) [1]. Recently approved direct-acting antivirals (DAAs) can achieve a >95% sustained viral response (SVR) for DAA-naïve patients with HCV [1]. However, it was reported that HCC develops or recurs in patients who achieve SVR [2,3]. In the guidelines, follow-up programs are recommended for SVR patients to detect the development of HCC earlier and to evaluate improvements in liver function [4,5]. Screening is recommended to be conducted every 6 months for high-risk patients and every 3–4 months for extremely high-risk patients [6]. Ultrasonography (US) and serum tumor markers are the primary screening modalities. In addition, dynamic computed tomography (CT) and dynamic magnetic resonance imaging (MRI) were combined with these screening methods. Properly stratifying high-risk patients is important for screening. Previous studies reported that older age, male sex, the lack of a SVR, habitual alcohol intake, higher alpha-fetoprotein levels, higher aspartate aminotransferase (AST) levels, lower platelet counts, and type 2 diabetes mellitus are risk factors [7–9]. In a large retrospective cohort study, the highest risk factor for post-SVR HCC development has been reported to be the presence of cirrhosis [10]. Therefore, liver fibrosis markers may be predictive markers for the development of post-SVR HCC. Wisteria floribunda agglutinin positive Mac-2 binding protein (M2BPGi), a glycoprotein marker for liver fibrosis, has been reported to be associated with HCC development [11–13].

Autotaxin (ATX) was discovered as an autocrine motility stimulating protein in a conditioned medium from A2058 human melanoma cell cultures [14]. Subsequently, ATX has been reported to have lysophospholipase D activity to generate lysophosphatidic acid (LPA) from lysophospholipids in the blood [15]. What was previously thought to be the function of ATX was actually the function of LPA. LPA is involved in cell migration, cell proliferation, neurogenesis, and angiogenesis [16,17]. In recent studies, serum ATX levels have been reported to correlate with liver fibrosis stage in patients with HCV [18,19], chronic hepatitis B virus (HBV) [20], and non-alcoholic fatty liver disease (NAFLD) [21]. ATX is metabolized by liver sinusoidal endothelial cells, and reduced clearance due to liver fibrosis increases serum ATX levels [22]. In addition, serum ATX levels are higher in women than in men [23].

Interestingly, ATX-LPA signaling has been reported to be associated with HCC development [24–26]. Kaffe et al. revealed that hepatocyte-specific ATX deletion in mice attenuated HCC development [24]. In addition, Nakagawa et al. established that histological liver fibrosis was attenuated and HCC development was reduced by an ATX inhibitor (AM063) [25]. Therefore, serum ATX levels could be a more useful predictive marker for post-SVR HCC development.

In the present study, we analyzed the association between serum ATX levels and the development of post-SVR HCC within 3 years after antiviral treatment. In addition, we determined whether ATX or M2BPGi was a more useful predictive marker for post-SVR HCC development.

2. Results

2.1. Comparisons of ATX and M2BPGi Levels by the Presence or Absence of Post-SVR HCC

We recruited 755 patients with HCV who had received interferon (IFN)-free DAA therapy. The patient selection criteria are shown in Figure 1. First, we analyzed the association between pretreatment ATX and M2BPGi levels and post-SVR HCC development using data from Cohort B. The pretreatment ATX levels in patients with post-SVR HCC were higher than those in patients without post-SVR HCC (median values: males, 1.56 mg/L vs. 1.14 mg/L; females, 2.37 mg/L vs. 1.67 mg/L; Figure 2A,B). The pretreatment M2BPGi levels in patients with post-SVR HCC were higher than those in patients without post-SVR HCC (males, 4.31 cutoff index (C.O.I.) vs. 1.82 C.O.I.; female, 3.67 C.O.I. vs. 2.52 C.O.I.; Figure 3A,B). Next, we examined the relationship between ATX and M2BPGi levels at 12/24 weeks after treatment and post-SVR HCC development. The post-treatment ATX levels were higher in patients with post-SVR HCC than in patients without post-SVR HCC (males, 1.39 mg/L vs. 0.95 mg/L; females, 1.74 mg/L vs. 1.37 mg/L; Figure 2C,D). The post-treatment M2BPGi levels were higher in the post-SVR HCC group (males, 2.43 C.O.I. vs. 1.12 C.O.I.; females, 2.76 C.O.I. vs. 1.35 C.O.I.; Figure 3C,D).

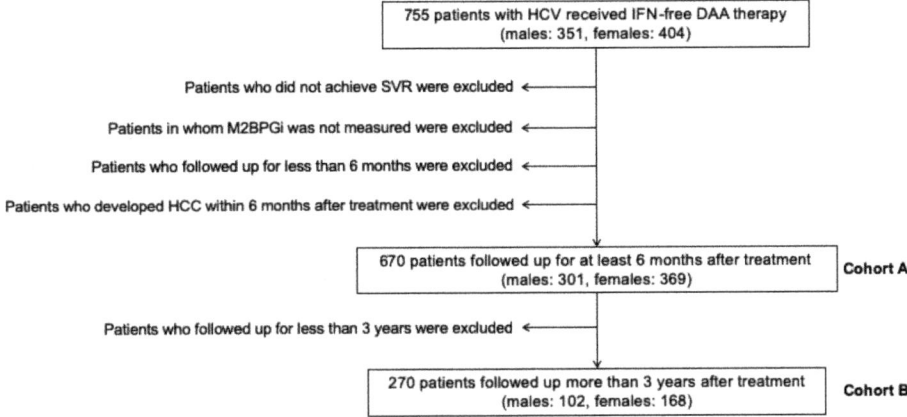

Figure 1. Selection of eligible patients. HCV: hepatitis C virus; IFN: interferon; DAA: direct-acting antiviral; SVR: sustained viral response; M2BPGi: Wisteria floribunda agglutinin positive Mac-2 binding protein; HCC: hepatocellular carcinoma.

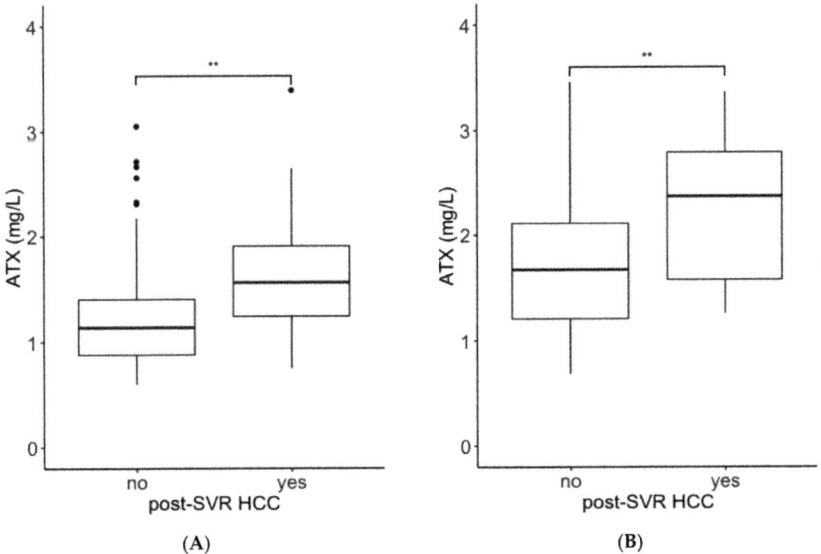

Figure 2. Cont.

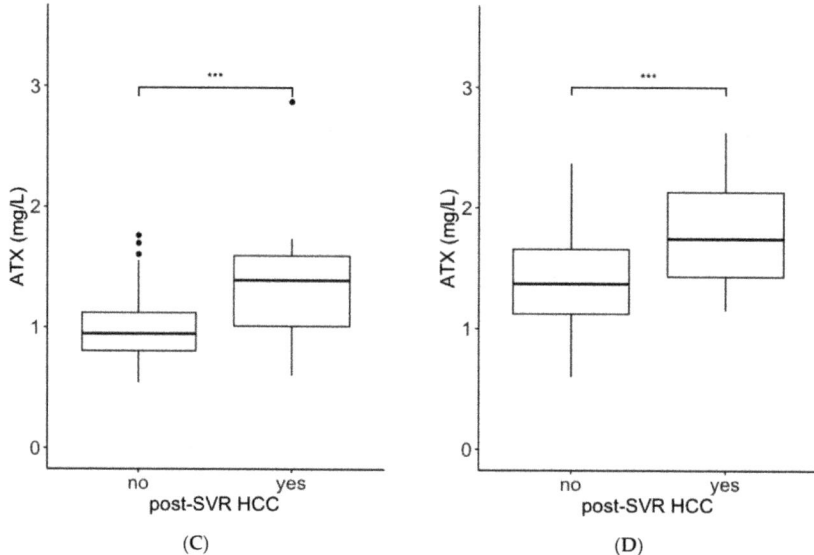

Figure 2. Comparisons of serum autotaxin (ATX) levels in patients with and without post-SVR HCC development. Data from Cohort B were used for the analysis. Data from male patients (**A**,**C**) and female patients (**B**,**D**) are shown. A and B indicate pretreatment levels, and C and D indicate those at 12/24 weeks after antiviral treatment. Boxes represent the interquartile range of the data. The horizontal lines in the boxes indicate the median values. The vertical lines connect the nearest values of 1.5 times the interquartile range from the quartile points. The dots indicate outliers. **: $p < 0.01$; ***: $p < 0.001$. ATX: autotaxin; SVR: sustained viral response; HCC: hepatocellular carcinoma.

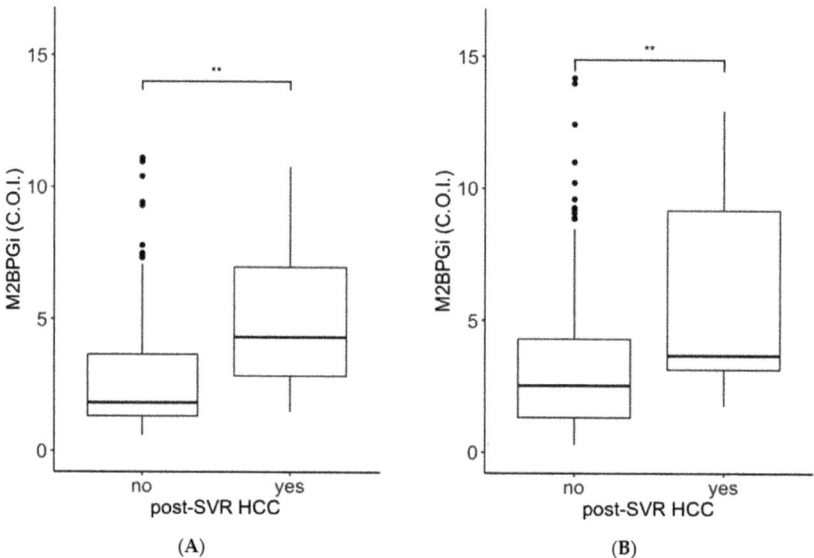

Figure 3. *Cont.*

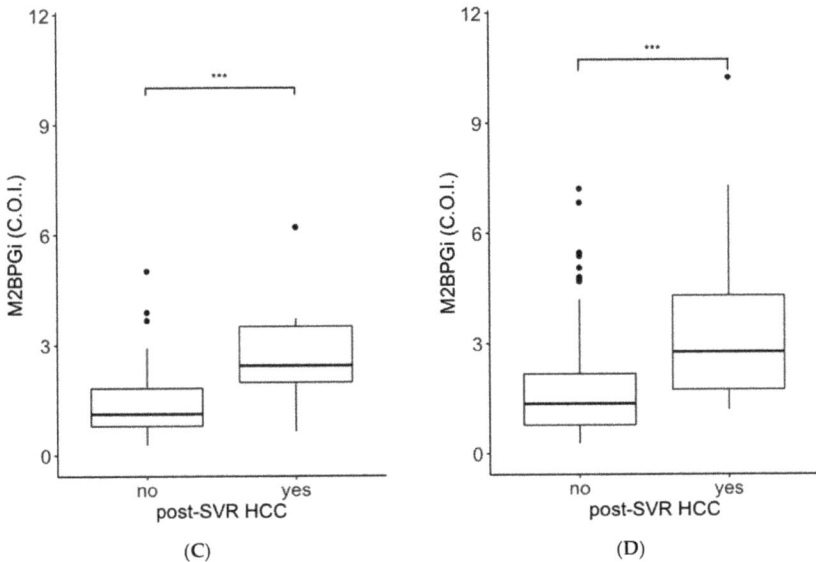

Figure 3. Comparisons of M2BPGi in patients with and without post-SVR HCC development. Data from Cohort B were used for the analysis. Data from male patients (**A**,**C**) and female patients (**B**,**D**) are shown. A and B indicate pretreatment levels, and C and D indicate those at 12/24 weeks after antiviral treatment. Boxes represent the interquartile range of the data. The horizontal lines in the boxes indicate the median values. The vertical lines connect the nearest values of 1.5 times the interquartile range from the quartile points. The dots indicate outliers. **: $p < 0.01$; ***: $p < 0.001$. M2BPGi: Wisteria floribunda agglutinin positive Mac-2 binding protein; SVR: sustained viral response; HCC: hepatocellular carcinoma.

2.2. Predictive Ability for Post-SVR HCC Development within 3 Years after Antiviral Treatment

Next, we analyzed the predictive ability for post-SVR HCC development using the area under the receiver operating characteristics (AUROCs). The AUROCs of pretreatment ATX levels were 0.70 for both male and female patients (Figure 4A,B), and those of pretreatment M2BPGi levels were 0.73 for both male and female patients (Figure 4A,B). The AUROCs of post-treatment ATX levels were 0.76 and 0.74 for male and female patients, respectively (Figure 4C,D), and those of post-treatment M2BPGi levels were 0.82 and 0.78 for male and female patients, respectively (Figure 4C,D). M2BPGi tended to be a more predictive marker than ATX for post-SVR HCC development, but this trend was not statistically significant. We also revealed cutoff values to predict post-SVR HCC development. The cutoff values of pretreatment ATX levels were 1.21 mg/L for male patients (sensitivity, 78.9%; specificity, 65.1%) and 2.26 mg/L for female patients (sensitivity, 57.9%; specificity, 79.9%). The cutoff values of pretreatment M2BPGi levels were 2.28 C.O.I. for male patients (sensitivity, 78.9%; specificity, 61.4%) and 2.23 C.O.I. for female patients (sensitivity, 94.7%; specificity, 45.0%). The cutoff values of post-treatment ATX levels were 1.37 mg/L for male patients (sensitivity, 57.9%; specificity, 94.0%) and 1.73 mg/L for female patients (sensitivity, 57.9%; specificity, 80.5%). The cutoff values of post-treatment M2BPGi levels were 1.89 C.O.I. for male patients (sensitivity, 78.9%; specificity, 78.3%) and 1.35 C.O.I. for female patients (sensitivity, 94.7%; specificity, 50.3%).

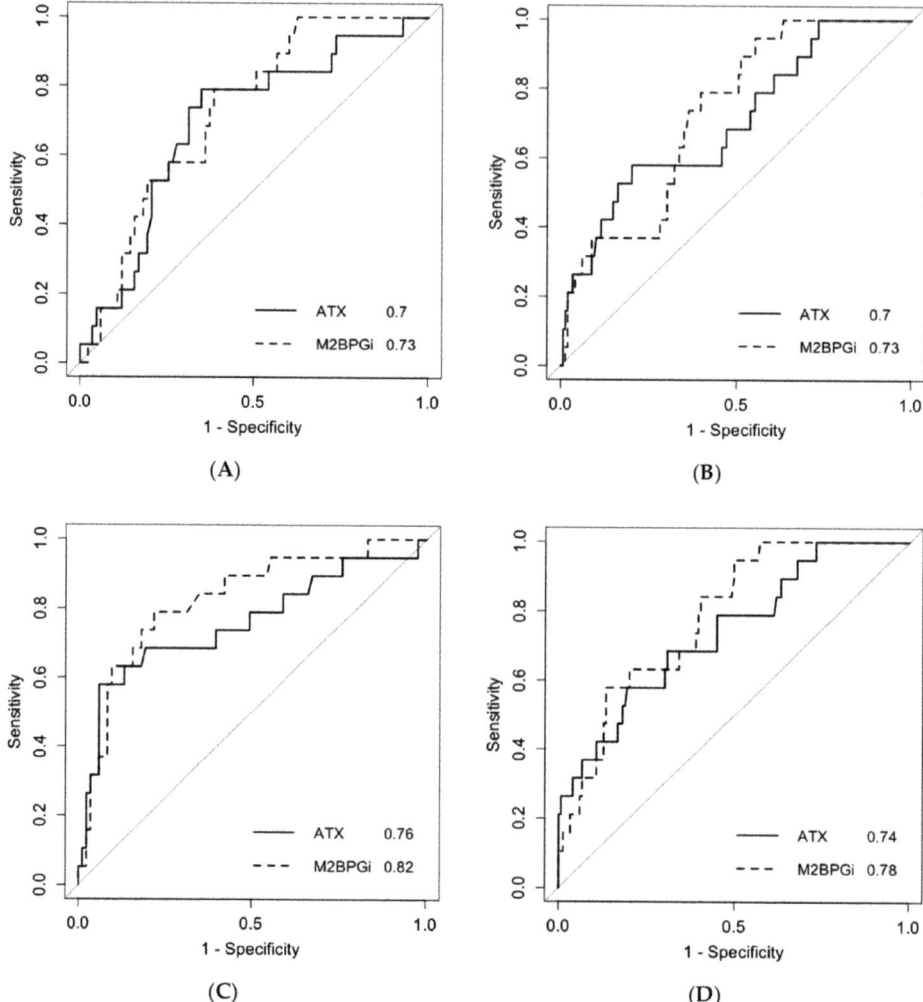

Figure 4. Area under the receiver operating characteristic curves for predicting post-SVR HCC development. Data from Cohort B were used for the analysis. Data from male patients (**A**,**C**) and female patients (**B**,**D**) are shown. A and B indicate pretreatment levels, and C and D indicate those at 12/24 weeks after antiviral treatment. The numbers at the bottom right are the area under the receiver operating characteristic of each liver fibrosis marker. SVR: sustained viral response; HCC: hepatocellular carcinoma; ATX: autotaxin; M2BPGi: Wisteria floribunda agglutinin positive Mac-2 binding protein.

2.3. Multivariate Analysis of Post-SVR HCC Development

Subsequently, we analyzed whether ATX or M2BPGi levels were useful predictive markers for post-SVR HCC development. We formed two groups using the cutoff values and conducted a multivariate analysis using data from Cohort A (Table 1). The multivariate analysis indicated that post-treatment ATX levels and post-treatment M2BPGi levels were significantly associated with post-SVR HCC development in male patients (hazard ratio, 3.75 and 6.43, respectively; Table 1).

In addition, pretreatment M2BPGi levels and post-treatment M2BPGi levels were significantly associated with post-SVR HCC development in female patients (hazard ratio, 11.76 and 13.07, respectively; Table 1).

Table 1. Factors associated with post-SVR HCC development.

		Factor	Category	Multivariate Analysis		
				Hazard Ratio	95% CI	p-Value
male	pretreatment	ATX	≥1.21 mg/L	3.26	0.82–12.89	0.092
		M2BPGi	≥2.28 C.O.I.	2.38	0.60–9.40	0.217
N = 301	post-treatment	ATX	≥1.37 mg/L	3.75	1.32–10.70	0.013
		M2BPGi	≥1.89 C.O.I.	6.43	1.83–22.52	0.004
female	pretreatment	ATX	≥2.26 mg/L	2.50	0.97–6.41	0.057
		M2BPGi	≥2.23 C.O.I.	11.76	1.47–94.07	0.02
N = 369	post-treatment	ATX	≥1.73 mg/L	2.34	0.92–5.97	0.08
		M2BPGi	≥1.35 C.O.I.	13.07	1.66–103.22	0.015

Data from Cohort A were used for the analysis. SVR: sustained viral response; HCC: hepatocellular carcinoma; ATX: autotaxin; M2BPGi: Wisteria floribunda agglutinin positive Mac-2 binding protein; 95% CI: 95% confidence interval.

2.4. Cumulative Non-Carcinogenic Rate after Antiviral Treatment

After antiviral treatment, 19 patients (both male and female) developed post-SVR HCC within 3 years. We evaluated the cumulative non-carcinogenic rate for markers that were found to be related in the multivariate analysis. The cumulative non-carcinogenic rates in male patients with post-treatment ATX levels ≥ 1.37 mg/L or post-treatment M2BPGi levels ≥ 1.89 C.O.I. were significantly lower than those in patients with post-treatment ATX levels < 1.37 mg/L or M2BPGi levels < 1.89 C.O.I. (Figure 5A,B). In addition, the cumulative non-carcinogenic rates in female patients with pretreatment M2BPGi levels ≥ 2.23 C.O.I. or post-treatment M2BPGi levels ≥ 1.35 C.O.I. were significantly lower than those in patients with pretreatment M2BPGi levels < 2.23 mg/L or post-treatment WFA+-M2BP levels < 1.35 C.O.I. (Figure 5C,D).

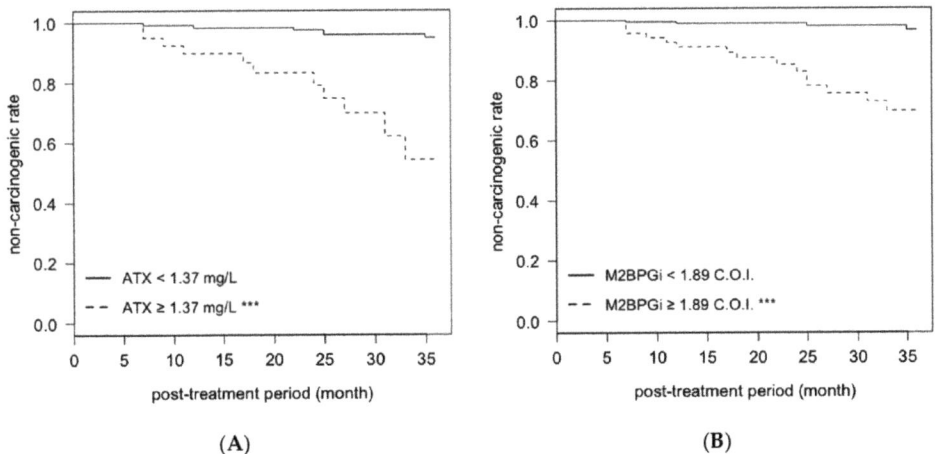

Figure 5. Cont.

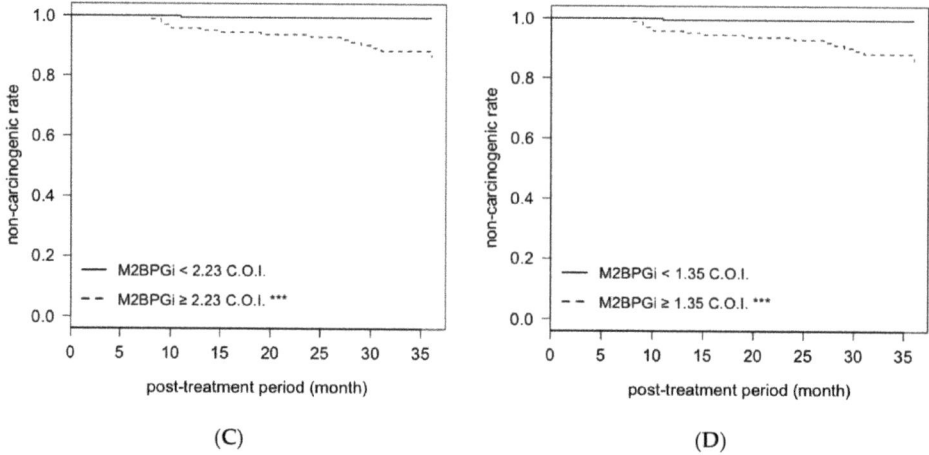

Figure 5. Cumulative non-carcinogenic rate after antiviral treatment. Data from Cohort A were used for the analysis. (**A**,**B**) indicate data by serum levels at 12/24 weeks after antiviral treatment in male patients. Data from female patients before treatment are shown in (**C**), and from female patients at 12/24 weeks after antiviral treatment are shown in (**D**). ***: $p < 0.001$. ATX: autotaxin; M2BPGi: Wisteria floribunda agglutinin positive Mac-2 binding protein.

2.5. Association between the Rate of ATX Change and Post-SVR HCC Development

Because ATX is a quantitative value and M2BPGi is a semi-quantitative value, we finally focused on the rate of ATX change before and after antiviral treatment. The pretreatment ATX levels and rate of ATX change were plotted, and we drew a regression line using data from Cohort B (Figure 6). The equations of the regression lines were as follows: $y = -17.61x + 7.38$ for males ($R^2 = 0.43$) and $y = -14.61x + 9.68$ for females ($R^2 = 0.41$). We divided the patients into two groups using the regression lines. The patients above the regression line were designated as Group A (group with a small reduction in ATX levels before and after antiviral treatment), and those below the regression line were Group B (group with a significant reduction in ATX levels). The proportion of both male and female patients with post-SVR HCC were significantly greater in group A than in group B (Table 2), and the trend was more pronounced in patients without a history of HCC (no HCC vs. first-onset; Table 2). Among patients with a history of HCC, post-SVR HCC also developed in Group B (no relapse vs. relapse; Table 2).

Table 2. Association between the rate of ATX change and post-SVR HCC development.

		No	First-Onset	No Relapse	Relapse	*p*-Value
male	Group A	28	6	7	7	0.006
N = 102	Group B	45	0	3	6	
female	Group A	57	8	8	5	0.034
N = 168	Group B	81	3	3	3	

Data from Cohort B were used for the analysis. ATX: autotaxin; SVR: sustained viral response; HCC: hepatocellular carcinoma; No: the patients with no HCC history and no carcinogenesis; First-onset: the patients with no HCC history and post-SVR HCC development; No relapse: the patients with HCC history and no carcinogenesis; Relapse: the patients with HCC history and post-SVR HCC development; Group A: group with a small reduction in ATX before and after antiviral treatment; Group B: group with a significant reduction in ATX before and after antiviral treatment.

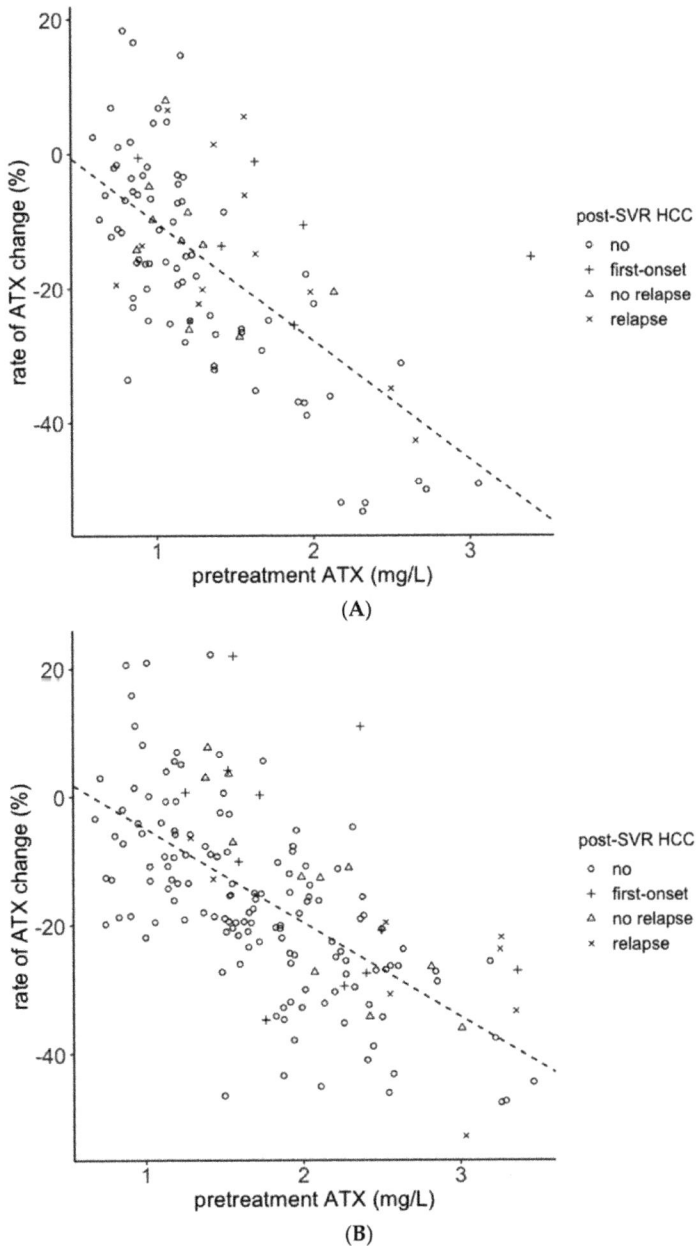

Figure 6. Association between pretreatment ATX levels and the rate of ATX change. Data from Cohort B were used for the analysis. Data from male patients (**A**) and female patients (**B**) are shown. Dotted lines represent the regression lines. no: the patients with no HCC history and no carcinogenesis; first-onset: the patients with no HCC history and post-SVR HCC development; no relapse: the patients with HCC history and no carcinogenesis; relapse: the patients with HCC history and post-SVR HCC development. ATX: autotaxin; SVR: sustained viral response; HCC: hepatocellular carcinoma.

3. Discussion

In the present study, we revealed an association between serum ATX levels and the development of post-SVR HCC within 3 years after antiviral treatment. First, we revealed that serum ATX levels before treatment and 12/24 weeks after antiviral treatment in patients with post-SVR HCC were higher than those without post-SVR HCC (Figure 2). The median values of pretreatment ATX levels in patients with post-SVR HCC were 1.56 mg/L in male patients and 2.37 mg/L in female patients, and these values were close to the cutoff values for predicting liver cirrhosis from reagent's attached document (male, 1.69 mg/L; female, 2.12 mg/L). Advanced hepatic cirrhosis is a main risk factor of HCC [10], and our results seemed to support this theory.

Next, we performed ROC analyses to predict post-SVR HCC development (Figure 4). AUROCs of serum ATX levels before treatment and 12/24 weeks after treatment were 0.7–0.76, and it was thought that ATX levels could stratify a high-risk group of post-SVR HCC patients to some extent. In addition, we revealed that AUROCs of M2BPGi were 0.73–0.82. Comparisons of the ability to predict post-SVR HCC showed that M2BPGi tended to be a better predictor than ATX, but this trend was not statistically significant. However, post-treatment ATX and post-treatment M2BPGi levels had higher predictive performance than pretreatment levels. It was suggested that the presence of HCV infection and/or hepatitis may affect the predictive capacity of post-SVR HCC development.

Previous studies reported that M2BPGi was associated with post-SVR HCC development [11–13]. However, studies reporting an association between ATX levels and post-SVR HCC development are rare. Therefore, we analyzed whether ATX or M2BPGi was a higher predictive capacity for post-SVR HCC development, and we revealed that M2BPGi was a more useful marker than ATX (Table 1). M2BPGi has also been reported to be a useful marker for HBV-related HCC [27,28], and NAFLD-related HCC [29]. It is unclear how M2BPGi is involved in HCC development, but it is suggested that it does more than simply indicate liver fibrosis.

M2BPGi is a semi-quantitative value [30]. We witnessed an approximate 10% change in C.O.I. when changing the reagent or calibrator lot (data not shown). Therefore, it is inappropriate to discuss differences of detailed value or degrees of change. In fact, when we analyzed the association between the rate of M2BPGi change and post-SVR HCC development, we found a significant difference only in female patients (data not shown). Because the levels of ATX is a quantitative value, we determined the rate of ATX change before and after antiviral treatment. There was a weak negative correlation between pretreatment ATX levels and rate of ATX change (Figure 6). Despite patients with high pretreatment ATX levels having a high risk of HCC development, all six male patients with ATX reduction rates of 43% or greater did not develop HCC more than 3 years after antiviral treatment (Figure 6A). In addition, 14 out of 15 female patients with ATX reduction rates of 35% or greater did not develop HCC (Figure 6B). According to a previous study, IFN-free DAA therapy decreases serum ATX levels [31]. The present study revealed that ATX changes varied from case to case and that the risk of post-SVR HCC development could be assessed by focusing on ATX changes (Figure 6 and Table 2). Several studies have reported on factors affecting serum ATX levels. The reference value of ATX in women is higher than that in men [23], and even higher in pregnant women [32]. Patients with follicular lymphoma have high ATX levels [33]. However, the patients with kidney disease, heart disease, and diabetes have few changes in ATX levels [34]. The determinations of factors that influence serum ATX levels will improve our understanding of them as predictive markers of HCC development.

The present study had several limitations. First, we analyzed post-SVR HCC development as early as 3 years after antiviral treatment. Therefore, it is unclear whether ATX can predict longer term carcinogenesis. Second, we did not separately analyze for HCC occurrence or HCC recurrence in the multivariate analysis, although patients with a history of HCC before IFN-free DAA therapy have been reported to have a high rate of HCC recurrence [35], because there were not enough patients with developing HCC to perform a multivariate analysis. Finally, validation analysis was not performed. However, the present study clearly showed the role of ATX in prediction for post-SVR HCC. To solve the problems, a larger number of cohorts with longer observation will be required. In addition, more robust cutoff values and predictive formulas that combining multiple biomarkers could be set by analyzing larger cohorts.

In conclusion, the present study revealed that M2BPGi levels especially 12/24 weeks after antiviral treatment were more useful than ATX levels as a predictive marker for post-SVR development within 3 years. However, the combination of pretreatment ATX levels and the rate of ATX change before and after antiviral treatment has the potential to predict post-SVR carcinogenesis. In the treatment of HCV, it is important to stratify high-risk patients and conduct appropriate HCC surveillance, and these results will help for clarifying prognosis.

4. Materials and Methods

4.1. Subjects

We recruited 755 patients with HCV who had received IFN-free DAA therapy at Osaka City University Hospital between August 2014 and April 2019. Written informed consent was obtained from all patients prior to DAA treatment. The patient selection criteria are shown in Figure 1. The following patients were excluded and defined as Cohort A (n = 670): patients who did not achieve SVR, those in whom M2BPGi was not measured, those who followed up for less than 6 months, and those who developed HCC within 6 months after antiviral treatment because HCC was thought to be present before antiviral treatment. Patients who followed up for less than 3 years were excluded and defined as Cohort B (n = 270). We diagnosed chronic HCV infection based on the presence of serum HCV antibody and detectable HCV RNA via the real-time PCR method. The clinical characteristics before antiviral treatment is summarized in Table 3. The median follow-up duration after antiviral treatment was 25 months in male and 34 months in female. A total of 41 male patients and 30 female patients received treatment for HCC before HCV treatment. A total of 19 male patients and 19 female patients developed post-SVR HCC within 3 years after antiviral treatment. In comparisons between Cohort A and Cohort B, significant differences in age, M2BPGi, PLT (platelet), and Fibrosis-4 (FIB-4) index in male patients were shown. FIB-4 index was calculated using Sterling's formula: {age (years) × AST (U/L)} / {platelet count ($\times 10^9$/L) × $\sqrt{\text{ALT (U/L)}}$}. The differences between the two cohorts might depend on the follow-up period, which the high-risk patients were followed up for longer term. This study was conducted according to the principals of the Declaration of Helsinki and was approved by the Ethics Committee of the Osaka City University Graduate School of Medicine (approval number: 4097).

4.2. Measurement of Serum ATX Levels

We measured serum ATX levels before treatment and 12/24 weeks after antiviral treatment. Serum samples were stored at −80°C until measurement. Before the analysis of ATX levels, serum samples were thawed at room temperature and centrifuged at 3500 g for 5 min. Serum ATX levels were measured by a two-site enzyme immunoassay with an AIA-2000 analyzer (Tosoh Co., Tokyo, Japan).

4.3. Laboratory Data

Platelet counts and routine biochemical tests were analyzed with standard procedures. M2BPGi was measured with a chemiluminescent enzyme immunoassay (not quantitative values) [30]. Laboratory data were obtained from the medical records. We used laboratory data within seven days before and after blood samples were collected.

Table 3. Baseline characteristics.

	Male			Female		
	Cohort A	Cohort B	p Value	Cohort A	Cohort B	p-Value
N	301	102	–	369	168	–
age (years)	67 (56–73)	70 (62–75)	0.01	70 (62–76)	71 (62–75)	0.95
therapy régimen [†] (A/B/C/D/E/F)	47/102/61/35/6/50	41/39/17/2/2/1	–	68/167/49/31/13/41	58/77/25/3/5/0	–
ATX (mg/L)	1.14 (0.86–1.47)	1.17 (0.91–1.56)	0.28	1.62 (1.20-2.10)	1.71 (1.27–2.25)	0.15
M2BPGi (C.O.I.)	1.82 (1.17–3.62)	2.15 (1.41–4.25)	0.04	2.10 (1.30–4.22)	2.63 (1.46–4.34)	0.10
PLT ($\times 10^4/\mu L$)	17.1 (12.9–21.8)	14.4 (10.6–20.1)	0.004	16.2 (11.5–21.4)	14.9 (10.7–19.5)	0.06
AST (U/L)	44 (30–68)	47 (33–72)	0.20	40 (28–61)	41 (32–61)	0.27
ALT (U/L)	41 (26–70)	42 (27–70)	0.67	35 (23–54)	37 (27–54)	0.31
FIB-4 index	2.67 (1.77–4.25)	3.28 (2.29-5.33)	<0.001	3.03 (1.86–4.95)	3.51 (2.09–5.26)	0.10
follow-up period (months)	25 (13–39)	–	–	34 (18–42)	–	–
HCC history before HCV treatment (Yes/No)	41/260	23/79	–	30/339	19/149	–
HCC development within 3 years after HCV treatment (Yes/No)	19/282	19/83	–	19/350	19/149	–

Data are presented as the median and interquartile range. Comparisons between Cohort A and Cohort B were performed with the Wilcoxon rank sum test. ATX: autotaxin; M2BPGi: Wisteria floribunda agglutinin positive Ma-2 binding protein; PLT: platelet; AST: aspartate aminotransferase; ALT: alanine aminotransferase; HCC: hepatocellular carcinoma; HCV: hepatitis C virus; [†] A: asunaprevir + daclatasvir, B: sofosbuvir + ledipasvir, C: sofosbuvir + ribavirin, D: elbasvir + grazoprevir, E: ombitasvir + paritaprevir + ritonavir, F: pibrentasvir + glecaprevir.

4.4. Surveillance after Antiviral Treatment and Diagnosis of HCC

For all patients who achieved SVR, US or dynamic CT with contrast media or gadolinium-ethoxybenzyl-diethylenetriamine pentaacetic acid-enhanced dynamic magnetic resonance imaging (Gd-EOB-DTPA-MRI) was performed every 3 to 6 months. HCC was diagnosed using contrast media and imaging modalities, such as dynamic CT or Gd-EOB-DTPA-MRI, and/or liver biopsy.

4.5. Statistical Analysis

All statistical analyses and data visualizations were performed by R software ver. 3.5.3 (The R Foundation for Statistical Computing, Vienna, Austria). Comparisons of serum liver fibrosis markers in patients with and without HCC development were performed with the Wilcoxon rank sum test. Diagnostic capacities were analyzed by the AUROCs. Cutoff values were identified by the Youden index. Factors associated with post-SVR HCC development were analyzed using Cox proportional hazards regression analysis. Kaplan–Meier curves were used to analyze the cumulative non-carcinogenic rate in the post-treatment period, and comparisons of two groups were performed with the log rank test. The regression lines were calculated with the least squares method. The comparisons of two groups separated by regression lines were performed with Fisher's exact test. A p-value of less than 0.05 was considered statistically significant. All the analyses were performed based on the patient's sex because ATX shows sex-related differences. We used Cox proportional hazards analysis (Table 1) and Kaplan–Meier curves (Figure 5) to analyze cohort A, which included cases whose follow-up was completed within 3 years after antiviral treatment, as the analyses involved a timeframe. The other analyses were performed in cohort B, which included cases followed up for more than 3 years, because of the analyses of carcinogenesis at the point of three years after antiviral treatment.

Author Contributions: Conceptualization, K.T. and A.T.; methodology, K.T. and A.T.; software, K.T.; validation, K.T. and A.T.; formal analysis, K.T.; investigation, K.T. and E.T.; resources, A.T., N.K., and M.H.; data curation, K.T.; writing—original draft preparation, K.T.; writing—review and editing, K.T., E.T., A.T., M.N., H.K., S.U.-K., M.E., N.K., and M.H.; visualization, K.T.; supervision, A.T.; project administration, A.T.; funding acquisition, A.T., N.K., and M.H. All authors have read and agreed to the published version of the manuscript.

Funding: We received reagents to measure serum autotaxin levels and borrow an AIA-2000 analyzer from Tosoh Corporation (Tokyo, Japan). This study is supported by research funding from Tosoh Corporation. The present study was supported in part by a Research Grant from the Japan Agency for Medical Research and Development (no. 19fk0210058h0001).

Acknowledgments: We thank the staff of the Hepatitis Research and Prevention Center, Osaka City University Hospital, for preparation of serum samples.

Conflicts of Interest: We receive reagents to measure serum autotaxin levels and borrow an AIA-2000 analyzer from Tosoh Corporation (Tokyo, Japan). This study is supported by research funding from Tosoh Corporation. The funders had no role in the design of the study; in the collection, analyses, or interpretation of data; in the writing of the manuscript, or in the decision to publish the results.

Abbreviations

HCV	Hepatitis C virus
HCC	Hepatocellular carcinoma
DAA	Direct-acting antiviral
SVR	Sustained viral response
US	Ultrasonography
CT	Computed tomography
MRI	Magnetic resonance imaging
AST	Aspartate aminotransferase
M2BPGi	Wisteria floribunda agglutinin positive Mac-2 binding protein
ATX	Autotaxin
LPA	Lysophosphatidic acid
HBV	Hepatitis B virus
NAFLD	Non-alcoholic fatty liver disease
IFN	Interferon
C.O.I.	Cutoff index
AUROC	Area under the receiver operating characteristic
FIB-4	Fibrosis-4
Gd-EOB-DTPA-MRI	Gadolinium-ethoxybenzyl-diethylenetriamine pentaacetic acid-enhanced dynamic magnetic resonance imaging

References

1. Spearman, C.W.; Dusheiko, G.M.; Hellard, M.; Sonderup, M. Hepatitis C. *Lancet* **2019**, *394*, 1451–1466. [CrossRef]
2. Waziry, R.; Hajarizadeh, B.; Grebely, J.; Amin, J.; Law, M.; Danta, M.; George, J.; Dore, G.J. Hepatocellular carcinoma risk following direct-acting antiviral HCV therapy: A systematic review, meta-analyses, and meta-regression. *J. Hepatol.* **2017**, *67*, 1204–1212. [CrossRef] [PubMed]
3. Li, D.K.; Ren, Y.; Fierer, D.S.; Rutledge, S.; Shaikh, O.S.; Lo Re, V., III; Simon, T.; Abou-Samra, A.-B.; Chung, R.T.; Butt, A.A. The short-term incidence of hepatocellular carcinoma is not increased after hepatitis C treatment with direct-acting antivirals: An ERCHIVES study. *Hepatology* **2018**, *67*, 2244–2253. [CrossRef] [PubMed]
4. AASLD-IDSA HCV Guidance Panel. Hepatitis C Guidance 2018 Update: AASLD-IDSA Recommendations for Testing, Managing, and Treating Hepatitis C Virus Infection. *Clin. Infect. Dis.* **2018**, *67*, 1477–1492. [CrossRef] [PubMed]
5. Pawlotsky, J.-M.; Negro, F.; Aghemo, A.; Berenguer, M.; Dalgard, O.; Dusheiko, G.; Marra, F.; Puoti, M.; Wedemeyer, H.; European Association for the Study of the Liver. EASL Recommendations on Treatment of Hepatitis C 2018. *J. Hepatol.* **2018**, *69*, 461–511. [CrossRef] [PubMed]

6. Kokudo, N.; Takemura, N.; Hasegawa, K.; Takayama, T.; Kubo, S.; Shimada, M.; Nagano, H.; Hatano, E.; Izumi, N.; Kaneko, S.; et al. Clinical practice guidelines for hepatocellular carcinoma: The Japan Society of Hepatology 2017 (4th JSH-HCC guidelines) 2019 update. *Hepatol. Res.* **2019**, *49*, 1109–1113. [CrossRef]
7. Ikeda, M.; Fujiyama, S.; Tanaka, M.; Sata, M.; Ide, T.; Yatsuhashi, H.; Watanabe, H. Risk factors for development of hepatocellular carcinoma in patients with chronic hepatitis C after sustained response to interferon. *J. Gastroenterol.* **2005**, *40*, 148–156. [CrossRef]
8. Arase, Y.; Kobayashi, M.; Suzuki, F.; Suzuki, Y.; Kawamura, Y.; Akuta, N.; Kobayashi, M.; Sezaki, H.; Saito, S.; Hosaka, T.; et al. Effect of type 2 diabetes on risk for malignancies includes hepatocellular carcinoma in chronic hepatitis C. *Hepatology* **2013**, *57*, 964–973. [CrossRef]
9. Yamashita, N.; Ohho, A.; Yamasaki, A.; Kurokawa, M.; Kotoh, K.; Kajiwara, E. Hepatocarcinogenesis in chronic hepatitis C patients achieving a sustained virological response to interferon: Significance of lifelong periodic cancer screening for improving outcomes. *J. Gastroenterol.* **2013**, *49*, 1504–1513. [CrossRef]
10. El-Serag, H.B.; Kanwal, F.; Richardson, P.; Kramer, J. Risk of Hepatocellular Carcinoma After Sustained Virological Response in Veterans with Hepatitis C Virus Infection. *Hepatology* **2016**, *64*, 130–137. [CrossRef]
11. Nagata, H.; Nakagawa, M.; Nishimura-Sakurai, Y.; Asano, Y.; Tsunoda, T.; Miyoshi, M.; Kaneko, S.; Goto, F.; Otani, S.; Kawai-Kitahata, F.; et al. Serial measurement of Wisteria floribunda agglutinin positive Mac-2-binding protein is useful for predicting liver fibrosis and the development of hepatocellular carcinoma in chronic hepatitis C patients treated with IFN-based and IFN-free therapy. *Hepatol. Int.* **2016**, *10*, 956–964. [CrossRef] [PubMed]
12. Yamasaki, K.; Tateyama, M.; Abiru, S.; Komori, A.; Nagaoka, S.; Saeki, A.; Hashimoto, S.; Sasaki, R.; Bekki, S.; Kugiyama, Y.; et al. Elevated serum levels of Wisteria floribundaagglutinin-positive human Mac-2 binding protein predict the development of hepatocellular carcinoma in hepatitis C patients. *Hepatology* **2014**, *60*, 1563–1570. [CrossRef] [PubMed]
13. Nagata, H.; Nakagawa, M.; Asahina, Y.; Sato, A.; Asano, Y.; Tsunoda, T.; Miyoshi, M.; Kaneko, S.; Otani, S.; Kawai-Kitahata, F.; et al. Effect of interferon-based and -free therapy on early occurrence and recurrence of hepatocellular carcinoma in chronic hepatitis C. *J. Hepatol.* **2017**, *67*, 933–939. [CrossRef] [PubMed]
14. Stracke, M.L.; Krutzsch, H.C.; Unsworth, E.J.; Arestad, A.; Cioce, V.; Schiffmann, E.; Liotta, L.A. Identification, Purification, and Partial Sequence Analysis of Autotaxin, a Novel Motility-stimulating Protein*. *J. Biol. Chem.* **1992**, *267*, 2524–2529. [PubMed]
15. Tokumura, A.; Majima, E.; Kariya, Y.; Tominaga, K.; Kogure, K.; Yasuda, K.; Fukuzawa, K. Identification of human plasma lysophospholipase D, a lysophosphatidic acid-producing enzyme, as autotaxin, a multifunctional phosphodiesterase. *J. Biol. Chem.* **2002**, *277*, 39436–39442. [CrossRef] [PubMed]
16. Moolenaar, W.H. Lysophospholipids in the limelight: Autotaxin takes center stage. *J. Cell Biol.* **2002**, *158*, 197–199. [CrossRef]
17. Aikawa, S.; Hashimoto, T.; Kano, K.; Aoki, J. Lysophosphatidic acid as a lipid mediator with multiple biological actions. *J. Biochem.* **2015**, *157*, 81–89. [CrossRef]
18. Watanabe, N.; Ikeda, H.; Nakamura, K.; Ohkawa, R.; Kume, Y.; Aoki, J.; Hama, K.; Okudaira, S.; Tanaka, M.; Tomiya, T.; et al. Both Plasma Lysophosphatidic Acid and Serum Autotaxin Levels are Increased in Chronic Hepatitis C. *J. Clin. Gastroenterol.* **2007**, *41*, 616–623. [CrossRef]
19. Yamazaki, T.; Joshita, S.; Umemura, T.; Usami, Y.; Sugiura, A.; Fujimori, N.; Shibata, S.; Ichikawa, Y.; Komatsu, M.; Matsumoto, A.; et al. Association of Serum Autotaxin Levels with Liver Fibrosis in Patients with Chronic Hepatitis C. *Sci. Rep.* **2017**, *7*, 1–10. [CrossRef]
20. Joshita, S.; Ichikawa, Y.; Umemura, T.; Usami, Y.; Sugiura, A.; Shibata, S.; Yamazaki, T.; Fujimori, N.; Komatsu, M.; Matsumoto, A.; et al. Serum Autotaxin Is a Useful Liver Fibrosis Marker in Patients with Chronic Hepatitis B Virus Infection. *Hepatol. Res.* **2017**, 1–28. [CrossRef]
21. Fujimori, N.; Umemura, T.; Kimura, T.; Tanaka, N.; Sugiura, A.; Yamazaki, T.; Joshita, S.; Komatsu, M.; Usami, Y.; Sano, K.; et al. Serum autotaxin levels are correlated with hepatic fibrosis and ballooning in patients with non-alcoholic fatty liver disease. *World J. Gastroenterol.* **2018**, *24*, 1239–1249. [CrossRef] [PubMed]
22. Jansen, S.; Andries, M.; Vekemans, K.; Vanbilloen, H.; Verbruggen, A.; Bollen, M. Rapid clearance of the circulating metastatic factor autotaxin by the scavenger receptors of liver sinusoidal endothelial cells. *Cancer Lett.* **2009**, *284*, 216–221. [CrossRef] [PubMed]

23. Nakagawa, H.; Ikeda, H.; Nakamura, K.; Ohkawa, R.; Masuzaki, R.; Tateishi, R.; Yoshida, H.; Watanabe, N.; Tejima, K.; Kume, Y.; et al. Autotaxin as a novel serum marker of liver fibrosis. *Clin. Chim. Acta* **2011**, *412*, 1201–1206. [CrossRef] [PubMed]
24. Kaffe, E.; Katsifa, A.; Xylourgidis, N.; Ninou, I.; Zannikou, M.; Harokopos, V.; Foka, P.; Dimitriadis, A.; Evangelou, K.; Moulas, A.N.; et al. Hepatocyte autotaxin expression promotes liver fibrosis and cancer. *Hepatology* **2017**, *65*, 1369–1383. [CrossRef]
25. Nakagawa, S.; Wei, L.; Song, W.M.; Higashi, T.; Ghoshal, S.; Kim, R.S.; Bian, C.B.; Yamada, S.; Sun, X.; Venkatesh, A.; et al. Molecular Liver Cancer Prevention in Cirrhosis by Organ Transcriptome Analysis and Lysophosphatidic Acid Pathway Inhibition. *Cancer Cell* **2016**, *30*, 879–890. [CrossRef]
26. Erstad, D.J.; Tager, A.M.; Hoshida, Y.; Fuchs, B.C. The autotaxin-lysophosphatidic acid pathway emerges as a therapeutic target to prevent liver cancer. *Mol. Cell. Oncol.* **2017**, *4*, 1–2. [CrossRef]
27. Liu, J.; Hu, H.-H.; Lee, M.-H.; Korenaga, M.; Jen, C.-L.; Batrla-Utermann, R.; Lu, S.-N.; Wang, L.-Y.; Mizokami, M.; Chen, C.-J.; et al. Serum Levels of M2BPGi as Short- Term Predictors of Hepatocellular Carcinoma in Untreated Chronic Hepatitis B Patients. *Sci. Rep.* **2017**, 1–10. [CrossRef]
28. Su, T.-H.; Peng, C.-Y.; Tseng, T.-C.; Yang, H.-C.; Liu, C.-J.; Liu, C.-H.; Chen, P.-J.; Chen, D.-S.; Kao, J.-H. Serum Mac-2-Binding Protein Glycosylation Isomer at Virological Remission Predicts Hepatocellular Carcinoma and Death in Chronic Hepatitis B-Related Cirrhosis. *J. Infect. Dis.* **2019**, *36*, 1755–1759. [CrossRef]
29. Kawanaka, M.; Tomiyama, Y.; Hyogo, H.; Koda, M.; Shima, T.; Tobita, H.; Hiramatsu, A.; Nishino, K.; Okamoto, T.; Sato, S.; et al. Wisteria floribundaagglutinin-positive Mac-2 binding protein predicts the development of hepatocellular carcinoma in patients with non-alcoholic fatty liver disease. *Hepatol. Res.* **2018**, *48*, 521–528. [CrossRef]
30. Kuno, A.; Sato, T.; Shimazaki, H.; Unno, S.; Saitou, K.; Kiyohara, K.; Sogabe, M.; Tsuruno, C.; Takahama, Y.; Ikehara, Y.; et al. Reconstruction of a robust glycodiagnostic agent supported by multiple lectin-assisted glycan profiling. *Prot. Clin. Appl.* **2013**, *7*, 642–647. [CrossRef]
31. Yamazaki, T.; Joshita, S.; Umemura, T.; Usami, Y.; Sugiura, A.; Fujimori, N.; Kimura, T.; Matsumoto, A.; Igarashi, K.; Ota, M.; et al. Changes in serum levels of autotaxin with direct-acting antiviral therapy in patients with chronic hepatitis C. *PLoS ONE* **2018**, *13*, e0195632-20. [CrossRef] [PubMed]
32. Masuda, A.; Fujii, T.; Iwasawa, Y.; Nakamura, K.; Ohkawa, R.; Igarashi, K.; Okudaira, S.; Ikeda, H.; Kozuma, S.; Aoki, J.; et al. Serum autotaxin measurements in pregnant women: Application for the differentiation of normal pregnancy and pregnancy-induced hypertension. *Clin. Chim. Acta* **2011**, *412*, 1944–1950. [CrossRef] [PubMed]
33. Masuda, A.; Nakamura, K.; Izutsu, K.; Igarashi, K.; Ohkawa, R.; Jona, M.; Higashi, K.; Yokota, H.; Okudaira, S.; Kishimoto, T.; et al. Serum autotaxin measurement in haematological malignancies: A promising marker for follicular lymphoma. *Br. J. Haematol.* **2008**, *143*, 60–70. [CrossRef] [PubMed]
34. Ikeda, H.; Kobayashi, M.; Kumada, H.; Enooku, K.; Koike, K.; Kurano, M.; Sato, M.; Nojiri, T.; Kobayashi, T.; Ohkawa, R.; et al. Performance of autotaxin as a serum marker of liver fibrosis. *Ann. Clin. Biochem.* **2018**, *55*, 469–477. [CrossRef]
35. Reig, M.A.; Mariño, Z.; Perelló, C.; Iñarrairaegui, M.; Ribeiro, A.; Lens, S.; Díaz, A.; Vilana, R.; Darnell, A.; Varela, M.; et al. Unexpected high rate of early tumor recurrence in patients with HCV-related HCC undergoing interferon-free therapy. *J. Hepatol.* **2016**, *65*, 719–726. [CrossRef]

© 2020 by the authors. Licensee MDPI, Basel, Switzerland. This article is an open access article distributed under the terms and conditions of the Creative Commons Attribution (CC BY) license (http://creativecommons.org/licenses/by/4.0/).

Article

Wisteria floribunda Agglutinin-Positive Mac-2 Binding Protein but not α-Fetoprotein as a Long-Term Hepatocellular Carcinoma Predictor

Leona Osawa [1,2], Nobuharu Tamaki [1,2], Masayuki Kurosaki [1], Sakura Kirino [1], Keiya Watakabe [1], Wan Wang [1], Mao Okada [1], Takao Shimizu [1], Mayu Higuchi [1,2], Kenta Takaura [1], Hitomi Takada [1,2], Shun Kaneko [1], Yutaka Yasui [1], Kaoru Tsuchiya [1], Hiroyuki Nakanishi [1], Jun Itakura [1], Yuka Takahashi [1], Nobuyuki Enomoto [2] and Namiki Izumi [1,*]

1. Department of Gastroenterology and Hepatology, Musashino Red Cross Hospital, Tokyo 180-8610, Japan; r.oosawa@musashino.jrc.or.jp (L.O.); tamaki@musashino.jrc.or.jp (N.T.); kurosaki@musashino.jrc.or.jp (M.K.); sa.kirino@musashino.jrc.or.jp (S.K.); wkkya1234567@gmail.com (K.W.); w.ou@musashino.jrc.or.jp (W.W.); m.okada@musashino.jrc.or.jp (M.O.); drtsss0415@gmail.com (T.S.); mayu.h@musashino.jrc.or.jp (M.H.); tuf029@gmail.com (K.T.); takadahi0107@gmail.com (H.T.); s.kaneko@musashino.jrc.or.jp (S.K.); yutakayas@hotmail.com (Y.Y.); tsuchiya@musashino.jrc.or.jp (K.T.); nakanisi@musashino.jrc.or.jp (H.N.); jitakura@musashino.jrc.or.jp (J.I.); y.takahashi@musashino.jrc.or.jp (Y.T.)
2. First Department of Internal Medicine, Faculty of Medicine, University of Yamanashi, Chuo, Yamanashi 409-3898, Japan; enomoto@yamanashi.ac.jp
* Correspondence: izumi012@musashino.jrc.or.jp; Tel.: +81-422-32-3111; Fax: +81-422-32-9551

Received: 11 May 2020; Accepted: 19 May 2020; Published: 21 May 2020

Abstract: Identification of high-risk patients for hepatocellular carcinoma (HCC) after sustained virological responses (SVR) is necessary to define candidates for long-term surveillance. In this study, we examined whether serum markers after 1 year of SVR could predict subsequent HCC development. Total 734 chronic hepatitis C patients without a history of HCC who achieved SVR with direct-acting antivirals were included. The regular surveillance for HCC started from 24 weeks after the end of treatment (SVR24). Factors at SVR24 and 1 year after SVR24 were analyzed for predicting HCC development. During the mean observation period of 19.7 ± 10 months, 24 patients developed HCC. At SVR24, *Wisteria floribunda* agglutinin-positive mac-2 binding protein (WFA±M2BP) ≥ 1.85 and α-fetoprotein (AFP) ≥ 6.0 ng/mL were independent factors of HCC development. However, at 1 year after SVR24, WFA±M2BP ≥ 1.85 was associated with subsequent HCC development (hazard ratio: 23.5, 95% confidence interval: 2.68–205) but not AFP. Among patients with WFA±M2BP ≥ 1.85 at SVR24, 42% had WFA±M2BP < 1.85 at 1 year after SVR24 (WFA±M2BP declined group). Subsequent HCC development was significantly lower in the declined group than in the non-declined group (1 year HCC rate: 0% vs. 9.4%, $p = 0.04$). In conclusion, WFA±M2BP but not AFP could identify high and no-risk cases of HCC at 1 year after SVR. Therefore, it was useful as a real-time monitoring tool to identify the candidates for continuous surveillance for HCC.

Keywords: hepatocellular carcinoma; WFA±M2BP; AFP; chronic hepatitis C; direct-acting antivirals

1. Introduction

Direct-acting antivirals (DAAs) treatment for chronic hepatitis C has enabled sustained virological responses (SVR) in several patients in recent years [1–6]. However, the number of patients with SVR has increased among the elderly and those with cirrhosis, and the number of patients who develop hepatocellular carcinoma (HCC) after SVR will increase in the future [7]. Therefore, it is clinically important to identify patients at a high risk of developing HCC after SVR and to perform appropriate screening.

Non-invasive fibrosis markers and α-fetoprotein (AFP) levels at 12 or 24 weeks after the end of treatment (SVR12 or 24) are reportedly associated with subsequent HCC development [8–13]. *Wisteria floribunda* agglutinin-positive mac-2 binding protein (WFA±M2BP) is a novel serum fibrosis marker [14,15], and WFA±M2BP at SVR is reported to be associated with HCC development [16,17]. Although WFA±M2BP and AFP can identify patients at high risk of HCC development at the time of SVR, it is difficult to continue screening for all cases judged high risk at the time of SVR. Liver fibrosis changes after the achievement of SVR differ from case to case [18], and subsequent changes in fibrosis lead to a different risk of HCC development [19,20]. Therefore, it is necessary to reevaluate the risk of HCC development over time.

Serum markers can be simply and repeatedly measured; therefore, it is considered possible to reevaluate the risk of HCC over time and further narrow down the high-risk cases. However, to our knowledge, no report has examined whether WFA±M2BP and AFP at 1 year after SVR are associated with HCC development. Further, it is unclear whether changes in the fibrosis markers alter the risk of carcinogenesis. Therefore, we examined whether WFA±M2BP and AFP after 1 year of achieving SVR are associated with HCC development and whether these changes could be used to evaluate the risk of HCC.

2. Results

2.1. Patient Characteristics

The clinical characteristics and laboratory data of patients are described at the time point of SVR24 and one year after SVR24 in Table 1. Average aspartate aminotransferase (AST) and alanine aminotransferase (ALT) at SVR24 were within the normal ranges because all patients achieved SVR. Twenty-one patients had liver nodules with intermediate probability of HCC (LR3) or probably of HCC (LR4) as defined by the liver imaging reporting and data system (LI-RADS) at entry [21]. There were 501 cases at 1 year after SVR24, excluding 18 patients with HCC development within 1 year. At 1 year after SVR24, AST and ALT were also within the normal ranges. The observation period began at the time of SVR24, and during the mean observation period of 19.7 ± 10 months, 24 patients developed HCC.

Table 1. Patients characteristics.

	At Entry (SVR24)	1 Year after SVR24
	$n = 734$	$n = 501$
Age (years)	65.9 ± 12	67.1 ± 12
Sex (male/female)	291/443	194/307
Albumin (g/dL)	4.32 ± 0.4	4.30 ± 0.4
Bilirubin (mg/dL)	0.67 ± 0.3	0.73 ± 0.3
AST (IU/L)	24.7 ± 8.1	23.7 ± 8.0
ALT (IU/L)	17.6 ± 9.0	17.5 ± 9.0
Platelet counts (×10^4/μL)	17.0 ± 5.6	17.7 ± 5.6
WFA±M2BP (COI)	1.52 ± 1.4	1.28 ± 1.1
AFP (ng/mL)	3.99 ± 3.4	3.51 ± 2.2
Presence of LR3/4 nodules	21 (2.9%)	9 (1.8%)
Histological fibrosis stage (1/2/3/4)	64/75/88/30	

AST, aspartate aminotransferase; ALT, alanine aminotransferase; WFA±M2BP, *Wisteria floribunda* agglutinin-positive mac-2 binding protein; COI, cut off index; AFP, alpha fetoprotein; LR, liver imaging reporting and data system; LR3, intermediate probability of HCC; LR4, probably of HCC.

Association between WFA±M2BP and Fibrosis Stage

Association between WFA±M2BP and fibrosis stage was examined. Median value of WFA±M2BP in F1, F2, F3, and F4 was 0.75, 1.16, 2.06, and 3.01, respectively, and WFA±M2BP increased as fibrosis stage increased ($p < 0.001$).

2.2. Prediction of HCC Development Using WFA±M2BP and AFP at SVR24

Serum WFA±M2BP and AFP at SVR24 were analyzed for predicting HCC development. ROC analysis was used to select WFA±M2BP of 1.85 cut off index (COI) as the optimal cutoff value for predicting HCC development within 1 year. WFA±M2BP of <1.85/≥1.85 were defined as low/high risk and low/high-risk patients were 567 (77.2%), and 167 (22.8%), respectively. The AFP level of 6.0 ng/mL was selected as the cutoff value and AFP of <6.0/≥6.0 ng/mL was defined as low/high risk of AFP. The 1-, 2-, and 3-year rate of HCC development in patients with low/high risk of WFA±M2BP were 1.2%/1.5%/1.5%, and 8.1%/13.1%/14.6%, respectively. The cumulative rate of HCC development was higher in patients with high risk than those with low risk ($p < 0.001$, Figure 1A). Similarly, the 1-, 2-, and 3-years rates of HCC development in patients with low/high risk of AFP were 0.9%/2.2%/2.2%, and 12.6%/13.8%/15.6%, respectively (Figure 1B). The cumulative rate of HCC development was high in high-risk groups ($p < 0.001$).

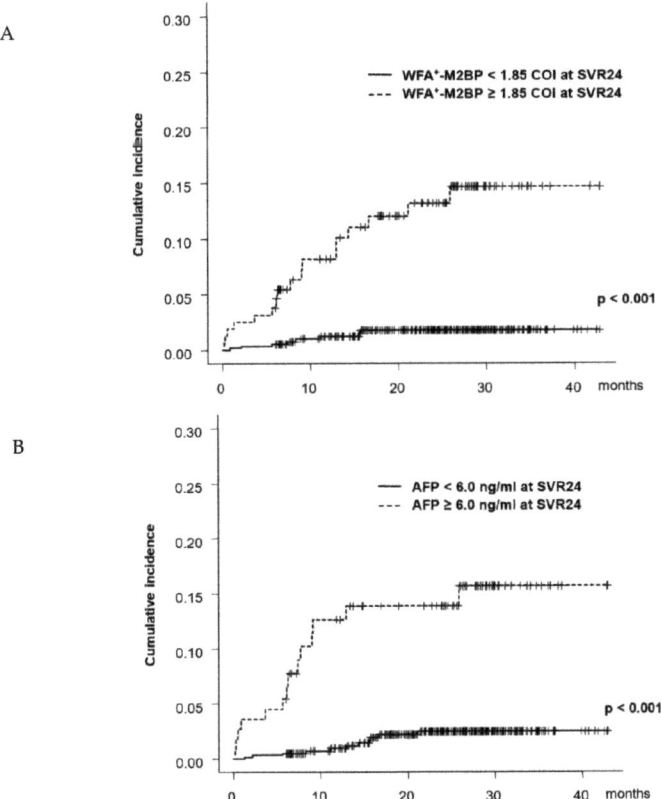

Figure 1. Cumulative incidence of hepatocellular carcinoma (HCC) development sustained virological responses after 24 weeks (SVR24). (**A**) patients were categorized into two groups as per *Wisteria floribunda* agglutinin-positive mac-2 binding protein (WFA±M2BP) at SVR24. (**B**) patients were categorized into two groups as per AFP at SVR24.

2.3. Prediction of HCC Development as Per WFA±M2BP and AFP at 1 Year after SVR24

Serum WFA±M2BP and AFP at 1 year after SVR24 (78 weeks post-treatment) were analyzed for predicting HCC development thereafter. Using the same cutoff values (WFA±M2BP of 1.85 COI and AFP level of 6.0 ng/mL), the cumulative incidence of HCC development was examined. Seven patients developed HCC after 1 year of SVR. The 1- and 2-year rate of HCC development, starting from the time point of 78 weeks post-treatment, in patients with low/high risk of WFA±M2BP at 1 year after SVR24 were 0.3%/0.3%, and 8.6%/11.3%, respectively ($p < 0.001$, Figure 2A). In contrast, the 1-, and 2-year rate of HCC development in patients with low/high risk of AFP at 1 year after SVR24 were 1.6%/1.6%, and 0.0%/2.9%, respectively and there was no significant difference between high and low-risk groups ($p = 0.8$, Figure 2B).

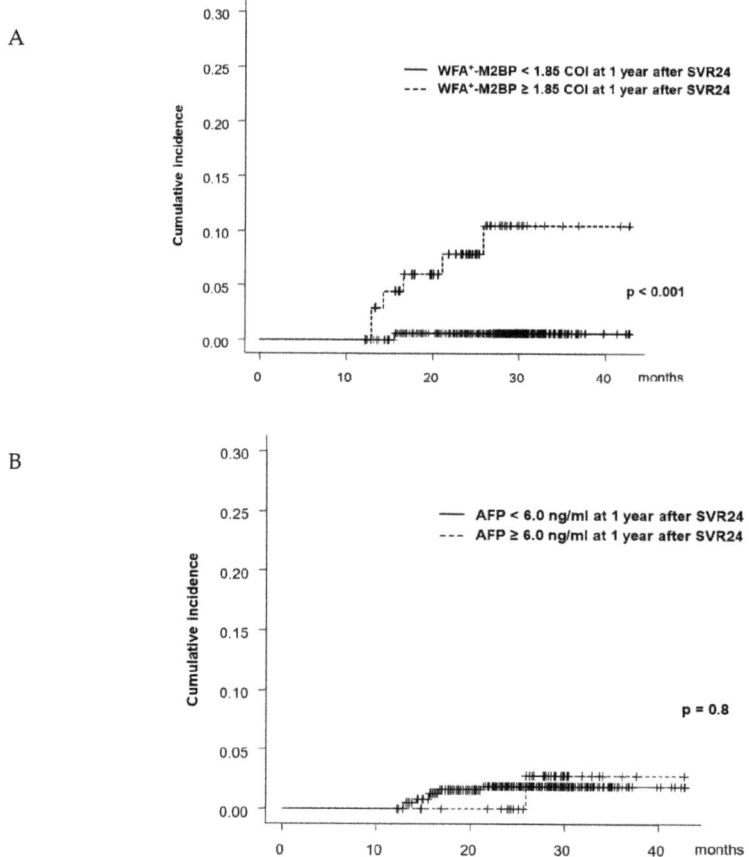

Figure 2. Cumulative incidence of HCC development from 1 year after SVR24 (**A**) patients were categorized into two groups as per the WFA±M2BP at 1 year after SVR24. (**B**) patients were categorized into two groups as per the AFP at 1 year after SVR24.

2.4. Time-Course Changes in WFA±M2BP and AFP and HCC Risk

Time-course changes in WFA±M2BP and AFP were examined. WFA±M2BP at SVR24 was 1.52 ± 1.4 COI that decreased significantly to 1.28 ± 1.1 COI at 1 year after SVR24 ($p < 0.001$). Similarly, the AFP level at SVR24 was 3.99 ± 3.4 ng/mL and decreased significantly to 3.51 ± 2.2 ng/mL 1 year after SVR24 ($p < 0.001$).

Among patients with a high risk of WFA±M2BP (≥1.85 COI) at SVR24, WFA±M2BP decreased to < 1.85 COI (low risk) at 1 year after SVR24 in 42 patients (42/102, 42%) (WFA±M2BP declined group) and remained ≥ 1.85 COI in 60 patients (60%) (WFA±M2BP non-declined group). Among patients with a high risk of AFP (≥6.0 ng/mL) at SVR24, AFP decreased to < 6.0 ng/mL at 1 year after SVR24 in 30% (20/67) patients (AFP declined group) and remained ≥ 6.0 ng/mL in 70% of the patients (AFP non-declined group). The 1- and 2-year rates of HCC development, starting from the time point of 78 weeks post-treatment, were 0% and 0%, respectively, in the WFA±M2BP declined group, while these rates were 9.4% and 12.4%, respectively, in the WFA±M2BP non-declined group. The cumulative incidence of HCC development was significantly higher in patients in the WFA±M2BP non-declined group (p = 0.04, Figure 3A). In contrast, there was no significant difference in the cumulative rate of HCC development between the AFP declined and non-declined group (Figure 3B).

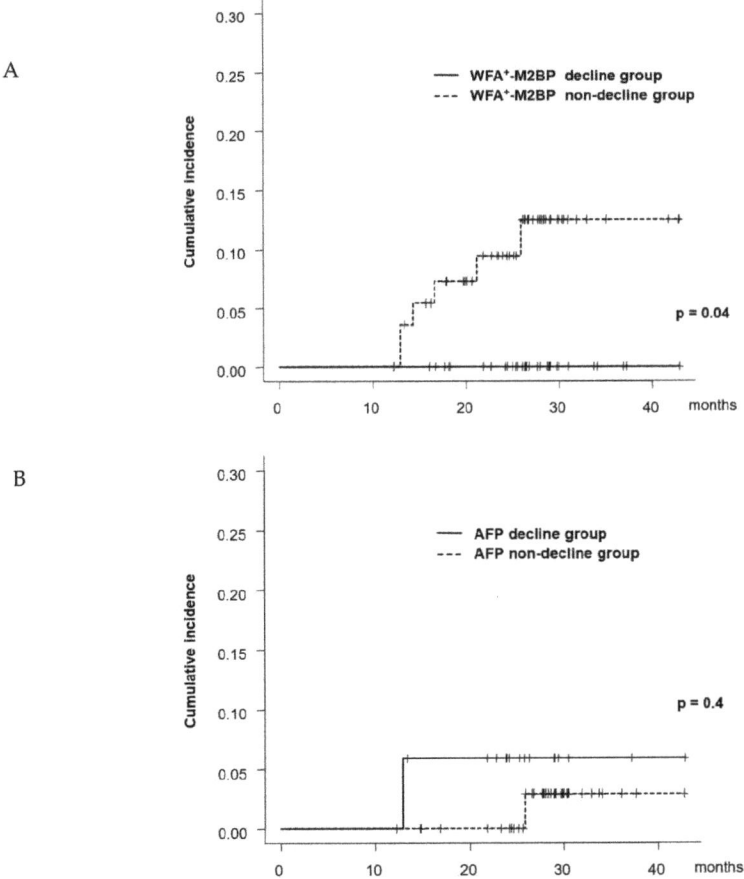

Figure 3. Cumulative incidence of HCC development as per change in the serum marker (**A**) patients were categorized into two groups as per the change in WFA±M2BP. Patients with WFA±M2BP ≥ 1.85 COI at SVR24 and WFA±M2BP < 1.85 at 1 year after SVR24 were defined as the declined group. (**B**) patients were categorized into two groups as per the change in AFP. The patients with AFP ≥ 6.0 ng/mL at SVR24 and AFP < 6.0 at 1 year after SVR24 were defined as the declined group.

2.5. Association between AFP and LR3/4 nodule

The association between serum AFP levels and the presence of LR3/4 nodule was analyzed at the time point of SVR24 and 1 year after SVR24. At SVR24, 2.1% (13/623) of patients with AFP at SVR24 < 6.0 ng/m had LR3/4 nodules and 7.2% (8/111) of patients with AFP ≥ 6.0 ng/m had LR3/4 nodules, and presence of LR3/4 nodules was significantly higher in patients with AFP ≥ 6.0 ng/mg ($p = 0.008$). However, at 1 year after SVR24, 0% of the patients with AFP ≥ 6.0 ng/m and 2.1% of those with AFP < 6.0 ng/m had LR3/4 nodules, with no significant difference.

2.6. Multivariable Analysis of Factors at SVR24 Associated with HCC Development

Factors at SVR24, including those other than WFA$^\pm$M2BP and AFP, were analyzed for their association with HCC development. Age (every 10 years), albumin, AST (every 30 IU/L), ALT (every 30 IU/L), platelet counts, WFA$^\pm$M2BP ≥ 1.85 COI (hazard ratio [HR]: 9.43, 95% confidence interval (CI): 3.91–22.7, $p < 0.001$, Table 2), AFP ≥ 6.0 ng/mL (HR: 8.17, 95%CI: 2.63–18.4, $p < 0.001$), and presence of LR3/4 nodules (HR: 15.4, 95%CI: 6.06–39.2, $p < 0.001$) were associated with HCC development in the univariate analysis. By using these factors, multivariate analysis revealed that WFA$^\pm$M2BP ≥ 1.85 COI (HR: 5.29, 95% CI: 2.07–13.0, $p < 0.001$), AFP ≥ 6.0 ng/mL (HR: 4.27, 95% CI: 1.84–9.94, $p < 0.001$), and the presence of LR3/4 nodules (HR: 8.49, 95%CI: 3.29–21.9, $p < 0.001$) were independently associated with HCC development.

Table 2. Factors associated with hepatocellular carcinoma (HCC) development.

	At SVR24					
	Univariate			Multivariate		
	HR	95%CI	p value	HR	95%CI	p value
Age (every 10 years)	1.90	1.20–2.99	0.006			
Sex (male)	1.31	0.59–2.93	0.5			
Albumin (g/dL)	0.22	0.09–0.56	0.001			
Bilirubin (mg/dL)	2.34	0.69–7.98	0.2			
AST (every 30 IU/L)	4.40	1.69–11.4	0.002			
ALT (every 30 IU/L)	3.42	1.40–8.35	0.007			
Platelet counts (×10^4/μL)	0.87	0.80–0.94	<0.001			
WFA$^\pm$M2BP ≥ 1.85 (COI)	9.43	3.91–22.7	<0.001	5.29	2.07–13.0	<0.001
AFP ≥ 6.0 (ng/mL)	8.17	3.63–18.4	<0.001	4.27	1.84–9.94	<0.001
Presence of LR3/4 nodules	15.4	6.06–39.2	<0.001	8.49	3.29–21.9	<0.001
	1 Year after SVR24					
	Univariate			Multivariate		
	HR	95%CI	p value	HR	95%CI	p value
Age (every 10 years)	2.40	0.91–6.31	0.08			
Sex (male)	0.64	0.12–3.30	0.6			
Albumin (g/dL)	0.17	0.04–0.65	0.01			
Bilirubin (mg/dL)	2.12	0.27–16.6	0.5			
AST (every 30 IU/L)	2.52	0.46–13.7	0.3			
ALT (every 30 IU/L)	1.18	0.11–12.1	0.9			
Platelet counts (×10^4/μL)	0.81	0.69–0.94	0.005			
WFA$^\pm$M2BP ≥ 1.85 (COI)	35.3	4.25–293	<0.001	23.5	2.68–205	0.004
AFP ≥ 6.0 (ng/mL)	1.23	0.15–10.2	0.9			
Presence of LR3/4 nodules	60.1	13.2–273	<0.001	24.1	5.02–116	<0.001

HCC, hepatocellular carcinoma; SVR, sustained virological response; HR, hazard ratio; CI, confidence interval, AST, aspartate aminotransferase; ALT, alanine aminotransferase; WFA±M2BP, *Wisteria floribunda* agglutinin-positive mac-2 binding protein; COI, cut off index; AFP, alpha-fetoprotein; LR, liver imaging reporting and data system; LR3, intermediate probability of HCC; LR4, probably of HCC.

2.7. Multivariable Analysis of Factors at 1 Year after SVR24 Associated with HCC Development

Similarly, factors at 1 year after SVR24, including those other than WFA$^±$M2BP and AFP, were analyzed for their association with HCC development. Similar to SVR24, WFA$^±$M2BP ≥ 1.85 COI (HR: 35.3, 95% CI: 4.25–293, p < 0.001), albumin, platelet counts, and presence of LR3/4 nodules (HR: 60.1, 95%CI: 13.2–273, p < 0.001) at 1 year after SVR24 were associated with HCC development in the univariate analysis. However, AFP ≥ 6.0 ng/mL at 1 year after SVR24 was not associated with subsequent HCC development (HR: 1.23, 95% CI: 0.15–10.2, p = 0.9). Multivariate analysis revealed that WFA$^±$M2BP ≥ 1.85 COI (HR: 23.5, HR: 2.68–205, p = 0.004) and presence of LR3/4 nodules (HR:24.1, 95%CI: 5.02–116, p < 0.001) were independent factors at 1 year after SVR24 for the prediction of HCC development thereafter.

3. Discussion

The present study revealed that WFA$^±$M2BP was useful for predicting HCC development at 1 year of SVR; however, AFP was not useful. In addition, even if WFA$^±$M2BP was high (≥ 1.85 COI) at SVR, the risk of HCC decreases in patients in whom WFA$^±$M2BP subsequently declines (<1.85 COI). However, AFP was useful for predicting HCC at the time of SVR, but not after one year. WFA$^±$M2BP could be easily measured and helped identify high cases of HCC development at any time after SVR; therefore, it was useful as a real-time monitor of HCC development risk in the long-term follow-up after SVR.

One of the novel findings of this study was that it confirmed that a high level of WFA$^±$M2BP after 1 year of SVR is associated with HCC development risk. The association between WFA$^±$M2BP at SVR and HCC risk has been reported by several studies, including our report [16,17]. Since WFA±M2BP at SVR was associated with histological fibrosis stage before DAA treatment, WFA±M2BP at SVR was a risk factor of HCC development after SVR. One advantage of WFA±M2BP is that it can assess the fibrosis stage instead of a liver biopsy and is easy to measure repeatedly. However, to our knowledge, no study has examined the association between WFA$^±$M2BP and HCC development risk after long-term follow-up. Early detection of HCC development after DAA treatment requires long-term follow-up. Therefore, not only the prediction of HCC development at SVR time point but also the prediction of HCC development at each follow-up time point is important. We found that WFA$^±$M2BP ≥ 1.85 COI at 1 year of SVR, as well as SVR24, were factors for HCC development.

Considering the changes in WFA$^±$M2BP after SVR, WFA$^±$M2BP generally declines over time. Patients with WFA$^±$M2BP ≥ 1.85 COI at SVR were at high-risk for subsequent HCC development; however, those with decreased WFA$^±$M2BP after 1 year had a reduced risk of HCC development. However, in some cases, WFA$^±$M2BP was still high, and in such cases, the risk of HCC development remained high. The advantage of WFA$^±$M2BP is that the change in the HCC risk can be identified by observing the time-dependent changes in WFA$^±$M2BP.

Although long-term follow-up is necessary to identify patients with HCC development after SVR, it is difficult to screen all patients frequently. However, the lack of screening after SVR is a known risk factor for the development of advanced HCC [22]. Therefore, there is an urgent need to construct a surveillance strategy after SVR. In surveillance, it is necessary to reevaluate the risk of HCC development not only at SVR but also at follow-up and to narrow down high-risk cases of HCC. WFA$^±$M2BP is useful as a real-time monitor for the prediction of HCC development in that WFA$^±$M2BP can assess the risk of HCC at any time point and assess changes in HCC risk by observing changes over time; further, clinically important information can be obtained noninvasively and conveniently.

Another novel finding of this study was that AFP after 1 year of SVR was not useful for predicting HCC development. It has been widely reported that AFP levels at SVR are associated with HCC risk [9–12,17]. This point was also confirmed in this study. However, it became clear that the AFP level 1 year after SVR was not associated with HCC development. It has been reported that high levels of AFP at the time of SVR are associated with the presence of LR3/4 nodules, and such patients are at a high risk of HCC development [23,24]. In this study, high levels of AFP at SVR were associated with the presence of LR3/4 nodules, and the cumulative incidence of HCC development was high in these patients; in particular, many HCC developments were observed within 1 year. Further, the AFP at 1 year after SVR decreased significantly, and no correlation was found when examining the association between AFP and LR3/4 nodules at 1 year after SVR. Although high AFP levels at SVR24 were associated with already existing HCC, high-risk nodules, and early development of HCC, no association between AFP and HCC development after 1 year of SVR, excluding that in these high-risk cases, is believed to exist. AFP was associated with the early development of HCC after SVR; however, one year thereafter, AFP was not useful for predicting HCC development; this was a novel finding of this study. AFP was not useful for predicting HCC development in the long-term follow-up; thus, WFA±M2BP, rather than AFP, was useful for HCC monitoring during long-term follow-up after SVR.

There are certain limitations to this study. At present, few cases have been followed up for 2 years. To verify the usefulness of WFA±M2BP over time, it is necessary to verify whether WFA±M2BP of 2 years after SVR24 and later is useful for prediction of HCC development, which is a future study subject. Moreover, there were few HCC cases; therefore, future long-term studies on a larger cohort are needed to examine the usefulness of WFA±M2BP over time. Several fibrosis markers have been confirmed as a predictive marker of HCC development after SVR [13,25]. The diagnostic accuracy of HCC development after SVR should be compared between WFA±M2BP and other markers in future studies.

In conclusion, WFA±M2BP but not AFP was useful as a real-time monitor of HCC prediction in long-term follow-up after SVR.

4. Materials and Methods

4.1. Patients

Between October 2014 and March 2018, 871 patients received DAAs at the Musashino Red Cross Hospital for the treatment of chronic hepatitis C and achieved SVR. Of these, 734 who met the following criteria were enrolled in this study: (1) those who were followed up for 6 months or more after SVR24, (2) had no history of HCC development, and (3) had no co-infection with hepatitis B virus or human immunodeficiency virus. The observation period began at the time of SVR24, and HCC development after SVR was followed up. Written informed consent was obtained from each patient. The study protocol conformed to the ethical guidelines of the Declaration of Helsinki and was approved by the institutional ethics review committee (approval number:28089, 4 April 2017).

4.2. Clinical and Laboratory Data

Age and sex of the patients were recorded at SVR24. Fasting blood counts and biochemical tests were also conducted on SVR24 and 1 year after SVR24 using standard methods.

4.3. HCC Surveillance and Diagnosis

Ultrasonography and blood tests, including tests for tumor markers, were performed every 3–6 months for HCC surveillance. When tumor marker levels rose abnormally and/or abdominal ultrasonography suggested a lesion suspicious of HCC, contrast-enhanced computed tomography, magnetic resonance imaging, or angiography was performed. HCC was diagnosed for tumors displaying vascular enhancement at the early phase and washout at the later phase as per the guidelines of the American Association for the Study of Liver Diseases, and the Japan Society of Hepatology [26,27]. Tumor biopsy was used to diagnose tumors with non-typical imaging findings.

Histological Evaluation

Of all patients enrolled in the study, liver biopsy was performed in 257 patients 1 month prior to the initiation of DAA treatment until the treatment. Liver biopsy specimens were obtained laparoscopically using 13G needles or by percutaneous ultrasound-guided liver biopsy using 15G needles. Specimens were fixed, paraffin-embedded, and stained using hematoxylin–eosin and Masson's trichrome. A minimum of a 15-mm biopsy sample was required for diagnosis. All liver biopsy samples were independently evaluated by two senior pathologists who were blinded to the clinical data. Fibrosis staging was assessed according to the METAVIR score: F0, no fibrosis; F1, portal fibrosis without septa; F2, portal fibrosis with few septa; F3, numerous septa without cirrhosis; and F4, cirrhosis.

4.4. Statistical Analyses

Receiver operating characteristic (ROC) curves and the Youden index were used to determine the optimal cutoff value of WFA±M2BP and AFP for predicting HCC development. Statistical significance was defined as a p-value < 0.05. Cumulative incidences of HCC development were calculated using the Kaplan–Meier method. The factors associated with HCC development were analyzed using the Cox-proportional hazard model. Correlated factors with a p-value < 0.05 in the univariate analysis were used for further multivariate analysis. Backward stepwise selection method was used for multivariate analyses. Association between WFA±M2BP and fibrosis stage was analyzed using Spearman's rank correlation test. Statistical analyses were performed using EZR (Saitama Medical Center, Jichi Medical University, Saitama, Japan) [28] and a graphical user interface for R (The R Foundation for Statistical Computing, Vienna, Austria).

Author Contributions: Study conception: L.O., N.T., M.K.; data collection: all authors; data analysis: L.O., N.T.; manuscript drafting: L.O., N.T.; clinical revision: M.K., N.E., N.I.; obtained funding: N.I.; study supervision: N.E., N.I., L.O. and N.T. have equally contributed to this study. All authors read and approved the published version of the manuscript.

Funding: This study was supported by a grant-in-aid from the Japan Agency for Medical Research and Development (grant number: JP19fk0210025h0003, URL: http://www.amed.go.jp/en/).

Conflicts of Interest: All authors have no conflict of interest to disclose.

Abbreviations

DAAs	direct-acting antivirals
SVR	sustained virological responses
HCC	hepatocellular carcinoma
AFP	α-fetoprotein
SVR24	24 weeks after the end of treatment
WFA±M2BP	*Wisteria floribunda* agglutinin-positive mac-2 binding protein
ROC	receiver operating characteristic
AST	aspartate aminotransferase
ALT	alanine aminotransferase
LR	the liver imaging reporting and data system
HR	hazard ratio
CI	95% confidence interval

References

1. Tsuji, K.; Kurosaki, M.; Itakura, J.; Mori, N.; Takaki, S.; Hasebe, C.; Akahane, T.; Joko, K.; Yagisawa, H.; Takezawa, J.; et al. Real-world efficacy and safety of ledipasvir and sofosbuvir in patients with hepatitis C virus genotype 1 infection: A nationwide multicenter study by the Japanese Red Cross Liver Study Group. *J. Gastroenterol.* **2018**, *53*, 1142–1150. [CrossRef] [PubMed]
2. Suda, G.; Ogawa, K.; Yamamoto, Y.; Katagiri, M.; Furuya, K.; Kumagai, K.; Konno, J.; Kimura, M.; Kawagishi, N.; Ohara, M.; et al. Retreatment with sofosbuvir, ledipasvir, and add-on ribavirin for patients who failed daclatasvir and asunaprevir combination therapy. *J. Gastroenterol.* **2017**, *52*, 1122–1129. [CrossRef] [PubMed]
3. Izumi, N.; Takehara, T.; Chayama, K.; Yatsuhashi, H.; Takaguchi, K.; Ide, T.; Kurosaki, M.; Ueno, Y.; Toyoda, H.; Kakizaki, S.; et al. Sofosbuvir-velpatasvir plus ribavirin in Japanese patients with genotype 1 or 2 hepatitis C who failed direct-acting antivirals. *Hepatol. Int.* **2018**, *12*, 356–367. [CrossRef] [PubMed]

4. Fujii, H.; Kimura, H.; Kurosaki, M.; Hasebe, C.; Akahane, T.; Yagisawa, H.; Kato, K.; Yoshida, H.; Itakura, J.; Sakita, S.; et al. Efficacy of daclatasvir plus asunaprevir in patients with hepatitis C virus infection undergoing and not undergoing hemodialysis. *Hepatol. Res.* **2018**, *48*, 746–756. [CrossRef] [PubMed]
5. Akahane, T.; Kurosaki, M.; Itakura, J.; Tsuji, K.; Joko, K.; Kimura, H.; Nasu, A.; Ogawa, C.; Kojima, Y.; Hasebe, C.; et al. Real-world efficacy and safety of sofosbuvir + ribavirin for hepatitis C genotype 2: A nationwide multicenter study by the Japanese Red Cross Liver Study Group. *Hepatol. Res.* **2019**, *49*, 264–270. [CrossRef] [PubMed]
6. Sho, T.; Suda, G.; Nagasaka, A.; Yamamoto, Y.; Furuya, K.; Kumagai, K.; Uebayashi, M.; Terashita, K.; Kobayashi, T.; Tsunematsu, I.; et al. Safety and efficacy of sofosbuvir and ribavirin for genotype 2 hepatitis C Japanese patients with renal dysfunction. *Hepatol. Res.* **2018**, *48*, 529–538. [CrossRef]
7. Kanwal, F.; Kramer, J.; Asch, S.M.; Chayanupatkul, M.; Cao, Y.; El-Serag, H.B. Risk of hepatocellular cancer in HCV patients treated with direct-acting antiviral agents. *Gastroenterology* **2017**, *153*, 996–1005. [CrossRef]
8. Higuchi, M.; Tamaki, N.; Kurosaki, M.; Watakabe, K.; Osawa, L.; Wang, W.; Okada, M.; Shimizu, T.; Takaura, K.; Takada, H.; et al. Prediction of hepatocellular carcinoma after sustained virological responses using magnetic resonance elastography. *Clin. Gastroenterol. Hepatol.* **2018**, *28*, 31323–31325. [CrossRef]
9. Asahina, Y.; Tsuchiya, K.; Nishimura, T.; Muraoka, M.; Suzuki, Y.; Tamaki, N.; Yasui, Y.; Hosokawa, T.; Ueda, K.; Nakanishi, H.; et al. α-fetoprotein levels after interferon therapy and risk of hepatocarcinogenesis in chronic hepatitis C. *Hepatology* **2013**, *58*, 1253–1262. [CrossRef]
10. Asahina, Y.; Tsuchiya, K.; Nishimura, T.; Muraoka, M.; Suzuki, Y.; Tamaki, N.; Yasui, Y.; Hosokawa, T.; Ueda, K.; Nakanishi, H.; et al. Genetic variation near interleukin 28B and the risk of hepatocellular carcinoma in patients with chronic hepatitis C. *J. Gastroenterol.* **2014**, *49*, 1152–1162. [CrossRef]
11. Tada, T.; Kumada, T.; Toyoda, H.; Kiriyama, S.; Tanikawa, M.; Hisanaga, Y.; Kanamori, A.; Kitabatake, S.; Yama, T.; Tanaka, J. Post-treatment levels of α-fetoprotein predict long-term hepatocellular carcinoma development after sustained virological response in patients with hepatitis C. *Hepatol. Res.* **2017**, *47*, 1021–1031. [CrossRef] [PubMed]
12. Yamada, R.; Hiramatsu, N.; Oze, T.; Urabe, A.; Tahata, Y.; Morishita, N.; Kodama, T.; Hikita, H.; Sakamori, R.; Yakushijin, T.; et al. Incidence and risk factors of hepatocellular carcinoma change over time in patients with hepatitis C virus infection who achieved sustained virologic response. *Hepatol. Res.* **2019**, *49*, 570–578. [CrossRef] [PubMed]
13. Tamaki, N.; Higuchi, M.; Kurosaki, M.; Kirino, S.; Osawa, L.; Watakabe, K.; Wang, W.; Okada, M.; Shimizu, T.; Takaura, K.; et al. Risk assessment of hepatocellular carcinoma development by magnetic resonance elastography in chronic hepatitis C patients who achieved sustained virological responses by direct-acting antivirals. *J. Viral Hepat.* **2019**, *26*, 893–899. [CrossRef] [PubMed]
14. Kuno, A.; Ikehara, Y.; Tanaka, Y.; Ito, K.; Matsuda, A.; Sekiya, S.; Hige, S.; Sakamoto, M.; Kage, M.; Mizokami, M.; et al. A serum "sweet-doughnut" protein facilitates fibrosis evaluation and therapy assessment in patients with viral hepatitis. *Sci. Rep.* **2013**, *3*, 1065. [CrossRef]
15. Tamaki, N.; Kurosaki, M.; Kuno, A.; Korenaga, M.; Togayachi, A.; Gotoh, M.; Nakakuki, N.; Takada, H.; Matsuda, S.; Hattori, N.; et al. Wisteria floribundaagglutinin positive human Mac-2-binding protein as a predictor of hepatocellular carcinoma development in chronic hepatitis C patients. *Hepatol. Res.* **2015**, *45*, E82–E88. [CrossRef]
16. Nagata, H.; Nakagawa, M.; Asahina, Y.; Sato, A.; Asano, Y.; Tsunoda, T.; Miyoshi, M.; Kaneko, S.; Otani, S.; Kawai-Kitahata, F.; et al. Effect of interferon-based and -free therapy on early occurrence and recurrence of hepatocellular carcinoma in chronic hepatitis C. *J. Hepatol.* **2017**, *67*, 933–939. [CrossRef]
17. Yasui, Y.; Kurosaki, M.; Komiyama, Y.; Takada, H.; Tamaki, N.; Watakabe, K.; Okada, M.; Wang, W.; Shimizu, T.; Kubota, Y.; et al. Wisteria floribunda agglutinin-positive Mac-2 binding protein predicts early occurrence of hepatocellular carcinoma after sustained virologic response by direct-acting antivirals for hepatitis C virus. *Hepatol. Res.* **2018**, *48*, 1131–1139. [CrossRef]
18. Shiratori, Y.; Imazeki, F.; Moriyama, M.; Yano, M.; Arakawa, Y.; Yokosuka, O.; Kuroki, T.; Nishiguchi, S.; Sata, M.; Yamada, G.; et al. Histologic improvement of fibrosis in patients with hepatitis C who have sustained response to interferon therapy. *Ann. Intern. Med.* **2000**, *132*, 517–524. [CrossRef]
19. Tamaki, N.; Kurosaki, M.; Tanaka, K.; Suzuki, Y.; Hoshioka, Y.; Kato, T.; Yasui, Y.; Hosokawa, T.; Ueda, K.; Tsuchiya, K.; et al. Noninvasive estimation of fibrosis progression overtime using the FIB-4 index in chronic hepatitis C. *J. Viral Hepat.* **2013**, *20*, 72–76. [CrossRef]

20. Tamaki, N.; Kurosaki, M.; Matsuda, S.; Muraoka, M.; Yasui, Y.; Suzuki, S.; Hosokawa, T.; Ueda, K.; Tsuchiya, K.; Nakanishi, H.; et al. Non-invasive prediction of hepatocellular carcinoma development using serum fibrosis marker in chronic hepatitis C patients. *J. Gastroenterol.* **2014**, *49*, 1495–1503. [CrossRef]
21. Elsayes, K.M.; Hooker, J.; Agrons, M.M.; Kielar, A.Z.; Tang, A.; Fowler, K.J.; Chernyak, V.; Bashir, M.R.; Kono, Y.; Do, R.K.; et al. 2017 version of LI-RADS for CT and MR imaging: An update. *Radiographics* **2017**, *37*, 1994–2017. [CrossRef] [PubMed]
22. Toyoda, H.; Tada, T.; Tsuji, K.; Hiraoka, A.; Tachi, Y.; Itobayashi, E.; Takaguchi, K.; Senoh, T.; Takizawa, D.; Ishikawa, T.; et al. Characteristics and prognosis of hepatocellular carcinoma detected in patients with chronic hepatitis C after the eradication of hepatitis C virus: A multicenter study from Japan. *Hepatol. Res.* **2016**, *46*, 734–742. [CrossRef] [PubMed]
23. Toyoda, H.; Kumada, T.; Tada, T.; Mizuno, K. Imaging basis of AFP and WFA(+)M2BP as indicators of the risk of HCC after SVR. *J. Hepatol.* **2018**, *68*, 606–607. [CrossRef] [PubMed]
24. Toyoda, H.; Kumada, T.; Tada, T.; Mizuno, K.; Sone, Y.; Kaneoka, Y.; Maeda, A.; Akita, T.; Tanaka, J. Impact of previously cured hepatocellular carcinoma (HCC) on new development of HCC after eradication of hepatitis C infection with non-interferon-based treatments. *Aliment. Pharmacol. Ther.* **2018**, *48*, 664–670. [CrossRef] [PubMed]
25. Ioannou, G.; Beste, L.A.; Green, P.K.; Singal, A.G.; Tapper, E.B.; Waljee, A.K.; Sterling, R.K.; Feld, J.J.; Kaplan, D.E.; Taddei, T.H.; et al. Increased risk for hepatocellular carcinoma persists up to 10 years after HCV eradication in patients with baseline cirrhosis or high FIB-4 scores. *Gastroenterology* **2019**, *157*, 1264–1278. [CrossRef] [PubMed]
26. Roberts, L.R.; Sirlin, C.B.; Zaiem, F.; Almasri, J.; Prokop, L.J.; Heimbach, J.K.; Murad, M.H.; Mohammed, K. Imaging for the diagnosis of hepatocellular carcinoma: A systematic review and meta-analysis. *Hepatology* **2018**, *67*, 401–421. [CrossRef] [PubMed]
27. Kokudo, N.; Hasegawa, K.; Akahane, M.; Igaki, H.; Izumi, N.; Ichida, T.; Uemoto, S.; Kaneko, S.; Kawasaki, S.; Ku, Y.; et al. Evidence-based clinical practice guidelines for hepatocellular carcinoma: The Japan society of hepatology 2013 update (3rd JSH-HCC guidelines). *Hepatol. Res.* **2015**, *45*, 12464. [CrossRef]
28. Kanda, Y. Investigation of the freely available easy-to-use software 'EZR' for medical statistics. *Bone Marrow Transplant.* **2013**, *48*, 452–458. [CrossRef]

© 2020 by the authors. Licensee MDPI, Basel, Switzerland. This article is an open access article distributed under the terms and conditions of the Creative Commons Attribution (CC BY) license (http://creativecommons.org/licenses/by/4.0/).

Article

Form-Vessel Classification of Cholangioscopy Findings to Diagnose Biliary Tract Carcinoma's Superficial Spread

Yoshimitsu Fukasawa, Shinichi Takano *, Mitsuharu Fukasawa, Shinya Maekawa, Makoto Kadokura, Hiroko Shindo, Ei Takahashi, Sumio Hirose, Satoshi Kawakami, Hiroshi Hayakawa, Tatsuya Yamaguchi, Yasuhiro Nakayama, Taisuke Inoue, Tadashi Sato and Nobuyuki Enomoto

First Department of Internal Medicine, Faculty of Medicine, University of Yamanashi, Chuo, Yamanashi 409-3898, Japan; ii258pp2@yahoo.co.jp (Y.F.); fmitsu@yamanashi.ac.jp (M.F.); maekawa@yamanashi.ac.jp (S.M.); makotok@yamanashi.ac.jp (M.K.); shindoh@yamanashi.ac.jp (H.S.); etakahashi@yamanashi.ac.jp (E.T.); sh99073@yahoo.co.jp (S.H.); k234_0516@yahoo.co.jp (S.K.); hhayakawa@yamanashi.ac.jp (H.H.); ytatsuya@yamanashi.ac.jp (T.Y.); ynakayama@yamanashi.ac.jp (Y.N.); tinoue@yamanashi.ac.jp (T.I.); tadashis@yamanashi.ac.jp (T.S.); enomoto@yamanashi.ac.jp (N.E.)
* Correspondence: stakano@yamanashi.ac.jp; Tel.: +81-55-273-9584

Received: 8 April 2020; Accepted: 5 May 2020; Published: 7 May 2020

Abstract: We aimed to evaluate a newly developed peroral cholangioscopy (POCS) classification system by comparing classified lesions with histological and genetic findings. We analyzed 30 biopsied specimens from 11 patients with biliary tract cancer (BTC) who underwent POCS. An original classification of POCS findings was made based on the biliary surface's form (F factor, 4 grades) and vessel structure (V-factor, 3 grades). Findings were then compared with those of corresponding biopsy specimens analyzed histologically and by next-generation sequencing to identify somatic mutations. In addition, the histology of postoperative surgical stumps and preoperative POCS findings were compared. Histological malignancy rate in biopsied specimens increased with increasing F- and V-factor scores (F1, 0%; F1, 25%; F3, 50%; F4, 62.5%; $p = 0.0015$; V1, 0%; V2, 20%; V3, 70%; $p < 0.001$). Furthermore, we observed a statistically significant increase of the mutant allele frequency of mutated genes with increasing F- and V-factor scores (F factor, $p = 0.0050$; V-factor, $p < 0.001$). All surgical stumps were accurately diagnosed using POCS findings. The F–V classification of POCS findings is both histologically and genetically valid and will contribute to the methods of diagnosing the superficial spread of BTC tumors.

Keywords: bile duct cancer; cholangioscope; genetic mutation; tumor spread; biopsy

1. Introduction

Biliary tract cancer (BTC), which arises from the biliary epithelium of the intrahepatic, extrahepatic, and gallbladder bile ducts, accounts for about 3% of all gastrointestinal cancers [1] and is the sixth leading cause of cancer death [2]. In Japan, perihilar bile duct, distal bile duct, and gallbladder cancers have overall 5-year survival rates of 24.2%, 39.1%, and 39.8%, respectively [3]. To date, surgery has been the exclusive curative therapy for BTC. In addition, survival post-surgery is short in cases involving positive resection margins, perineural invasion, lymph node metastasis, and undifferentiated adenocarcinoma in resected tissues [4].

To avoid unnecessary invasive procedures and determine the appropriate therapy, a precise diagnosis of tumor spread is important. Currently, more extensive surgery made possible by accumulated experience and recent technical advances has allowed for complete resection of BTC lesions (e.g., hepatopancreatoduodenectomy) [5]. By conducting a thorough examination pre-surgery, a positive resected margin is avoidable, improving risk factors related to postoperative survival. Earlier studies have reported the primary tumor's superficial spread or extension in 31.6–39.3% of BTC cases, with more than 20-mm length of superficial spread in 14.6–17.9% cases [6,7]. These lesions can be identified using ultrasonography [8], multi detector-row computed tomography (MDCT) [9], and magnetic resonance imaging [10]. Intraductal ultrasonography (IDUS) during endoscopic retrograde cholangiopancreatography (ERCP) has been shown to be beneficial for both qualitative diagnosis and the diagnosis of the main tumor's superficial spread [11,12]. However, these methods have a limited diagnostic accuracy in terms of the superficial tumor spread. In contrast, superficial spread of tumor can be diagnosed using peroral cholangioscopy (POCS), which has the advantage of allowing direct visualization of the bile duct lumen [13]. The diagnostic accuracy has been reported to increase when POCS is used with bile duct biopsy [14–16]. Furthermore, recent improvements in image resolution and the development of narrow-band imaging have enabled the detailed observation of surface structures and the fine vasculature of bile ducts [17]. Several POCS studies, focusing on surface and vessel structures, have reported on benign and malignant bile ducts findings [16,18–20]. However, to date, there are no reports systematically classifying POCS findings.

Recent advances in next-generation sequencing (NGS) have enabled rapid and comprehensive gene sequencing, which have allowed the identification of gene alterations in numerous tumors, including BTC [21,22]. Of note, targeted deep sequencing has a high sensitivity in detecting multiple gene mutations. The variant allele frequency (VAF) of genes reflect the fraction of tumor cells per sample and can be used to determine the tumor grade [23].

In this study, we developed a classification system based on POCS findings in surface and vessel structures to diagnose BTC tumor spread. The validity of this classification system was evaluated using histological diagnosis and gene mutation analysis in biopsy specimens. Furthermore, we examined the effectiveness of this classification in determining the extent of resection.

2. Results

2.1. Patient Characteristics and Assessment of Biopsied Samples

A total of 11 patients (8 men and 3 women) were enrolled in this study, with their median age being 70 (range, 59–79) years. Lesions were in the following regions: intrahepatic bile duct ($n = 1$), perihilar bile duct ($n = 2$), and distal bile duct ($n = 8$). Macroscopic classification revealed 5, 4, and 2 cases of papillary type, nodular type, and flat type, respectively. Histological tumor invasion around the bile duct (pT) and histological lymph node metastasis (pN) were evaluated according to the TNM Classification of Malignant Tumors (7th edition) [24]. Staging revealed 4 early-stage (<pT3) cases and 7 more advanced cases (≥pT3), with 7 pN0 cases and 4 pN1 cases (Table 1). Endoscopic procedures resulted in no complications. Surgical resection after POCS examination was performed in all patients.

The median amount of DNA extracted from 18 biopsied samples was 13.0 (range, 2.5–34.0) ng. However, the amount of DNA extracted from the other 12 samples was below the detection sensitivity. The median sequence read depth was 7570 (range, 261–16,055) (Table S1). Specimens of 12, 8, 2, and 8 parts in the bile ducts were biopsied from areas with F1, F2, F3, and F4, respectively. Specimens of 15, 5, and 10 were from areas with V1, V2, and V3, respectively.

Table 1. Baseline characteristics of patients.

Characteristics	Values ($n = 11$)
Age, mean ± SD (years)	69.9 ± 6.9
Sex (n)	
Male	8
Female	3
Location of main lesions in CBD (n)	
Bh	1
Bp	2
Bd	8
Macroscopic tumor type (n)	
Papillary	5
Nodular	4
Infiltrating	2
Histology (n)	
Well	5
Moderate	6
Depth of invasion (n)	
<pT3	4
≥pT3	7
Lymph node metastasis (n)	
pN0	7
pN1	4

CBD, common bile duct; Bh, intrahepatic bile duct; Bp, perihilar bile duct; Bd, distal bile duct.

2.2. Association between the F–V Classification and the Histological Assessment of Biopsied Samples

We observed a positive correlation between F factor and V-factor scores (correlation coefficient: 0.91; Figure S1). The pathological malignancy rates with respect to the F factor were as follows: F1, 0%; F2, 25%; F3, 50%; and F4, 62.5% (Figure 1A). Similarly, those with respect to the V-factor were as follows: V1, 0%; V2, 20%; and V3, 70% (Figure 1B). We found that higher F–V scores significantly corresponded with higher histological malignancies of the biopsied specimens (F factor, $p = 0.0015$; V-factor, $p < 0.001$). However, no malignancy of the biopsied specimens was observed in POCS findings in terms of F1V1 and F2V1. Surgical margins were negative in 9 of 11 cases, and all stumps of these 9 cases were F1V1 in POCS findings. In 2 cases, surgical margins were positive with carcinoma in situ, and these cases had a positive surgical margin with F2V3 in POCS findings.

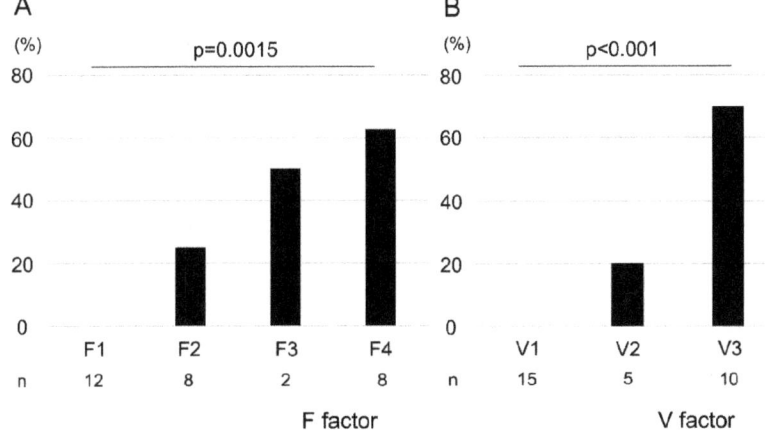

Figure 1. Association between pathological malignancy rate and F–V factors. Pathological malignancy rates increased with increasing F- and V-factor scores (**A**, F factor; **B**, V-factor). Statistical significance was determined using the Cochran–Armitage trend test.

2.3. Association between the F–V Classification and Genetic Mutations

In the present study, of the 50 cancer-related genes that were examined, *TP53* (36%), *RB1* (27%), and *KIT* (18%) were the most frequently mutated ones. Of the tested samples, 13 (43.3%) had at least one gene mutation (Figure S2). The fraction of samples with a gene mutation according to the F factor was as follows: F1, 16.7%; and F2–F4, 61.1% (Figure 2A), whereas those with a mutation according to the V-factor were as follows: V1, 13.3%; V2–V3, 73.3% (Figure 2B). We observed that the differences between V-factor categories were statistically significant (F factor, $p = 0.0423$; V-factor, $p = 0.0032$). Furthermore, we found an increase in VAF of the mutated genes with increasing F- and V-factor scores (Figure 2C,D, $p = 0.005$ and <0.001, respectively).

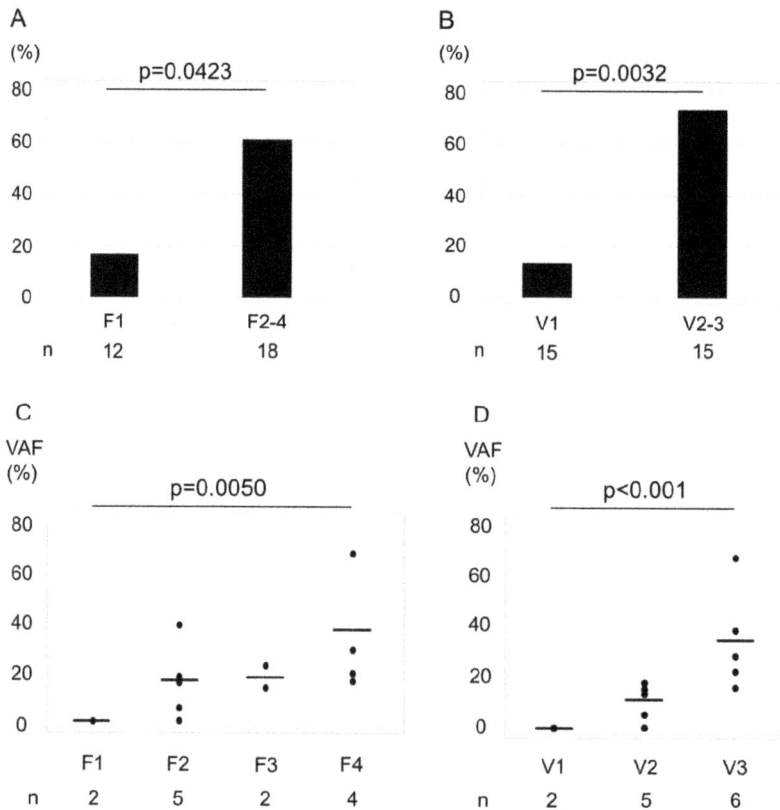

Figure 2. Association between the percentage of cases with a gene mutation and F–V-factor scores. Bar graphs represent the percentage of cases with a gene mutation by F factor score (**A**) and V-factor score (**B**). The rate of genetic mutations of F2–F4 was higher than F1 (A). The rate of genetic mutations of V2–V3 was higher than V1 (B). Statistical significance was assessed using χ^2 test. The variant allele frequencies (VAFs) increased with increasing F- and V-factor scores (**C**, F factor; **D**, V-factor). Horizontal bars indicate the mean. Increasing trends were analyzed using the Jonckheere–Terpstra trend test. VAFs were plotted only for specimens with a confirmed gene mutation.

2.4. Association between the Histological Assessment and Genetic Mutations in F–V Classification

We assessed the association between F–V classification and histological diagnosis (Figure 3A) or VAFs (Figure 3B) of biopsied specimens. The group evaluated as F1V1 or F2V1 in POCS were all histologically benign, had a low rate of genetic mutation, and a low gene mutation VAF. On the contrary, the groups evaluated as F4V3 or F3V3 or F2V3 in POCS were histologically malignant, had a high rate of genetic mutation, and had a high gene mutation VAF. The group evaluated as F3V2 or F2V2 in POCS were histologically benign, had a high rate of genetic mutation, and had a low gene mutation VAF.

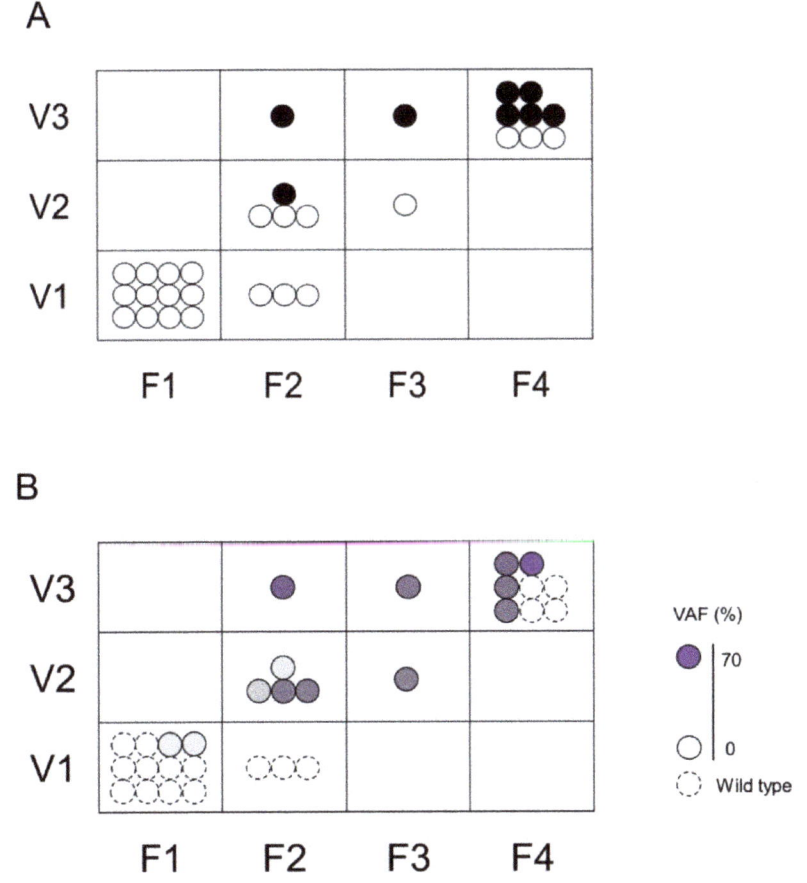

Figure 3. Association between the histological assessment and genetic mutations in F–V classification. The upper Figure (**A**) shows the association between F–V classification and histological assessment. Black circle (•) indicates malignancy and white circle (○) indicates non-malignant lesions. The lower Figure (**B**) shows the association between F–V classification and genetic mutation. Dotted circles represent specimens without genetic mutation, and solid circles represent specimens with genetic mutation. The color density in the circle indicates the VAF.

Figure 4 shows a representative case. Specifically, this case highlights the relationship among F–V classification of POCS findings, histology, and genetic mutations. In this case, the main tumor lies in the middle bile duct. It is classified as F3V3 according to POCS findings, malignant pathology, and gene mutations (Figure 4C). In addition, the perihilar and inferior bile duct has a benign lesion. The benign lesion in the inferior bile duct is classified as F1V1 according to POCS findings, with no gene mutation (Figure 4A,D). The tumor extends into the superior bile duct, categorized as F3V2 with a gene mutation, with a benign pathology (Figure 4B). These findings were consistent with those of the resected tissues that were pathologically diagnosed.

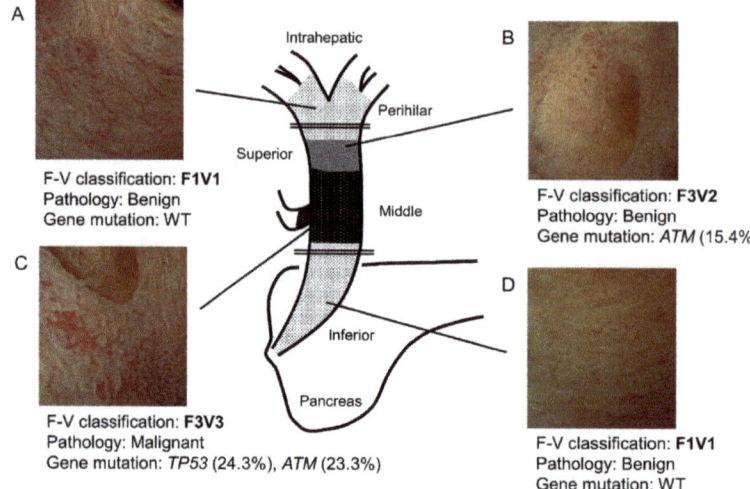

Figure 4. Schema of a representative bile duct carcinoma case. (**A**) In the perihilar bile duct, POCS showed the presence of a flat bile duct epithelium with a network of thin vessels (F1V1). In this region's biopsied specimens, neither a tumor nor a genetic mutation was identified. (**B**) In the superior bile duct, POCS revealed a papillary bile duct epithelium with irregular, non-dilated vessels (F3V2). In this region's biopsied specimens, no tumor was observed. However, a genetic mutation in *ATM* was found (VAF; 15.4%). (**C**) In the main lesion of the middle bile duct, POCS demonstrated the presence of a papillary bile duct epithelium with an irregular, dilated, and tortuous vessel (F3V3). The biopsied specimens showed adenocarcinoma. Genetic mutations in *TP53* (VAF, 24.3%) and *ATM* (VAF, 23.3%) were identified. (**D**) In the inferior bile duct, POCS revealed a flat bile duct epithelium, with a network of thin vessels (F1V1). In this region's biopsied specimens, neither a tumor nor genetic mutation was observed. VAF, variant allele frequency; WT, wild type. The double line shows the resection line.

2.5. Association between F–V Classification and Pathology Diagnosis of Resected Stump

In total, 11 patients underwent the following procedures: pancreatoduodenectomy ($n = 7$), hepatectomy ($n = 3$), and extrahepatic bile tract resection ($n = 1$, Table 2). Of the 15 resected stumps, 13 were F1V1 and 2 were F2V3 according to the F–V classification. Histologically, the F1V1 stumps had no carcinoma and the F2V3 stumps had carcinoma in situ.

Table 2. Relationship between F–V classification and pathology diagnosis of resected stump.

Case	Operation	Findings of Ductal Margin (Duodenum Side)		Findings of Ductal Margin (Liver Side)	
		F–V Classification	Pathological Diagnosis	F–V Classification	Pathological Diagnosis
1	PD	-	-	F2V3	CIS
2	Hepatectomy	F2V3	CIS	F1V1	negative
3	PD	-	-	F1V1	negative
4	*	F1V1	negative	F1V1	negative
5	Hepatectomy	F1V1	negative	F1V1	negative
6	PD	-	-	F1V1	negative
7	PD	-	-	F1V1	negative
8	Hepatectomy	F1V1	negative	F1V1	negative
9	PD	-	-	F1V1	negative
10	PD	-	-	F1V1	negative
11	PD	-	-	F1V1	negative

*, Extrahepatic bile tract resection; PD, Pancreatoduodenectomy; CIS, Carcinoma in situ.

3. Discussion

In the present study, we classified the POCS findings of BTC cases based on the form of the bile duct surface (F factor) and vascular structures (V-factor). This new system is called "the F–V classification of POCS findings." The system was validated by comparing it to the histological diagnosis and genetic mutation analysis in simultaneously biopsied specimens. Comparison with the histological diagnosis revealed a statistically significant increase of the malignancy rate with increasing F- and V-factor scores. Comparison with the mutation status showed an increased frequency of mutant variants in samples with an increase in the F- and V-factor scores. In addition, the F–V classifications of resected margins according to POCS findings were all accurate.

F–V classification is the first reported system to quantify and classify BTC based on POCS findings. Several reports have quantified POCS findings according to bile duct malignancies [16,19,20,25]. However, none of these have reported methods for stratification according to malignancy. We found that this approach is confusing when applied to diagnosis. On the contrary, we noticed that the reported observations of POCS findings could be categorized into 2 groups. The first group comprised surface structures of the bile duct such as "irregular fine granular pattern" [16], "irregular papillogranular surface" [19], "nodular elevated surface-like submucosal tumor" [19], "irregular surface or papillary projections" [20], and "luminal narrowing that was continuous with the main cancerous lesion" [20]. The second group comprised vascular structures such as "fish-egg-like appearance" [16,19], "irregularly dilated and tortuous vessels" [20], and "irregular or spider vascularity" [25]. Therefore, we decided to develop a classification system by further scoring these POCS findings according to the degree of malignancy. Specifically, our F–V classification of POCS findings is based on these systematic studies. Its validity was verified by comparing it with histological diagnosis and genetic mutation analysis in biopsied specimens.

Recent advances in NGS have enabled the identification of comprehensive gene profiles of numerous cancers, including BTC, which has been reported to have frequent alterations in *TP53*, *KRAS*, *SMAD4*, and *BAP1* genes [22]. Characteristic gene alterations vary depending on the main tumor site. For example, alterations in *TP53*, *KRAS*, *BAP1*, *ARID1A*, *IDH*, and *SMAD4* are generally observed in intrahepatic cholangiocarcinoma, whereas *TP53*, *KRAS*, *SMAD4*, and *ERBB2* mutations are associated with extrahepatic cholangiocarcinoma [22,26]. *TP53* alterations are characteristic of extrahepatic cholangiocarcinoma. In our study, *TP53* mutations were the most frequently observed one in extrahepatic cholangiocarcinoma. For other mutations, we did not observe the same tendency as reported. We believe that this discrepancy may be because of the small sample size in our study, not accurately reflecting distribution of gene alterations. The VAF, also known as the mutant allele frequency, indicates tumor cellularity from extracted DNA. The VAF has been used to predict the degree of malignancy [23] and the reactivity to drugs [27] in certain tumors. Thus, we used the VAFs of biopsied bile duct specimens to classify the degree of malignancy. We found a correlation between the fraction of cases with a mutation and the F–V classification of POCS findings. The same was true for the histological diagnosis.

To select the appropriate surgical procedure, the superficial spread of a tumor should be precisely diagnosed by POCS. This is because BTC is often accompanied by superficial spread in the bile duct [6,7]. Postoperative 5-year survival rate is unaffected by positive surgical margins with carcinoma in situ [6,28]. However, because positive margins are reported to affect longer post-surgical survival, we should aim for negative surgical margins [29]. On the contrary, more extensive biliary resection may greatly increase surgical stress. Specifically, resection of the upstream bile duct requires hepatectomy, whereas the resection of the downstream bile duct requires pancreatectomy. These expanded surgical procedures are associated with the risk of surgery-related death [30]. Thus, an adequate surgery, neither excessive nor insufficient, should be chosen based on the disease extent, patient's general condition, and the imposed surgical risks. Currently, the final resection margin in BTC surgery is determined by intraoperative frozen-section diagnosis, which is not always correct [31,32]. Reports show that the epithelial layer's correct diagnosis rate is considerably lower than subepithelial layer [31]. POCS can directly visualize the bile duct lumen with biopsy, thereby aiding the diagnosis of BTC's spread [18,20]. Here, assuming that F2V3 in F–V classification is malignant, the correct diagnosis rate of the F–V classification in stump evaluation was 100%. Therefore, we believe that the F–V classification may be more effective in the diagnosis of BTC superficial spread versus intraoperative frozen sections. Furthermore, in the future, it may become possible to determine the range of resection by POCS findings and genetic variation of the biopsy specimen. In summary, the F–V classification of POCS findings, together with intraoperative frozen-section diagnosis, may enable the precise diagnosis of a surgical stump.

Multiple clinical implications were fostered by the findings of this study. First, the F–V classification of POCS findings may guide in the assessment of the potential risks in diagnosed bile duct tumors. In a prospective multicenter study, the diagnostic accuracy of BTC superficial spread has been reported to be 83.7% (41/49) for POCS findings and 92.9% (39/42) for POCS with biopsy [19]. However, even with the addition of biopsy to the POCS diagnosis, the accuracy remains to be imperfect, probably because biopsy specimens were too small for histological diagnosis and the gray zones of the histologic characteristics that exist precluded differentiation between benignity and malignancy. As shown in Figure 4, some samples with mutations but without histological confirmation of malignancy had V2 findings by the F–V classification. In other words, a V2 finding in the F–V classification may be equivalent to a histologic diagnosis of malignancy or to a potential risk of malignancy because only this finding can allow the identification of mutated bile duct epithelium without histological confirmation of malignancy. Furthermore, in another study, we recently reported similar concepts about the relation between the endoscopic findings of colorectal tumors and genetic abnormalities [33]. Accumulated gene alterations in the adenoma components of colorectal carcinoma could be diagnosed based on irregular surface pattern findings on magnifying endoscopy. this means that a gray zone with accumulated genetic changes exists that cannot be diagnosed as malignant tumor via histology. Second, in accordance with the preceding discussion, we believe that the F–V classification may be useful in determining whether the surgical margins for the papillary and nodular expanding types of BTC are distal or perihilar. The papillary and nodular expanding types of BTC tend to show extensive spread on histology [6,28,34] and often require hepatectomy, in addition to pancreatoduodenectomy [6]. The F–V classification of POCS findings may be beneficial, especially for the gray zone that cannot be diagnosed even by biopsy.

There are several limitations in our study. First, this was a single-centered retrospective study with a small sample size. Although 36 patients underwent resection, 22 of them underwent POCS during the study period and only 11 patients who had available POCS findings and mutational analysis of the biopsied samples were included in our study. Second, no correlation was found between F-factors and mutation frequency in tissue samples, which might be because of insufficient sampling, especially of the main lesions. This could have likely reduced the chances of detecting target gene mutations. Thus, the rate of malignancy in histological diagnosis and that of genetic mutation are not high in BTC main lesions. Alternatively, different gene mutations other than those analyzed in this study might have existed in our biopsied samples. Third, there are inflammatory biliary diseases such as IgG4-related sclerosing cholangitis, which should be differentiated from BTC. We did not assess whether our POCS classification would be useful for the diagnosis of such inflammatory biliary diseases. Therefore, future prospective studies with a large sample size and the selection of more appropriate target genes may improve the correlation between the POCS findings and analysis of the biopsied specimens.

In conclusion, we classified POCS findings of BTC as "the classification of POCS findings." In addition, we evaluated its validity by performing histological diagnosis and genetic mutation analysis on biopsied specimens. Although the findings of this pilot study need further verification, we hope that this classification would help stratify the grade of malignancy around the tumor lesion and enable the selection of an appropriate surgical procedure by precisely diagnosing the superficial spread of BTC tumors.

4. Materials and Methods

4.1. Patients and Samples

We retrospectively reviewed the medical records of 11 patients who underwent POCS examination to diagnose BTC and its superficial spread before surgery at Yamanashi University Hospital between January 2013 and December 2017. We assessed 2 to 5 regions up- and downstream of the main lesion (Figure 4) and took 2–3 biopsies from each region of the bile duct using POCS, which yielded a total of 70 specimens from 11 patients. Of these specimens, 30 good quality specimens were included in the study (Table S2). The remaining 40 samples were excluded because of inability to extract DNA ($n = 3$), poor quality of the extracted DNA ($n = 10$), or duplication of collection sites ($n = 27$). When several samples were obtained from the same region, we chose those with the best size, quantity, and quality of the extracted DNA. The Human Ethics Review Committee of Yamanashi University Hospital approved this study (Receipt number: 1523, From January 2017 to March 2019).

4.2. Bile Duct Biopsies Using POCS

A video cholangioscope (CHF-B260, Olympus Medical Systems, Tokyo, Japan) with outer diameters of 3.4 and 1.2 mm was used as the baby scope. It was passed through the side-viewing mother scope (TJF-240, Olympus Medical Systems) with a 4.2-mm working channel into the bile duct using a 0.025-inch guide wire. Before inserting the baby scope into the bile duct, endoscopic sphincterotomy, or endoscopic papillary balloon dilation was performed. The bile duct was irrigated with sterile saline solution during the POCS procedure through a working channel. Furthermore, the bile duct surface was observed. Tissues were sampled according to bile duct assessment using thin biopsy forceps (Spybite Biopsy Forceps, Boston Scientific, Marlborough, MA, USA) (Figure S3). A pathologist performed histological diagnosis on hematoxylin-eosin-stained slides. Malignancy was noted as suspicious or definite. Patients were under conscious sedation using intravenous flunitrazepam (5–10 mg) during all endoscopic procedures, and all 11 cases in this study underwent ERCP with the introduction of a plastic stent or an endoscopic nasobiliary drainage tube, days before POCS. No cases of cholangitis were observed when performing POCS.

4.3. Form-Vessel Classification of Bile Duct Carcinoma POCS Findings and Its Diagnostic Accuracy of Surgical Margins

POCS findings of bile duct surface were evaluated according to the form of the bile duct surface (F factor) and vessel structure (V-factor) in the following regions: left and right hepatic duct, the confluence of the hepatic ducts, and the superior, middle, and inferior parts of the bile duct lumen in order to determine whether pancreatoduodenectomy or hepatectomy was required. We used 4 grades to classify the bile duct surface form: F1, flat pattern; F2, granular pattern; F3, papillary pattern; and F4, nodular pattern. Vessel structures were classified into 3 grades: V1, network of thin vessels; V2, irregular non-dilated vessel; and V3, irregular dilated and tortuous vessels (Figure 5). Atypicality was worse and more severe with a higher score. This classification system was named "the F–V classification of POCS findings." At least 3 gastroenterologists specialized in the bile ducts evaluated the classified findings.

In additionally, we evaluated whether the POCS findings could accurately diagnose the pathology of resected margins. We correlated the POCS findings with the site of resection by measuring the distance from the boundary line of bile duct carcinoma to the point of confirmation, such as the junction of the cystic duct and the confluence of the hepatic ducts, on both POCS examination and surgery. Moreover, the pathology of surgical stumps was evaluated on the frozen section during surgery and after resection using formalin-fixed paraffin-embedded tissues. There were 15 resected stumps in 11 cases. All of them had liver side stump. Moreover, 4 patients who had undergone hepatectomy or extrahepatic bile tract resection had duodenal side stump. The histology of resected stumps was compared with preoperative assessment by the POCS findings.

A, Form factor (F factor)

F1 : Flat pattern
F2 : Granular pattern
F3 : Papillary pattern
F4 : Nodular pattern

B, Vessel factor (V factor)

V1 : Network of thin vessel
V2 : Irregular undilated vessel
V3 : Irregular dilated and tortuous vessel

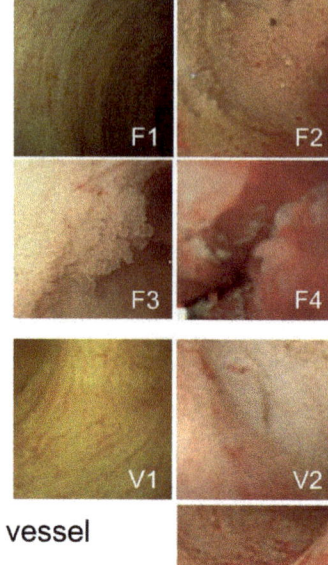

Figure 5. F–V classification of bile duct POCS findings. Bile duct epithelium POCS findings were classified into 4 surface structure groups (F1–F4) (**A**) and 3 vessel pattern groups (V1–V3) (**B**).

4.4. Genetic Mutational Analysis of Biopsied Specimens

DNA extraction and mutational analysis of biopsied specimens were performed as previously reported [35]. Briefly, biopsied specimens were laser-capture microdissected using the ArcturusXT Laser-Capture Microdissection System (Life Technologies, Carlsbad, CA, USA). Tissue was obtained from 8-µm thick sections of formalin-fixed paraffin-embedded (FFPE) samples. DNA was extracted using the GeneRead DNA FFPE Kit (QIAGEN, Hilden, Germany), following the manufacturer's instructions. Extracted DNA quantity and quality were assessed using NanoDrop (Thermo Fisher, Waltham, MA, USA) and Qubit (Thermo Fisher) platforms. Extracted DNA (10 ng) was amplified using barcode adaptors (Ion Xpress Barcode Adapters 1-96 Kit, Life Technologies) by the Ion AmpliSeq Cancer Horspot panel v.2 (Thermo Fisher), which contains 207 primer pairs and targets approximately 2800 hotspot mutations located in the following 50 cancer-related genes: *ABL1, AKT1, ALK, APC, ATM, BRAF, CDH1, CDKN2A, CSF1R, CTNNB1, EGFR, ERBB2, ERBB4, EZH2, FBXW7, FGFR1, FGFR2, FGFR3, FLT3, GNA11, GNAS, GNAQ, HNF1A, HRAS, IDH1, JAK2, JAK3, IDH2, KDR/VEGFR2, KIT, KRAS, MET, MLH1, MPL, NOTCH1, NPM1, NRAS, PDGFRA, PIK3CA, PTEN, PTPN11, RB1, RET, SMAD4, SMARCB1, SMO, SRC, STK11, TP53,* and *VHL*. Such genes are available in the COSMIC database [36]. The barcoded libraries were amplified by emulsion PCR on Ion Sphere particles. Sequencing was then performed on an Ion Chef System and an Ion Proton Sequencer (Life Technologies) using the Ion PI Hi-Q Chef Kit (Life Technologies), based on the manufacturer's instructions. Variants were identified using Ion reporter software version 5.10 (Thermo Fisher), and those with a VAF > 2% (with a sequence read depth >100) were considered true variants. The highest VAF among several mutated genes in the same sample was used as the respective sample's VAF.

4.5. Statistical Analysis

Statistical analysis was performed to validate our classification system. Specifically, we used the Cochran–Armitage trend test to determine the rates of histological malignancy and gene mutation. The Jonckheere–Terpstra trend test was used to compare the VAFs between F and V factors. A P value of <0.05 was considered statistically significant. All statistical analyses of recorded data were performed using the Excel statistical software package (Ekuseru–Toukei 2012; Social Survey Research Information Co., Ltd., Tokyo, Japan).

Supplementary Materials: Supplementary materials can be found at http://www.mdpi.com/1422-0067/21/9/3311/s1.

Author Contributions: Conceptualization, S.T. and M.F.; Methodology, S.T.; Software, S.M.; Validation, E.T., H.S. and M.K.; Formal Analysis, Y.F.; Investigation, Y.F.; Resources, S.H., S.K., H.H.; Data Curation, H.S., E.T.; Writing—Original Draft Preparation, S.T.; Writing—Review & Editing, S.M.; Visualization, Y.F.; Supervision, T.Y., Y.N., T.I., T.S.; Project Administration, N.E.; Funding Acquisition, S.T., N.E. All authors have read and agreed to the published version of the manuscript.

Funding: This study was supported by grants from Japan Society for the Promotion of Science (JSPS KAKENHI Grant Numbers: 26670380 and 18K07999; http://www.jsps.go.jp/j-grantsinaid/).

Acknowledgments: We thank Tomoko Nakajima and Takako Ohmori for their valuable technical assistance and Hiroko Amemiya for her secretarial assistance. Statistical analyses were performed under the advice from Hiroshi Yokomichi (BMath, MD, MPH, PhD: Department of Health Sciences, Interdisciplinary Graduate School of Medicine and Engineering, University of Yamanashi). The authors would like to thank Enago (www.enago.jp) for the English language review.

Conflicts of Interest: The authors declare no conflict of interest.

References

1. Vauthey, J.N.; Blumgart, L.H. Recent advances in the management of cholangiocarcinomas. *Semin. Liver Dis.* **1994**, *14*, 109–114. [CrossRef] [PubMed]
2. Matsuda, T.; Ajiki, W.; Marugame, T.; Ioka, A.; Tsukuma, H.; Sobue, T. Population-based survival of cancer patients diagnosed between 1993 and 1999 in Japan: A chronological and international comparative study. *Jpn. J. Clin. Oncol.* **2011**, *41*, 40–51. [CrossRef] [PubMed]
3. Ishihara, S.; Horiguchi, A.; Miyakawa, S.; Endo, I.; Miyazaki, M.; Takada, T. Biliary tract cancer registry in Japan from 2008 to 2013. *J. Hepato-Biliary-Pancreat. Sci.* **2016**, *23*, 149. [CrossRef] [PubMed]
4. Wellner, U.F.; Shen, Y.; Keck, T.; Jin, W.; Xu, Z. The survival outcome and prognostic factors for distal cholangiocarcinoma following surgical resection: A meta-analysis for the 5-year survival. *Surg. Today* **2017**, *47*, 271–279. [CrossRef] [PubMed]
5. Ebata, T.; Yokoyama, Y.; Igami, T.; Sugawara, G.; Mizuno, T.; Nagino, M. Review of hepatopancreatoduodenectomy for biliary cancer: An extended radical approach of Japanese origin. *J. Hepato-Biliary-Pancreat. Sci.* **2014**, *21*, 550–555. [CrossRef]
6. Igami, T.; Nagino, M.; Oda, K.; Nishio, H.; Ebata, T.; Yokoyama, Y.; Shimoyama, Y. Clinicopathologic study of cholangiocarcinoma with superficial spread. *Ann. Surg.* **2009**, *249*, 296–302. [CrossRef]
7. Nakanishi, Y.; Zen, Y.; Kawakami, H.; Kubota, K.; Itoh, T.; Hirano, S.; Tanaka, E.; Nakanuma, Y.; Kondo, S. Extrahepatic bile duct carcinoma with extensive intraepithelial spread: A clinicopathological study of 21 cases. *Mod. Pathol.* **2008**, *21*, 807–816. [CrossRef]
8. Albu, S.; Tantau, M.; Sparchez, Z.; Branda, H.; Suteu, T.; Badea, R.; Pascu, O. Diagnosis and treatment of extrahepatic cholangiocarcinoma: Results in a series of 124 patients. *Rom. J. Gastroenterol.* **2005**, *14*, 33–36.
9. Unno, M.; Okumoto, T.; Katayose, Y.; Rikiyama, T.; Sato, A.; Motoi, F.; Oikawa, M.; Egawa, S.; Ishibashi, T. Preoperative assessment of hilar cholangiocarcinoma by multidetector row computed tomography. *J. Hepatobiliary Pancreat Surg.* **2007**, *14*, 434–440. [CrossRef]
10. Huang, X.Q.; Shu, J.; Luo, L.; Jin, M.L.; Lu, X.F.; Yang, S.G. Differentiation grade for extrahepatic bile duct adenocarcinoma: Assessed by diffusion-weighted imaging at 3.0-T MR. *Eur. J. Radiol.* **2016**, *85*, 1980–1986. [CrossRef]

11. Tamada, K.; Tomiyama, T.; Wada, S.; Ohashi, A.; Satoh, Y.; Ido, K.; Sugano, K. Endoscopic transpapillary bile duct biopsy with the combination of intraductal ultrasonography in the diagnosis of biliary strictures. *Gut* **2002**, *50*, 326–331. [CrossRef] [PubMed]
12. Tamada, K.; Nagai, H.; Yasuda, Y.; Tomiyama, T.; Ohashi, A.; Wada, S.; Kanai, N.; Satoh, Y.; Ido, K.; Sugano, K. Transpapillary intraductal US prior to biliary drainage in the assessment of longitudinal spread of extrahepatic bile duct carcinoma. *Gastrointest. Endosc.* **2001**, *53*, 300–307. [CrossRef]
13. Seo, D.W.; Lee, S.K.; Yoo, K.S.; Kang, G.H.; Kim, M.H.; Suh, D.J.; Min, Y.I. Cholangioscopic findings in bile duct tumors. *Gastrointest. Endosc.* **2000**, *52*, 630–634. [CrossRef] [PubMed]
14. Siddiqui, A.A.; Mehendiratta, V.; Jackson, W.; Loren, D.E.; Kowalski, T.E.; Eloubeidi, M.A. Identification of cholangiocarcinoma by using the Spyglass Spyscope system for peroral cholangioscopy and biopsy collection. *Clin. Gastroenterol. Hepatol.* **2012**, *10*, 466–471. [CrossRef] [PubMed]
15. Nagakawa, Y.; Kasuya, K.; Bunso, K.; Hosokawa, Y.; Kuwabara, H.; Nakagima, T.; Osakabe, H.; Tsuchiya, T.; Itoi, T.; Tsuchida, A. Usefulness of multi-3-dimensional computed tomograms fused with multiplanar reconstruction images and peroral cholangioscopy findings in hilar cholangiocarcinoma. *J. Hepato-Biliary-Pancreat. Sci.* **2014**, *21*, 256–262. [CrossRef] [PubMed]
16. Kawakami, H.; Kuwatani, M.; Etoh, K.; Haba, S.; Yamato, H.; Shinada, K.; Nakanishi, Y.; Tanaka, E.; Hirano, S.; Kondo, S.; et al. Endoscopic retrograde cholangiography versus peroral cholangioscopy to evaluate intraepithelial tumor spread in biliary cancer. *Endoscopy* **2009**, *41*, 959–964. [CrossRef]
17. Itoi, T.; Sofuni, A.; Itokawa, F.; Tsuchiya, T.; Kurihara, T.; Ishii, K.; Tsuji, S.; Moriyasu, F.; Gotoda, T. Peroral cholangioscopic diagnosis of biliary-tract diseases by using narrow-band imaging (with videos). *Gastrointest. Endosc.* **2007**, *66*, 730–736. [CrossRef]
18. Itoi, T.; Osanai, M.; Igarashi, Y.; Tanaka, K.; Kida, M.; Maguchi, H.; Yasuda, K.; Okano, N.; Imaizumi, H.; Yokoyama, T.; et al. Diagnostic peroral video cholangioscopy is an accurate diagnostic tool for patients with bile duct lesions. *Clin. Gastroenterol. Hepatol.* **2010**, *8*, 934–938. [CrossRef]
19. Osanai, M.; Itoi, T.; Igarashi, Y.; Tanaka, K.; Kida, M.; Maguchi, H.; Yasuda, K.; Okano, N.; Imaizumi, H.; Itokawa, F. Peroral video cholangioscopy to evaluate indeterminate bile duct lesions and preoperative mucosal cancerous extension: A prospective multicenter study. *Endoscopy* **2013**, *45*, 635–642. [CrossRef]
20. Nishikawa, T.; Tsuyuguchi, T.; Sakai, Y.; Sugiyama, H.; Kishimoto, T.; Ohtsuka, M.; Miyazaki, M.; Yokosuka, O. Preoperative assessment of longitudinal extension of cholangiocarcinoma with peroral video-cholangioscopy: A prospective study. *Dig. Endosc.* **2014**, *26*, 450–457. [CrossRef]
21. Jiao, Y.; Pawlik, T.M.; Anders, R.A.; Selaru, F.M.; Streppel, M.M.; Lucas, D.J.; Niknafs, N.; Guthrie, V.B.; Maitra, A.; Argani, P.; et al. Exome sequencing identifies frequent inactivating mutations in BAP1, ARID1A and PBRM1 in intrahepatic cholangiocarcinomas. *Nat. Genet.* **2013**, *45*, 1470–1473. [CrossRef] [PubMed]
22. Nakamura, H.; Arai, Y.; Totoki, Y.; Shirota, T.; Elzawahry, A.; Kato, M.; Hama, N.; Hosoda, F.; Urushidate, T.; Ohashi, S.; et al. Genomic spectra of biliary tract cancer. *Nat. Genet.* **2015**, *47*, 1003–1010. [CrossRef]
23. Libbrecht, L.; Baldin, P.; Dekairelle, A.F.; Jouret-Mourin, A. Evaluation of the correlation between KRAS mutated allele frequency and pathologist tumorous nuclei percentage assessment in colorectal cancer suggests a role for zygosity status. *J. Clin. Pathol.* **2018**, *71*, 743–744. [CrossRef] [PubMed]
24. Sobin, L.H.; Gospodarowicz, M.K.; Wittekind, C.; International Union against Cancer. *TNM Classification of Malignant Tumours*, 7th ed.; Wiley-Blackwell: Chichester, UK; Hoboken, NJ, USA, 2010; p. 309.
25. Robles-Medranda, C.; Valero, M.; Soria-Alcivar, M.; Puga-Tejada, M.; Oleas, R.; Ospina-Arboleda, J.; Alvarado-Escobar, H.; Baquerizo-Burgos, J.; Robles-Jara, C.; Pitanga-Lukashok, H. Reliability and accuracy of a novel classification system using peroral cholangioscopy for the diagnosis of bile duct lesions. *Endoscopy* **2018**, *50*, 1059–1070. [CrossRef]
26. Churi, C.R.; Shroff, R.; Wang, Y.; Rashid, A.; Kang, H.C.; Weatherly, J.; Zuo, M.; Zinner, R.; Hong, D.; Meric-Bernstam, F.; et al. Mutation profiling in cholangiocarcinoma: Prognostic and therapeutic implications. *PLoS ONE* **2014**, *9*, e115383. [CrossRef]
27. Ono, A.; Kenmotsu, H.; Watanabe, M.; Serizawa, M.; Mori, K.; Imai, H.; Taira, T.; Naito, T.; Murakami, H.; Nakajima, T.; et al. Mutant allele frequency predicts the efficacy of EGFR-TKIs in lung adenocarcinoma harboring the L858R mutation. *Ann. Oncol.* **2014**, *25*, 1948–1953. [CrossRef]
28. Nakanishi, Y.; Kondo, S.; Zen, Y.; Yonemori, A.; Kubota, K.; Kawakami, H.; Tanaka, E.; Hirano, S.; Itoh, T.; Nakanuma, Y. Impact of residual in situ carcinoma on postoperative survival in 125 patients with extrahepatic bile duct carcinoma. *J. Hepato-Biliary-Pancreat. Sci.* **2010**, *17*, 166–173. [CrossRef]

29. Sasaki, T.; Kondo, S.; Ambo, Y.; Hirano, S.; Sichinohe, T.; Kaga, K.; Sugiura, H.; Shimozawa, E. Local recurrence at hepaticojejunostomy 9 years after resection of bile duct cancer with superficial flat spread. *J. Hepatobiliary Pancreat Surg* **2006**, *13*, 458–462. [CrossRef]
30. Mizushima, T.; Yamamoto, H.; Marubashi, S.; Kamiya, K.; Wakabayashi, G.; Miyata, H.; Seto, Y.; Doki, Y.; Mori, M. Validity and significance of 30-day mortality rate as a quality indicator for gastrointestinal cancer surgeries. *Ann. Gastroenterol. Surg.* **2018**, *2*, 231–240. [CrossRef]
31. Shiraki, T.; Kuroda, H.; Takada, A.; Nakazato, Y.; Kubota, K.; Imai, Y. Intraoperative frozen section diagnosis of bile duct margin for extrahepatic cholangiocarcinoma. *World J. Gastroenterol.* **2018**, *24*, 1332–1342. [CrossRef]
32. Mantel, H.T.; Westerkamp, A.C.; Sieders, E.; Peeters, P.M.; de Jong, K.P.; Boer, M.T.; de Kleine, R.H.; Gouw, A.S.; Porte, R.J. Intraoperative frozen section analysis of the proximal bile ducts in hilar cholangiocarcinoma is of limited value. *Cancer Med.* **2016**, *5*, 1373–1380. [CrossRef] [PubMed]
33. Kuno, T.; Tsukui, Y.; Takano, S.; Maekawa, S.; Yamaguchi, T.; Yoshida, T.; Kobayashi, S.; Iwamoto, F.; Ishida, Y.; Kawakami, S.; et al. Genetic alterations related to endoscopic treatment of colorectal tumors. *JGH Open* **2020**, *4*, 75–82. [CrossRef]
34. Sakamoto, E.; Nimura, Y.; Hayakawa, N.; Kamiya, J.; Kondo, S.; Nagino, M.; Kanai, M.; Miyachi, M.; Uesaka, K. The pattern of infiltration at the proximal border of hilar bile duct carcinoma: A histologic analysis of 62 resected cases. *Ann. Surg.* **1998**, *227*, 405–411. [CrossRef] [PubMed]
35. Takano, S.; Fukasawa, M.; Kadokura, M.; Shindo, H.; Takahashi, E.; Hirose, S.; Maekawa, S.; Mochizuki, K.; Kawaida, H.; Itakura, J.; et al. Next-Generation Sequencing Revealed TP53 Mutations to Be Malignant Marker for Intraductal Papillary Mucinous Neoplasms That Could Be Detected Using Pancreatic Juice. *Pancreas* **2017**, *46*, 1281–1287. [CrossRef] [PubMed]
36. Forbes, S.A.; Bindal, N.; Bamford, S.; Cole, C.; Kok, C.Y.; Beare, D.; Jia, M.; Shepherd, R.; Leung, K.; Menzies, A.; et al. COSMIC: Mining complete cancer genomes in the Catalogue of Somatic Mutations in Cancer. *Nucleic Acids Res.* **2011**, *39*, D945–D950. [CrossRef]

© 2020 by the authors. Licensee MDPI, Basel, Switzerland. This article is an open access article distributed under the terms and conditions of the Creative Commons Attribution (CC BY) license (http://creativecommons.org/licenses/by/4.0/).

Article

Possible Relevance of PNPLA3 and TLL1 Gene Polymorphisms to the Efficacy of PEG-IFN Therapy for HBV-Infected Patients

Hirayuki Enomoto [1,*], Nobuhiro Aizawa [1], Kunihiro Hasegawa [1], Naoto Ikeda [1], Yoshiyuki Sakai [1], Kazunori Yoh [1], Ryo Takata [1], Yukihisa Yuri [1], Kyohei Kishino [1], Yoshihiro Shimono [1], Noriko Ishii [1], Tomoyuki Takashima [1], Takashi Nishimura [1,2], Hiroki Nishikawa [1,3], Yoshinori Iwata [1], Hiroko Iijima [1,2] and Shuhei Nishiguchi [1]

[1] Division of Hepatobiliary and Pancreatic Disease, Department of Internal Medicine, Hyogo College of Medicine Division of Hepatobiliary and Pancreatic Disease, Department of Internal Medicine, Hyogo College of Medicine, Nishinomiya, Hyogo 663-8501, Japan; nobu23hiro@yahoo.co.jp (N.A.); hiro.red1230@gmail.com (K.H.); nikeneko@hyo-med.ac.jp (N.I.); sakai429@hyo-med.ac.jp (Y.S.); mm2wintwin@ybb.ne.jp (K.Y.); chano_chano_rt@yahoo.co.jp (R.T.); gyma27ijo04td@gmail.com (Y.Y.); hcm.kyohei@gmail.com (K.K.); yoshihiro19870729@yahoo.co.jp (Y.S.); ishinori1985@yahoo.co.jp (N.I.); tomo0204@yahoo.co.jp (T.T.); tk-nishimura@hyo-med.ac.jp (T.N.); nishikawa_6392_0207@yahoo.co.jp (H.N.); yo-iwata@hyo-med.ac.jp (Y.I.); hiroko-i@hyo-med.ac.jp (H.I.); nishiguc@hyo-med.ac.jp (S.N.)

[2] Ultrasound Imaging Center, Hyogo College of Medicine, Nishinomiya, Hyogo 663-8501, Japan

[3] Center for Clinical Research and Education, Hyogo College of Medicine, Nishinomiya, Hyogo 663-8501, Japan

* Correspondence: enomoto@hyo-med.ac.jp; Tel.: +81-798-45-6111

Received: 24 March 2020; Accepted: 24 April 2020; Published: 27 April 2020

Abstract: Lifestyle changes have led to an increase in the number of patients with nonalcoholic fatty liver disease (NAFLD). However, the effects of NAFLD-associated single-nucleotide gene polymorphisms (SNPs) in HBV-infected patients have not been adequately investigated. Methods: We investigated the association of the NAFLD-related SNPs patatin-like phospholipase domain-containing protein 3 (PNPLA3; rs738409), transmembrane 6 superfamily member 2 (TM6SF2; rs58542926), 17-beta hydroxysteroid dehydrogenase 13 (HSD17B13; rs72613567, rs6834314 and rs62305723), membrane-bound O-acyltransferase domain containing 7 (MBOAT7; rs641738) and glucokinase regulatory protein (GCKR; rs1260326) with the presence of histologically proven hepatic steatosis (HS) in HBV-infected patients ($n = 224$). We also investigated tolloid-like 1 (TLL1) SNP (rs17047200), which has been reported to be involved in the disease progression in Japanese NAFLD patients, and evaluated the association of HS and various SNPs with the treatment efficacy of pegylated-interferon (PEG-IFN) monotherapy following nucleotide/nucleoside (NA) treatment (NA/PEG-IFN sequential therapy; $n = 64$). Among NAFLD-associated SNPs evaluated, only the PNPLA3 SNP was significantly associated with the presence of hepatic steatosis in a total of 224 HBV-infected patients ($P = 1.0 \times 10^{-4}$). Regarding the sequential therapy, PNPLA3 SNP and TLL1 SNP were related to the treatment efficacy, and patients without minor alleles of these SNPs showed favorable results with a high virologic response and significant reduction in their HBsAg titer. A multivariate analysis showed that HBeAg positivity (odds ratio 5.810, $p = 0.016$) and the absence of a risk allele in PNPLA3 and TLL1 SNPs (odds ratio 8.664, $p = 0.0042$) were significantly associated with treatment efficacy. The PNPLA3 SNP might be associated with the presence of HS, and the combination of the PNPLA3 and TLL1 SNPs might be related to the efficacy of PEG-IFN monotherapy following NA treatment.

Keywords: hepatic steatosis; single nucleotide polymorphism; HBs antigen; sequential therapy

1. Introduction

Hepatitis B virus (HBV) infection is a major cause of chronic liver disease (CLD) [1–3]. The management of HBV-infection is extremely important, particularly in areas with a high prevalence of HBV, such as Asia [3]. Many viral and host factors can affect the clinical manifestations of HBV-infection, and HBV-infected patients show varied clinical courses.

Lifestyle changes have led to an increase in the number of patients with metabolic disorder-related diseases, including nonalcoholic fatty liver disease (NAFLD)/hepatic steatosis (HS). Although NAFLD/HS itself is a major cause of CLD [4,5], it can also develop in patients who already have various CLDs. HS is reported to be a major factor causing ALT elevation in HBV-infected patients with a low viral load [6,7], and a meta-analysis suggested that the presence of HS may influence the efficacy of antiviral therapy, especially in nucleotide/nucleoside analogue (NA) treatment; this effect is less commonly observed in patients undergoing pegylated-interferon (PEG-IFN) treatment [8].

Although HS is closely related to patients' lifestyle, some genetic characteristics are known to be associated with the development of NAFLD/HS [9]. Among NAFLD-associated genetic polymorphisms, patatin-like phospholipase domain-containing protein 3 (PNPLA3) is regarded as the most important, as the single-nucleotide polymorphism (SNP) has been shown to be universally associated with the development of NAFLD [9]. Recent studies have suggested that, in addition to influencing several clinical features in patients with NAFLD [9], the PNPLA3 SNP is also related to the development of HS in HBV-infected patients [10–12]. HCV infection (typically genotype 3 virus) is known to cause HS, and the role of HS in patients with viral hepatitis has been mainly studied in patients with HCV infection [13–16]. In contrast to HCV infection, HBV infection is less relevant to the development of HS [17], so HBV-infected patients may be a good model for assessing the clinical role of NAFLD-associated SNPs in CLDs. However, the impact of NAFLD-related SNPs on antiviral treatment in HBV-infected patients has been poorly investigated.

In the present study, we evaluated the association of NAFLD-associated SNPs with the presence of histologically-proven HS in HBV-infected patients and their influence on the efficacy of antiviral treatment, including a reduction in the quantitative HBV surface antigen (HBsAg) titer.

2. Results

2.1. The Association of NAFLD-Associated Gene Polymorphisms with HS in HBV-Infected Patients

As mentioned in the "Patients and Methods" section, we consecutively enrolled a total of 224 patients who received a liver biopsy and evaluated seven genetic polymorphisms associated with the development of NAFLD: PNPLA3 rs738409, transmembrane 6 superfamily member 2 (TM6SF2) rs58542926 [18], 17-beta hydroxysteroid dehydrogenase 13 (HSD17B13) rs72613567, HSD17B13 rs6834314, HSD17B13 rs62305723, membrane-bound O-acyltransferase domain containing 7 (MBOAT7) rs641738 and glucokinase regulatory protein (GCKR) rs1260326 [19–21]. The basic characteristics of the patients are shown in Table 1.

With regard to the PNPLA3 SNP, the frequency of HS was significantly different among the groups with different genotypes. In addition, the G (minor) allele frequency in patients with HS was significantly higher than that in patients without HS (Table 2). Furthermore, the genetic variants showed a statistically significant association with the presence of HS (Table 3). However, the SNPs of the remaining genes (TM6SF2, HSD17B13, MBOAT7 and GCKR) were not related to the frequency of HS in HBV-infected patients of our cohort (Table 2). The HSD17B13 rs72613567 SNP was reported to be highly linked with rs6834314 SNP ($r^2 = 0.94$) [20], and the genotypes of two HSD17B13 SNPs (rs72613567 and rs6834314) were completely matched in all HBV-infected patients of the current study.

Table 1. Characteristics of the HBV-Infected Patients who Underwent a Liver Biopsy ($n = 224$).

Gender (Male/Female)	128/96
Age (years)	45 (18–78)
Body Mass Index	22.7 (16.3–42.7)
AST (IU/L)	24.5 (11–242)
ALT (IU/L)	24 (7–513)
GGT (IU/L)	22 (7–349)
ALP (IU/L)	202 (71–655)
Total bilirubin (mg/dL)	0.8 (0.2–2.9)
Albumin (g/dL)	4.0 (2.7–5.1)
Platelets ($\times 10^3/\mu L$)	186 (43–379)
Prothrombin time (%)	88.7 (57.4–132.3)
Glucose (mg/dL)	89 (71–163)
Triglyceride (mg/dL)	90 (31–333)
Total Cholesterol (mg/dL)	175 (88–311)
HBV Genotype (A/B/C/D/ND)	9/24/174/2/15
HBV-DNA (Log copies/mL)	3.2 (<2.1–≥9.1)
HBeAg (-/+)	158/66
Histological stage of liver fibrosis (F0-1/F2/F3/F4)	126/51/38/9

Quantitative variables are expressed as the median (range). GGT: γ-glutamyl transferase, ALP: alkaline phosphatase, HBV: hepatitis B virus.

Table 2. The Relationship of NAFLD-Associated Gene Polymorphisms with Hepatic Steatosis in a Total of 224 HBV-Infected Patients who Underwent a Liver Biopsy.

		Presence of HS	p-Value	HS (-) 169 Cases (338 Alleles)	HS(+) 55 Cases (110 Alleles)	p-Value
PNPLA3 rs738409	CC	9/68	* 3.5×10^{-4}	Frequency of G allele		* 9.9×10^{-5}
	CG	24/107		137/338	68/110	
	GG	22/49				
TM6SF2 rs58542926	CC	43/181	0.570	Frequency of T allele		0.591
	CT	12/43		31/338	12/110	
HSD17B13 rs72613567	TT	24/107	0.334	Frequency of TA allele		0.269
	T/TA	25/102		95/338	37/110	
	TA/TA	6/15				
HSD17B13 rs6834314	AA	24/107	0.334	Frequency of G allele		0.269
	AG	25/102		95/338	37/110	
	GG	6/15				
HSD17B13 rs62305723	GG	49/208	0.232	Frequency of A allele		0.239
	GA	6/16		10/338	6/110	
MBOAT7 rs641738	CC	31/138	0.849	Frequency of T allele		0.391
	CT	22/79		67/338	26/110	
	TT	2/7				
GCKR rs1260326	CC	10/44	0.070	Frequency of T allele		0.091
	CT	20/106		184/338	70/110	
	TT	25/74				

Please note the following points: There were no patients with the minor type (TT) of the TM6SF2 (rs58542926) SNP in the current cohort. Consistent with the previous report [20], the genotypes of rs72613567 and rs6834314 were completely equal in all patients in the current cohort. There were no patients with the minor type (AA) of the HSD17B13 (rs62305723) SNP in the current cohort. HS: Hepatic steatosis, PNPLA3: patatin-like phospholipase domain-containing protein 3, TM6SF2: transmembrane 6 superfamily member 2, HSD17B13: 17-beta hydroxysteroid dehydrogenase 13, MBOAT7: membrane-bound O-acyltransferase domain containing 7, GCKR: glucokinase regulatory protein. *: $p < 0.05$.

Table 3. The Association of the Genetic Variants of PNPLA3 with the Presence of Hepatic Steatosis.

	Odds Ratio (95% CI)	p-Value
PNPLA3 rs738409 (single-unit increments)	2.367 (1.517–3.786)	* 0.0001

The genotypes were entered as a continuous variable (0, 1 and 2 for major homozygotes, heterozygotes, and minor homozygotes, respectively), and change in single-unit increments was shown. PNPLA3: patatin-like phospholipase domain-containing protein 3, CI: confidence interval *: $p < 0.05$.

2.2. The Association of HS and NAFLD-Associated SNPs with the Response to PEG-IFN Therapy

We next assessed the impact of histologically confirmed HS and NAFLD-associated SNPs in patients receiving PEG-IFN therapy. With regard to the virologic response (VR) after 48 weeks of PEG-IFN therapy, the overall response rates at 24 and 48 weeks after the off-treatment phase were 29/64 (45.3%) and 21/64 (32.8%), respectively. Patients with HS showed a lower VR rate at 48 weeks after the off-treatment phase than those without HS, although the difference did not reach a statistical significance (Table 4). Regarding the PNPLA3 SNP, patients with the CC type had a higher response rate than those with other types, and the difference reached statistical significance (Table 4 and Supplementary Figure S1). The PNPLA3 SNP also showed a statistically significant association with the VR ratios (Supplementary Table S1). In addition, the responders and non-responders showed significant differences in two factors: the effects of preceding NA treatment and HBeAg positivity. However, unlike HCV treatment [22], the interleukin 28B (IL28B) SNP (rs8099917) was not shown to be related to the efficacy of anti-HBV therapy in our cohort. Several NAFLD-related gene SNPs other than PNPLA3 SNP were also not significantly associated with the treatment response to PEG-IFN therapy (Table 4).

Table 4. The Comparison of the Clinical Characteristics of HBV-Infected Patients Based on the Sustained Virologic Response at 48 Weeks After the Off-Treatment Phase.

	Responder ($n = 21$)	Non-Responder ($n = 43$)	p-Value
Gender (Male/Female)	11/10	31/12	0.119
Age (years)	40 (26–74)	43 (30–71)	0.238
Treatment period of NA (years)	2.6 (1.0–10.9)	3.30 (1.0–11.3)	0.177
Treatment efficacy of NA (+/−) §	20/1	30/13	* 0.025
HBeAg (−/+)	18/3	20/23	* 3.0×10^{-3}
HBV Genotype (A/B/C/ND)	1/1/13/0	3/0/32/1	0.987
Significant fibrosis (≥F2) (−/+)	12/9	25/18	0.940
Hepatic steatosis (−/+)	18/3	30/13	0.167
ALT (IU/L) ¶	18 (6–43)	19 (8–80)	0.177
Glucose (mg/dL)	83 (79–104)	89 (79–145)	0.530
Triglyceride (mg/dL)	78 (45–128)	87 (37–264)	0.527
Total Cholesterol (mg/dL)	156 (137–253)	163 (118–240)	0.181
IL28B rs8099917 (TT/Non-TT)	15/6	35/8	0.520
PNPLA3 rs738409 (CC/Non-CC)	9/12	8/35	* 0.039
TM6SF2 rs58542926 (CC/Non-CC)	19/2	36/7	0.706
HSD17B13 rs72613567 (TT/Non-TT)	7/14	21/22	0.240
HSD17B13 rs6834314 (AA/Non-AA)	7/14	21/22	0.240
HSD17B13 rs62305723 (GG/Non-GG)	19/2	41/2	0.592
MBOAT7 rs641738 (CC/Non-CC)	13/8	24/19	0.643
GCKR rs1260326 (CC/Non-CC)	3/18	14/29	0.120

Quantitative variables are expressed as the median (range). Responders were defined as those with a low HBV DNA titer (<4.0 log copies/mL: equivalent to 2000 IU/mL) and HBeAg negativity at 48 weeks after the off-treatment phase. § Treatment efficacy was defined by an HBV-DNA titer lower than the quantitative limit (2.1 log copies/mL) at the initiation of PEG-IFN (after previous NA treatment). ¶ ALT values at the initiation of PEG-IFN therapy are shown. ND: Not determined. IL28B: interleukin 28B, PNPLA3: patatin-like phospholipase domain-containing protein 3, TM6SF2: transmembrane 6 superfamily member 2, HSD17B13: 17-beta hydroxysteroid dehydrogenase 13, MBOAT7: membrane-bound O-acyltransferase domain containing 7, GCKR: glucokinase regulatory protein. *: $p < 0.05$.

We also assessed the reduction in the HBsAg titer in response to PEG-IFN treatment. Before the initiation of PEG-IFN therapy, the presence of HS and the types of PNPLA3 SNPs did not significantly affect the HBsAg titer (Supplementary Figure S2). However, patients without HS showed a significant reduction in the HBsAg titer at the end of PEG-IFN treatment, while those with HS did not show any such reduction (Figure 1A). Furthermore, the patients with the CC type showed a statistically significant reduction in HBsAg, while those with the non-CC types did not (Figure 1B). Although the HBsAg titers of the patients with non-CC types did not show a significant reduction, some patients with the CG type responded to PEG-IFN treatment and showed reduced HBsAg values, while the reduction in HBsAg values was limited in patients with the GG type (Supplementary Figure S3).

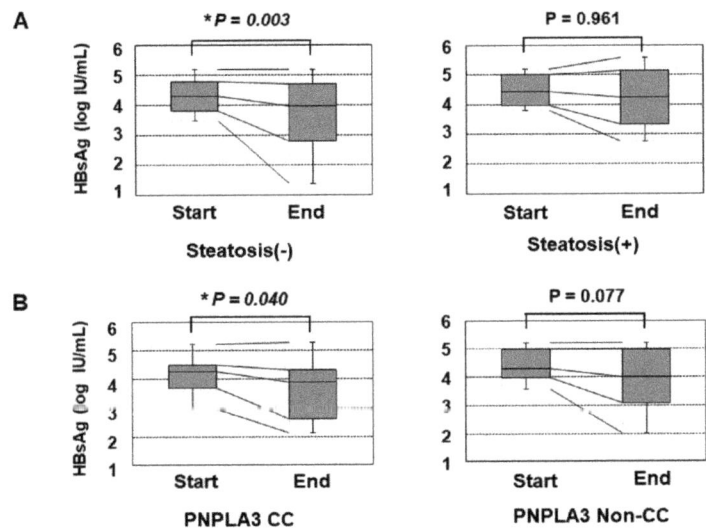

Figure 1. The transition of the HBsAg values in patients over 48 weeks of PEG-IFN. (**A**) a comparison of the HBsAg values at the initiation and termination of PEG-IFN treatment. The left and right panels show the HBsAg values of patients without HS ($n = 48$) and with HS ($n = 16$), respectively. (**B**) the association of the PNPLA3 SNP with the decrease in the HBsAg titer in response to PEG-IFN treatment. The left and right panels show the HBsAg values of patients with the CC type ($n = 17$) and non-CC types ($n = 47$), respectively. *: $p < 0.05$.

2.3. Role of the TLL1 SNP and Its Combination with the PNPLA3 SNP

We further determined the TLL1 gene SNP rs17047200, which was shown to be related to the development of hepatocellular carcinoma (HCC) in HCV-eradicated patients [23,24], since the combination of PNPLA3 and TLL1 SNPs was recently suggested to be associated with disease progression in Japanese NAFLD patients [25]. The TLL1 SNP was not related to the frequency of histologically evaluated HS in HBV-infected patients (Supplementary Figure S4); however, patients with the major (AA) type had a higher rate of VR than those with other types (Figure 2A). We also found that patients with the AA type showed a statistically significant reduction in HBsAg values, while those with the non-AA types did not (Figure 2B).

In line with a previous paper [25], we also classified the patients according to the number of risk alleles of the two SNPs (G allele of PNPLA3 or T allele of TLL1), and the numbers of patients with 0/1/2/3/4 risk alleles were 12/31/20/1/0, respectively. As only one patient had ≥3 risk alleles, we categorized the patients into the three groups: 'Genetic risk score 0 (with no risk allele)', 'Genetic risk score 1 (with one risk allele)', and 'Genetic risk score ≥2 (with two or three risk alleles)'. The classifications of the genetic risk score were significantly associated with the VR ratios (Figure 3A and Table 5). In addition, the HBsAg titer was significantly decreased in the group with 'score 0' but not in the other groups (Figure 3B).

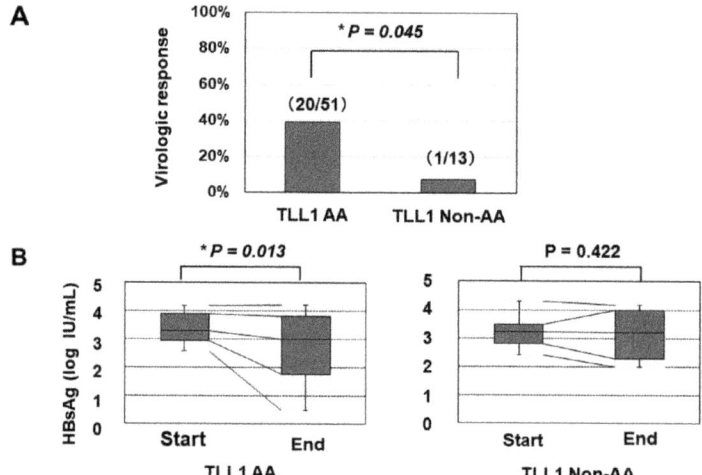

Figure 2. The association of the TLL1 SNP with the virologic response and decrease in the HBsAg titer in response to PEG-IFN treatment. (**A**) The response rates in patients with the AA and non-AA types of the TLL1 SNPs were 53.8% (20/51) and 9.1% (1/13), respectively (*: $p < 0.05$). (**B**) the association of the TLL1 SNP with the decrease in the HBsAg titer in response to PEG-IFN treatment. The HBsAg values at the initiation and termination of PEG-IFN treatment were compared. *: $p < 0.05$.

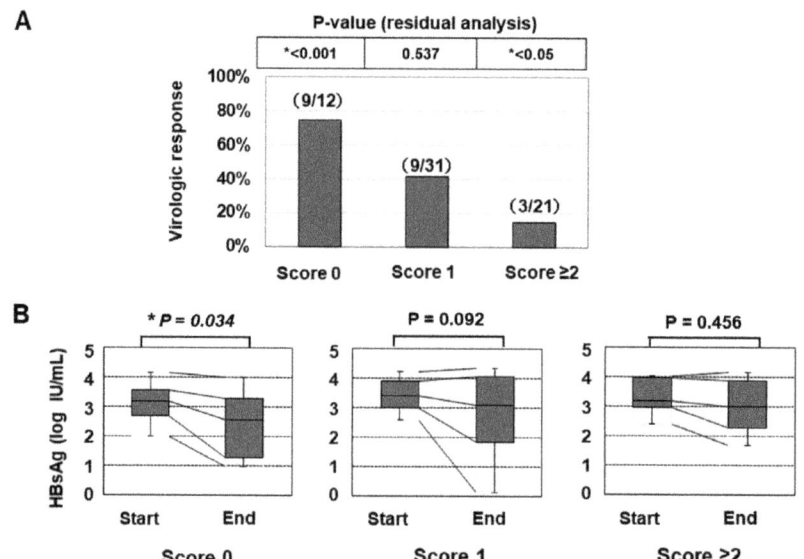

Figure 3. The association of the genetic risk score with the treatment efficacy of PEG-IFN therapy. (**A**) the virologic response rates of patients were shown (*: $p < 0.05$). (**B**) the association of the genetic risk score with the decrease in the HBsAg titer in response to PEG-IFN treatment. The HBsAg values at the initiation and termination of PEG-IFN treatment were compared (*: $p < 0.05$).

Table 5. The Association of the Genetic Risk Score with the Virologic Response Rates of PEG-IFN Therapy.

Genetic Risk Score	Odds Ratio (95% CI)	p-Value
0	1 [Reference]	
1	0.136 (0.229–0.623)	* 0.0102
≥2	0.056 (0.009–0.332)	* 0.0015

The classifications of the genetic risk score (score 0, 1 and ≥2) were entered as categorical variables, and the odds ratios were determined (*: $p < 0.05$). CI: confidence interval.

Given the favorable response noted among patients with 'score 0', we included the genetic score as a clinical characteristic in addition to the factors listed in Table 4 and performed a multivariate analysis. A genetic risk score of 0 and HBeAg positivity were found to be independently associated with the VR (Table 6 and Supplementary Table S2).

Table 6. Results of a Multivariate Analysis for the Factors Associated with a Sustained Virologic Response at 48 Weeks After the Off-Treatment Phase of PEG-IFN.

Multivariate Analysis	Odds Ratio (95% CI)	p-Value
Treatment efficacy of NA (+/−) §	2.594 (0.347–53.18)	0.378
HBeAg (−/+)	5.810 (1.363–34.24)	* 0.016
Genetic risk score (0/≥1) ¶	8.666 (1.915–54.26)	* 0.0042

§ Treatment efficacy was defined by an HBV-DNA titer lower than the quantitative limit (2.1 log copies/mL) at the initiation of PEG-IFN (after previous NA treatment). ¶ The genetic risk score was determined as the total number of risk alleles of the two SNPs (G allele of PNPLA3 or T allele of TLL1). PNPLA3: patatin-like phospholipase domain-containing protein 3, TLL1: tolloid-like 1. *: $p < 0.05$.

Since many non-responders needed to resume NA treatment (including tenofovir), it was not easy to evaluate the long-term changes in the HBsAg titer of all patients after PEG-IFN monotherapy. However, when we assessed the patients who did not receive any antiviral treatment after the off-treatment phase, HBsAg loss (dropping below the lower limit of detection) occurred within 48 weeks in six patients (6/64: 9.3%). None of these patients had histologically confirmed HS. HBsAg loss was observed in three patients in the 'Genetic risk score 0' group (3/12: 25.0%) and in three patients in the 'Genetic risk score 1' (3/31: 9.7%) group. However, none of the patients with a 'Genetic risk score ≥2' achieved HBsAg loss (0/21: 0.0%) (Table 7).

Table 7. Cases in which the HBsAg Titer Decreased to an Undetectable Level within 48 Weeks After the Off-Treatment Phase.

Case No.	Gender	Age (yr)	HBV Genotype	Fibrosis Stage	Hepatic Steatosis	PNPLA3 SNP	TLL1 SNP	Genetic Score
#1	Male	39	C	F2	(−)	CC	AA	0
#2	Female	42	C	F2	(−)	CG	AA	1
#3	Male	46	A	F2	(−)	CC	AA	0
#4	Male	51	C	F3	(−)	CC	AA	0
#5	Male	28	C	F1	(−)	CG	AA	1
#6	Male	41	ND	F1	(−)	CG	AA	1

ND: Not determined.

3. Discussion

HBV infection is a major health concern worldwide. NAs are excellent drugs for suppressing the replication of HBV, but many patients need to receive long-term treatment. PEG-IFN is a possible therapeutic tool for successfully withdrawing NA treatment in HBV-infected patients, and we participated in two clinical studies on this point in Japan; however, the VR ratios were not high, being around 30% in both [26,27]. We therefore explored new factors associated with the treatment efficacy of PEG-IFN following NA treatment.

NAFLD is a major lifestyle-associated health concern. However, the effect of HS in antiviral treatment for HBV has varied among studies. For instance, a recent paper suggested that complication with NAFLD/HS was associated with the promising efficacy of anti-HBV treatment in 80 pediatric patients [28], while a recent meta-analysis of studies in adult patients suggested that HS may reduce the efficacy of antiviral therapy for HBV infection [8]. Our data agreed with the recent meta-analysis of studies in adult patients [8] and suggested that NAFLD/HS and its associated gene polymorphisms might be involved in the response to NA/PEG-IFN sequential therapy in HBV-infected Japanese patients.

Unlike HCV infection, the relevance of IL28B SNPs to the treatment efficacy of PEG-IFN in patients with HBV infection remains controversial [29,30], and no genetic factors have been confirmed to influence the effects of PEG-IFN therapy in HBV-infected Asian patients [3]. Our results may provide some new insights into factors predicting the effects of PEG-IFN therapy for HBV infection, although the precise mechanism remains to be clarified.

Several limitations associated with the present study warrant mention. First, our treatment protocol was designed to administer PEG-IFN therapy to patients who had already been treated with NA ('sequential therapy'). Although the duration of the preceding NA treatment was not related to the VR (Table 4), and its treatment efficacy was not found to be an independently associated factor (Table 6), our findings cannot be directly compared to those of previous studies regarding PEG-IFN monotherapy without the administration of NA. Second, this study was a retrospective analysis that included 64 patients. When we divided the cases into two groups according to the timing of the initiation of PEG-IFN (N=32, each group), mildly significant differences ($p < 0.05$) were found in some clinical characteristics between the patients in the first-half group and those in the second-half group (Supplementary Table S3). Nevertheless, in both cohorts, the patients with a 'genetic risk score 0' had a significantly higher response rate than other groups (Supplementary Table S4), suggesting the clinical relevance of the genetic risk factor to the treatment efficacy. However, the VR rate in the 'score ≥ 1' group was 23.1% (12/52), while the rate in the 'score 0' group was 75.0% (9/12) in the current study (Figure 3A). When conducting a new study with reference to these ratios, 15 patients in the 'score 0' group should be planned for inclusion (significance level: 0.05, and power: 0.8). Therefore, further validation in another study with a larger cohort is still required in order to draw conclusions regarding the clinical impact of genetic risk factors. Third, the susceptibility to HS may vary among ethnic and geographic backgrounds. Recent studies have also suggested that the clinical impact of TLL1 SNP may differ to some degree between Japanese and Caucasian [24,31]. Thus, the role of PNPLA3 and TLL1 SNPs in HBV-infected patients should be further evaluated using the data from patients outside Japan. A larger-scale study of HBV-infected patients, including NA/PEG-IFN sequential therapy with a defined NA and PEG-IFN treatment schedule, is warranted. Finally, as described above, our research results did not clarify the mechanisms underlying how these gene SNPs affect the efficacy of anti-HBV therapy. The expression of genes located downstream of PNPLA3 and TLL1 should be verified by further experiments to better understand the role of HS and its related genes in HBV-infected patients.

In summary, our results suggested that NAFLD-related SNPs may be associated with not only with the presence of HS but also the efficacy of antiviral therapy in HBV-infected patients.

4. Patients and Methods

4.1. Patients

Chronic HBV infection was defined as a positive HBsAg status for more than six months. The following exclusion criteria were applied: alcohol intake ≥ 20 g/day, hepatocellular carcinoma, receiving immunosuppressive therapy, HIV co-infection, and HCV co-infection. The current study was conducted under the approval of the ethics committee of the institutional review board (Nos. 1831, 3321 and

Hi-92). Written informed consent regarding the liver biopsy and the research use of the clinical data and genomic analyses was obtained from all of the patients.

4.2. Genotyping of Genetic Polymorphisms

Among the genetic polymorphisms associated with HS, we first evaluated the gene polymorphisms PNPLA3 C>G (rs738409) and TM6SF2 C>T (rs58542926), based on a recent review article concerning Japanese NAFLD patients [18]. We also evaluated recently reported NAFLD-related HSD17B13 gene SNPs [19–21]. Of the three SNPs with a suggested relationship to NAFLD histology (rs72613567, rs6834314 and rs62305723), rs6834314, and rs62305723 were determined with commercially available kits. For the rs72613567 SNP (T>TA; minor allele: an insertion of an adenine), we used the probe set described in the previous report [21]. In addition, the SNPs of the MBOAT7 C>T (rs641738) and the GCKR SNP C>T (rs1260326) were also determined [21]. We further determined the TLL1 gene SNP (rs17047200), which was shown to be related to the development of HCC in HCV-eradicated patients [23,24] and was recently reported to influence the clinical features in Japanese NAFLD patients in combination with the PNPLA3 C>G (rs738409) SNP [25].

Genomic DNA was isolated from peripheral mononuclear cells and stored until use at −20 °C [22]. The SNPs of PNPLA3 (rs738409), TM6SF27 (rs58542926), HSD17B13 (rs6834314 and rs62305723), MBOAT7 (rs641738), GCKR (rs1260326), and TLL1 (rs17047200) were determined with real-time polymerase chain reaction (PCR) using TaqMan® SNP Assays (Thermo Fisher Scientific Japan, Tokyo: Catalogue No. 4351379; Assay ID rs738409: C__7241_10, rs58542926: C__89463510_10, rs6834314: C__30687619_10, rs62305723: C__89666454_10, rs641738: C___8716820_10, rs1260326: C___2862880_1, and rs17047200: C__33773674_10) according to the manufacturer's instructions. With respect to the treatment efficacy of the PEG-IFN therapy, we also determined the IL28B gene SNP T>G (rs8099917), which has been reported to be significantly associated with the efficacy of IFN treatment for HCV infection according to the methods previously described [22].

4.3. The Liver Biopsy and Laboratory Data

We retrospectively evaluated a total of 224 HBV-positive patients who underwent a percutaneous liver biopsy between August 2010 and June 2017. We histologically estimated the fibrosis stages and the degree of HS, as described previously (histologically confirmed HS was defined as ≥ 5% HS) [4,7]. Recent studies have reported the clinical significance of the coexistence of NASH in HBV-infected patients [32,33]. However, the histological definition of NASH in HBV-infected patients has not been accurately defined, and the Asia-Pacific guidelines exclude HBV-infected patients from the definition of NAFLD [34]. Thus, the present study focused only on the presence of HS.

The histological findings were externally assessed by expert pathologists without any clinical information (SMC Laboratories, Inc., Tokyo, Japan). In addition to common laboratory variables, given the current clinical importance of quantitative HBsAg [35], we measured the HBsAg titer as well as the HBeAg and HBV-DNA titers [7]. All blood samples were collected on the day of the liver biopsy under fasting conditions.

4.4. PEG-IFN Therapy and Its Efficacy

We previously participated in two prospective cohort studies regarding PEG-IFN monotherapy following NA treatment [26,27]. As mentioned in a previous study, the analysis of one study arm was considered to include minimal bias [26]. In the present study, we retrospectively analyzed the pooled patients who had been enrolled in these studies from our institute and whose liver histology had been assessed before PEG-IFN.

In brief, patients who had been treated with NA for more than one year received PEG-IFN therapy (Chugai Pharmaceutical Co., Ltd., Tokyo, Japan). NA treatment was discontinued within four weeks after the initiation of PEG-IFN treatment, and PEG-IFN (180 µg per body, once a week) was administered for 48 weeks. Patients with a low HBV DNA titer (<4.0 log copies/mL: equivalent to

2000 IU/mL) and HBeAg negativity at 48 weeks after the off-treatment phase were defined as having a sustained VR [3].

4.5. Statistical Analyses

Quantitative variables are shown as the median (range). The statistical significance of differences between two groups was determined using the Mann–Whitney U test. In the multivariate analysis, logistic regression models were generated with potential associated factors selected from among those with p-values of <0.05. Differences in the frequency between groups were assessed using the chi-squared test or Fisher's exact test. To compare the frequency among three groups, the group with a significantly higher or lower ratio than the other groups was determined using a residual analysis. To analyze the associations of PNPLA3 genetic variants with the presence of HS and the treatment efficacy of PEG-IFN, the genotypes were entered as a continuous variable (0, 1, and 2 for major homozygotes, heterozygotes and minor homozygotes, respectively), and the linear trend across genotypes was analyzed. To determine the risk score with the combination of the two gene SNPs (PNPLA3 rs738409 and TLL1 rs17047200), we used the group with 'genetic risk score ≥2'. We therefore entered the classifications of the genetic risk score (score 0, 1 and ≥2) as a categorical variable and determined the odds ratios. In addition, p-values of <0.05 were considered to be statistically significant. The JMP 13 software (SAS Institute Inc., Cary, NC, USA) was used for the statistical analysis.

5. Conclusions

The PNPLA3 SNP might be associated with the presence of HS, and the combination of the PNPLA3 and TLL1 SNPs might be related to the efficacy of PEG-IFN monotherapy following NA treatment.

Supplementary Materials: Supplementary materials can be found at http://www.mdpi.com/1422-0067/21/9/3089/s1

Author Contributions: S.N. and H.E. designed the research. Y.I., N.A., Y.S. (Yoshiyuki Sakai), R.T., N.I. (Naoto Ikeda), K.H., T.N., K.Y., K.K., Y.S. (Yoshihiro Shimono), N.I. (Noriko Ishii), Y.Y., T.T., H.N., and H.I. participated in the sample collection and data acquisition. N.A., K.H., and H.E. analyzed the data. H.E. and S.N. wrote and edited the manuscript. All authors have read and agreed to the published version of the manuscript.

Funding: This research was supported in part by the Japan Agency for Medical Research and Development (Nos. JP17fk0210306 and JP19fk0210034).

Acknowledgments: We thank Nozomi Kanazawa, Sachiko Inui, Yoko Kasuya, Sayaka Fujii, Hiromi Kido and Kana Minemoto (Hyogo College of Medicine) for their technical and secretarial assistance.

Conflicts of Interest: Shuhei Nishiguchi received research grants from Chugai Pharmaceutical and lecture fees from Gilead Sciences. The remaining authors declare no conflicts of interest in association with the present study.

Abbreviations

ALP	alkaline phosphatase
CLD	chronic liver disease
GCKR	glucokinase regulatory protein
GGT	γ-glutamyl transferase
HBsAg	hepatitis B virus surface antigen
HBV	hepatitis B virus
HCC	hepatocellular carcinoma
HCV	hepatitis C virus
HS	hepatic steatosis
HSD17B13	17-beta hydroxysteroid dehydrogenase 13
IL28B	interleukin 28B
MBOAT7	membrane-bound O-acyltransferase domain containing 7
NA	nucleotide/nucleoside analogue
NAFLD	nonalcoholic fatty liver disease

PCR	polymerase chain reaction
PEG-IFN	pegylated-interferon
PNPLA3	patatin-like phospholipase domain-containing protein 3
PT	prothrombin time
SNP	single nucleotide polymorphism
TLL1	tolloid-like 1
TM6SF2	transmembrane 6 superfamily member 2
VR	virologic response

References

1. Terrault, N.A.; Lok, A.S.F.; McMahon, B.J.; Chang, K.M.; Hwang, J.P.; Jonas, M.M.; Brown, R.S., Jr.; Bzowej, N.H.; Wong, J.B. Update on prevention; diagnosis; and treatment of chronic hepatitis B: AASLD 2018 hepatitis B guidance. *Hepatology* **2018**, *67*, 1560–1599. [CrossRef]
2. European Association for the Study of the Liver. EASL 2017 Clinical Practice Guidelines on the management of hepatitis B virus infection. *J. Hepatol.* **2017**, *67*, 370–398. [CrossRef] [PubMed]
3. Sarin, S.K.; Kumar, M.; Lau, G.K.; Abbas, Z.; Chan, H.L.; Chen, C.J.; Chen, D.S.; Chen, H.L.; Chen, P.J.; Chien, R.N.; et al. Asian-Pacific clinical practice guidelines on the management of hepatitis B: A 2015 update. *Hepatol. Int.* **2016**, *10*, 1–98. [CrossRef] [PubMed]
4. Chalasani, N.; Younossi, Z.; Lavine, J.E.; Charlton, M.; Cusi, K.; Rinella, M.; Harrison, S.A.; Brunt, E.M.; Sanyal, A.J. The diagnosis and management of nonalcoholic fatty liver disease: Practice guidance from the American Association for the Study of Liver Diseases. *Hepatology* **2018**, *67*, 328–357. [CrossRef] [PubMed]
5. European Association for the Study of the Liver (EASL); European Association for the Study of Diabetes (EASD); European Association for the Study of Obesity (EASO). EASL-EASD-EASO Clinical Practice Guidelines for the management of non-alcoholic fatty liver disease. *J. Hepatol.* **2016**, *64*, 1388–1402. [CrossRef]
6. Spradling, P.R.; Bulkow, L.; Teshale, E.H.; Negus, S.; Homan, C.; Simons, B.; McMahon, B.J. Prevalence and causes of elevated serum aminotransferase levels in a population-based cohort of persons with chronic hepatitis B virus infection. *J. Hepatol.* **2014**, *61*, 785–791. [CrossRef]
7. Enomoto, H.; Aizawa, N.; Nishikawa, H.; Ikeda, N.; Sakai, Y.; Takata, R.; Hasegawa, K.; Nakano, C.; Nishimura, T.; Yoh, K.; et al. Relationship Between Hepatic Steatosis and the Elevation of Aminotransferases in HBV-Infected Patients With HBe-Antigen Negativity and a Low Viral Load. *Medicine (Baltimore)* **2016**, *95*, e3565. [CrossRef]
8. Zhu, Y.; Yang, Q.; Lv, F.; Yu, Y. The Effect of Hepatosteatosis on Response to Antiviral Treatment in Patients with Chronic Hepatitis B: A Meta-Analysis. *Gastroenterol. Res. Pract.* **2017**, *2017*, 1096406. [CrossRef]
9. Eslam, M.; Valenti, L.; Romeo, S. Genetics and epigenetics of NAFLD and NASH: Clinical impact. *J. Hepatol.* **2018**, *68*, 268–279. [CrossRef]
10. Ghalamkari, S.; Sharafi, H.; Alavian, S.M. Association of PNPLA3 rs738409 polymorphism with liver steatosis but not with cirrhosis in patients with HBV infection: Systematic review with meta-analysis. *J Gene Med.* **2018**, *20*, e3001. [CrossRef]
11. Viganò, M.; Valenti, L.; Lampertico, P.; Facchetti, F.; Motta, B.M.; D'Ambrosio, R.; Romagnoli, S.; Dongiovanni, P.; Donati, B.; Fargion, S.; et al. Patatin-like phospholipase domain-containing 3 I148M affects liver steatosis in patients with chronic hepatitis B. *Hepatology* **2013**, *58*, 1245–1252. [CrossRef] [PubMed]
12. Zampino, R.; Coppola, N.; Cirillo, G.; Boemio, A.; Grandone, A.; Stanzione, M.; Capoluongo, N.; Marrone, A.; Macera, M.; Sagnelli, E.; et al. Patatin-Like Phospholipase Domain-Containing 3 I148M Variant Is Associated with Liver Steatosis and Fat Distribution in Chronic Hepatitis B. *Dig. Dis. Sci.* **2015**, *60*, 3005–3010. [CrossRef] [PubMed]
13. Roingeard, P. Hepatitis C virus diversity and hepatic steatosis. *J. Viral Hepat.* **2013**, *20*, 77–84. [CrossRef] [PubMed]
14. Stättermayer, A.F.; Scherzer, T.; Beinhardt, S.; Rutter, K.; Hofer, H.; Ferenci, P. Review article: Genetic factors that modify the outcome of viral hepatitis. *Aliment. Pharmacol. Ther.* **2014**, *39*, 1059–1070. [CrossRef]
15. Negro, F. Facts and fictions of HCV and comorbidities: Steatosis, diabetes mellitus, and cardiovascular diseases. *J. Hepatol.* **2014**, *61*, S69–S78. [CrossRef]

16. Adinolfi, L.E.; Rinaldi, L.; Guerrera, B.; Restivo, L.; Marrone, A.; Giordano, M.; Zampino, R. NAFLD and NASH in HCV Infection: Prevalence and Significance in Hepatic and Extrahepatic Manifestations. *Int. J. Mol. Sci.* **2016**, *17*, 803. [CrossRef]
17. Wang, C.C.; Tseng, T.C.; Kao, J.H. Hepatitis B virus infection and metabolic syndrome: Fact or fiction? *J. Gastroenterol. Hepatol.* **2015**, *30*, 14–20. [CrossRef]
18. Yoneda, M.; Imajo, K.; Takahashi, H.; Ogawa, Y.; Eguchi, Y.; Sumida, Y.; Yoneda, M.; Kawanaka, M.; Saito, S.; Tokushige, K.; et al. Clinical strategy of diagnosing and following patients with nonalcoholic fatty liver disease based on invasive and noninvasive methods. *J. Gastroenterol.* **2018**, *53*, 181–196. [CrossRef]
19. Abul-Husn, N.S.; Cheng, X.; Li, A.H.; Xin, Y.; Schurmann, C.; Stevis, P.; Liu, Y.; Kozlitina, J.; Stender, S.; Wood, G.C.; et al. A Protein-Truncating HSD17B13 Variant and Protection from Chronic Liver Disease. *N. Engl. J. Med.* **2018**, *378*, 1096–1106. [CrossRef]
20. Ma, Y.; Belyaeva, O.V.; Brown, P.M.; Fujita, K.; Valles, K.; Karki, S.; de Boer, Y.S.; Koh, C.; Chen, Y.; Du, X.; et al. 17-Beta Hydroxysteroid Dehydrogenase 13 Is a Hepatic Retinol Dehydrogenase Associated With Histological Features of Nonalcoholic Fatty Liver Disease. *Hepatology* **2019**, *69*, 1504–1519. [CrossRef]
21. Gellert-Kristensen, H.; Nordestgaard, B.G.; Tybjaerg-Hansen, A.; Stender, S. High Risk of Fatty Liver Disease Amplifies the Alanine Transaminase–Lowering Effect of a HSD17B13 Variant. *Hepatology* **2020**, *71*, 56–66. [CrossRef] [PubMed]
22. Aizawa, N.; Enomoto, H.; Takashima, T.; Sakai, Y.; Iwata, K.; Ikeda, N.; Tanaka, H.; Iwata, Y.; Saito, M.; Imanishi, H.; et al. Thrombocytopenia in pegylated interferon and ribavirin combination therapy for chronic hepatitis C. *J. Gastroenterol.* **2014**, *49*, 1253–1263. [CrossRef] [PubMed]
23. Matsuura, K.; Sawai, H.; Ikeo, K.; Ogawa, S.; Iio, E.; Isogawa, M.; Shimada, N.; Komori, A.; Toyoda, H.; Kumada, T.; et al. Japanese Genome-Wide Association Study Group for Viral Hepatitis. Genome-Wide Association Study Identifies TLL1 Variant Associated With Development of Hepatocellular Carcinoma After Eradication of Hepatitis C Virus Infection. *Gastroenterology* **2017**, *152*, 1383–1394. [CrossRef]
24. Iio, E.; Matsuura, K.; Shimada, N.; Atsukawa, M.; Itokawa, N.; Abe, H.; Kato, K.; Takaguchi, K.; Senoh, T.; Eguchi, Y.; et al. TLL1 variant associated with development of hepatocellular carcinoma after eradication of hepatitis C virus by interferon-free therapy. *J. Gastroenterol.* **2019**, *54*, 339–346. [CrossRef]
25. Seko, Y.; Yamaguchi, K.; Mizuno, N.; Okuda, K.; Takemura, M.; Taketani, H.; Hara, T.; Umemura, A.; Nishikawa, T.; Moriguchi, M.; et al. Combination of PNPLA3 and TLL1 polymorphism can predict advanced fibrosis in Japanese patients with nonalcoholic fatty liver disease. *J. Gastroenterol.* **2018**, *53*, 438–448. [CrossRef] [PubMed]
26. Matsumoto, A.; Nishiguchi, S.; Enomoto, H.; Kang, J.H.; Tanaka, Y.; Shinkai, N.; Kurosaki, M.; Enomoto, M.; Kanda, T.; Yokosuka, O.; et al. Combinational use of hepatitis B viral antigens predicts responses to nucleos(t)ide analogue/peg-interferon sequential therapy. *J. Gastroenterol.* **2018**, *53*, 247–257. [CrossRef] [PubMed]
27. Enomoto, M.; Nishiguchi, S.; Tamori, A.; Kozuka, R.; Fujii, H.; Uchida-Kobayashi, S.; Fukunishi, S.; Tsuda, Y.; Higuchi, K.; Saito, M.; et al. Sequential therapy involving an early switch from entecavir to pegylated interferon-α in Japanese patients with chronic hepatitis B. *Hepatol. Res.* **2018**, *48*, 459–468. [CrossRef]
28. Wang, L.; Wang, Y.; Liu, S.; Zhai, X.; Zhou, G.; Lu, F.; Zhao, J. Nonalcoholic fatty liver disease is associated with lower hepatitis B viral load and antiviral response in pediatric population. *J. Gastroenterol.* **2019**, *54*, 1096–1105. [CrossRef]
29. Sonneveld, M.J.; Wong, V.W.; Woltman, A.M.; Wong, G.L.; Cakaloglu, Y.; Zeuzem, S.; Buster, E.H.; Uitterlinden, A.G.; Hansen, B.E.; Chan, H.L.; et al. Polymorphisms near IL28B and serologic response to peginterferon in HBeAg-positive patients with chronic hepatitis B. *Gastroenterology* **2012**, *142*, 513–520. [CrossRef]
30. Wei, L.; Wedemeyer, H.; Liaw, Y.F.; Chan, H.L.; Piratvisuth, T.; Marcellin, P.; Jia, J.; Tan, D.; Chow, W.C.; Brunetto, M.R.; et al. No association between IFNL3 (IL28B) genotype and response to peginterferon alfa-2a in HBeAg-positive or -negative chronic hepatitis B. *PLoS ONE* **2018**, *13*, e0199198. [CrossRef]
31. Degasperi, E.; Galmozzi, E.; Facchetti, F.; Farina, E.; D'Ambrosio, R.; Soffredini, R.; Iavarone, M.; Lampertico, P. TLL1 variants do not predict hepatocellular carcinoma development in HCV cirrhotic patients treated with direct-acting antivirals. *J. Viral. Hepat.* **2019**, *26*, 1233–1236. [CrossRef] [PubMed]

32. Brouwer, W.P.; van der Meer, A.J.; Boonstra, A.; Pas, S.D.; de Knegt, R.J.; de Man, R.A.; Hansen, B.E.; ten Kate, F.J.; Janssen, H.L. The impact of PNPLA3 (rs738409 C>G) polymorphisms on liver histology and long-term clinical outcome in chronic hepatitis B patients. *Liver Int.* **2015**, *35*, 438–447. [CrossRef] [PubMed]
33. Choi, H.S.J.; Brouwer, W.P.; Zanjir, W.M.R.; de Man, R.A.; Feld, J.J.; Hansen, B.E.; Janssen, H.L.A.; Patel, K. Nonalcoholic Steatohepatitis Is Associated With Liver-Related Outcomes and All-Cause Mortality in Chronic Hepatitis B. *Hepatology* **2020**, *71*, 539–548. [CrossRef] [PubMed]
34. Wong, V.W.; Chan, W.K.; Chitturi, S.; Chawla, Y.; Dan, Y.Y.; Duseja, A.; Fan, J.; Goh, K.L.; Hamaguchi, M.; Hashimoto, E.; et al. Asia-Pacific Working Party on Non-alcoholic Fatty Liver Disease guidelines 2017-Part 1: Definition; risk factors and assessment. *J. Gastroenterol. Hepatol.* **2018**, *33*, 70–85. [CrossRef] [PubMed]
35. Tseng, T.C.; Liu, C.J.; Yang, H.C.; Su, T.H.; Wang, C.C.; Chen, C.L.; Kuo, S.F.; Liu, C.H.; Chen, P.J.; Chen, D.S.; et al. High levels of hepatitis B surface antigen increase risk of hepatocellular carcinoma in patients with low HBV load. *Gastroenterology* **2012**, *142*, 1140–1149. [CrossRef] [PubMed]

© 2020 by the authors. Licensee MDPI, Basel, Switzerland. This article is an open access article distributed under the terms and conditions of the Creative Commons Attribution (CC BY) license (http://creativecommons.org/licenses/by/4.0/).

MDPI
St. Alban-Anlage 66
4052 Basel
Switzerland
Tel. +41 61 683 77 34
Fax +41 61 302 89 18
www.mdpi.com

International Journal of Molecular Sciences Editorial Office
E-mail: ijms@mdpi.com
www.mdpi.com/journal/ijms

www.ingramcontent.com/pod-product-compliance
Lightning Source LLC
LaVergne TN
LVHW070548100526
838202LV00012B/411